D0513879

INJUSTICE

INJUSTICE

STATE TRIALS FROM SOCRATES TO NUREMBERG

BRIAN HARRIS

FOREWORD BY THE HON. MICHAEL BELOFF

SUTTON PUBLISHING

First published in the United Kingdom in 2006 by
Sutton Publishing Limited · Phoenix Mill
Thrupp · Stroud · Gloucestershire · GL5 2BU

British Library Cataloguing in Publication Data
A catalogue record for this book is available from the British Library.

ISBN 0-7509-4021-2

Typeset in 10/12pt New Baskerville.
Typesetting and origination by
Sutton Publishing Limited.
Printed and bound in England by
J.H. Haynes & Co. Ltd, Sparkford.

For Neil and Jane
No one could want better

Contents

List of Illustrations

Foreword

Justice is both the father and the son of the law. The law's substance is –
or should be – informed by a sense of justice: the law's procedures should
produce a just outcome. Brian Harris's absorbing book is about cases
when very diverse legal systems have – or may have – produced the wrong
result; the conviction of the innocent or, at any rate, of those about
whose guilt a reasonable doubt exists.

The author has trawled history with discrimination for some of the
most famous perceived miscarriages of justice from the trial of Socrates
in fourth-century BC Athens to that of the Rosenbergs in twentieth-
century AD United States. His subtitle 'State Trials' does not bear its
conventional sense. For him, state trials are the machinery that the state
uses (or, in respect of the Nuremberg trials, a collection of states use) in
self-defence against perceived threats to its (or their) authority. And he
dissolves the boundary between Church and State to embrace the trials of
Galileo and Joan of Arc.

Brian Harris's achievement is to sweeten his research with a relaxed
and readable style. He provides vivid sketches of the characters who
people his narrative – the Lincoln conspirators, the Nazi war criminals;
and acutely analyses the psychology of such disparate martyrs to their
causes as Sir Thomas More and Sir Roger Casement. He conducts a
balanced audit of the verdicts reached; and recognises that not all the
victims of injustice were necessarily blameless. For every Galileo there was
a Lord Haw-Haw too.

Common themes emerge from case histories so distinct in terms of
time and context; injustice occurs when the offence charged may be of
dubious basis in law, if soundly based in morality. Arguably, the crimes
against peace and humanity that were found proven at Nuremberg were
offences that did not exist at the time of their alleged commission;
treason for which Charles I stood trial should be a crime against a king
but not by a king. It occurs when distorted constructions are given to
known offences. Both 'Lord Haw-Haw' and Sir Roger Casement posed
threats to the security of the British nation; the complex issue was
whether it was to that nation that they owed allegiance. It occurs when
charges are framed in obscure and unspecific terms: a criticism that the
author makes of those levelled against Socrates and the Lincoln
conspirators. It occurs when the tribunal that determines the case (a
military commission in the case of the Lincoln conspirators) lacks

constitutional validity or fails the tests now enshrined in the European Convention of independence and impartiality, actual and perceived. It occurs when the punishment does not fit, because it is grossly disproportionate to the crime: as in the case of the Tolpuddle Martyrs or the Rosenbergs.

The book has a theme both perennial and topical. The principle of the common law that it is better that a hundred guilty men go free than that one innocent man is convicted is, in the opinion of many, put at risk at a time when governments, sensitive to populist opinion that sees both results as forms of injustice, dismantle many of the traditional procedural safeguards such as trial by jury or the privilege against self-incrimination. Indeed, the terrorist threat has led many governments to bypass the criminal process altogether and to deprive persons, presumed to be (whatever the actual facts) innocent, partially or wholly of their liberty without any trial at all.

There are, of course, counter trends. The fair trial provisions of the Human Rights Act have been interpreted by a liberal judiciary to mean that no verdict obtained in proceedings conducted in breach of those standards can stand. Whereas in the cases, for example, of Lord Haw-Haw and the Rosenbergs, a single judge stood out in rejecting the claims of the state, in the recent case of the Belmarsh detainees, there was only one Law Lord out of nine who was prepared to support them. Extreme cases may make bad law; but Brian Harris reminds us of the risks of departing from due process, and of blindly accepting that the interests of the state and those of justice necessarily coincide. For this alone it merits a wide and attentive readership, whom it will not disappoint.

Michael Beloff QC

Acknowledgements

I am grateful to Alison Cooper of Leicester University, Andrew Carnes and Andrew Tabachnik of 4/5 Gray's Inn Square, Jack Maurice, barrister and Dr Tom McMorrow for reading the text and correcting its more egregious errors. Nor must I overlook the services of Olney library, whose ability to obtain even the most recondite works suggests a reach almost as extensive as that of the Roman Empire in its prime.

Is not injustice the greatest of all threats of the state?
Plato, *The Republic*

Introduction

The popular image of the state trial is of a cynical attempt by the authorities to silence an awkward individual at all costs, often with poignantly tragic consequences – and this book contains its fair share of such cases. But state trials are not always like this. In the cold glare of the legal process some accused, though acting from the highest motives, are manifestly guilty; while others, though innocent, prove to have been far from blameless. Even where the trial is flawlessly conducted, the man in the public gallery can be left with the uneasy feeling that justice has not been entirely served, either because the whole truth has not come out or because the line between right and wrong has been imperfectly drawn. With uncertainties and moral ambiguities like these abounding, the state trial can be a fascinating petri dish of human behaviour.

I can – just – remember the fuss at the end of the Second World War when William Joyce, or 'Lord Haw-Haw' as he was better known, was hanged for treason. At the time I understood little of the issues at stake and even less about the man at the centre of them, a lack of understanding that I have been able to remedy, in part at least, in preparing this book about state trials and their potential for injustice.

People tend to think of state trials as the trial of a political offence, but few countries have – or are willing to admit to having – political offences. I prefer to think of state trials simply as something that men in power do to people they feel threatened by. An advantage of this approach is that I have been able to include in this book, not only such obvious crimes as treason, espionage and insurrection, but also such diverse matters as inattention to duty, cowardice, robbery for political purposes, impiety and industrial unrest. And, by treating that great supranational institution the Catholic Church as a state, I have been able to take in the worlds of heresy and witchcraft also.

I cannot pretend that my selection of cases is in any sense methodical. I have chosen them, whether famous or relatively unknown, simply because they interested me as examples of real or supposed injustice. This has resulted in a motley cast of defendants, ranging from admiral to actor, royal to rustic, fish peddler to philosopher. Their stories are sometimes horrifying, sometimes ennobling, often both; which is no doubt why such trials have inspired so many works of fiction. But fiction can distort our understanding of events – often the greater the writer the greater the distortion. On examination, the real stories of Joan of Arc,

1

Galileo and Sir Thomas More turn out to be every bit as moving as those that have come from the pens of Bernard Shaw, Bertolt Brecht and Robert Bolt.

Some of these trials disclose a deplorable determination on the prosecutor's part to secure a conviction by any means; and the prosecutor's misconduct has sometimes proved to be the judge's temptation. While most courts try, in the old phrase, to 'let justice be done though the heavens fall', we should not allow our proper respect for the law to be carried over into an uncritical acceptance of the courts. Judges are human like the rest of us. The good judges know this and struggle to achieve that dispassionate conduct of the proceedings which their duty demands. Unfortunately, as these pages can testify, not all have been successful. (Of course, jurors can fall into the same trap, but they have a better excuse.)

Conversely, we should not assume that every allegation of 'injustice' is well founded. When I looked into a number of notorious cases of supposed injustice I found them to be nothing of the kind. It is, for example, difficult to fault the *conviction* of the Tolpuddle Martyrs; the injustice in that case was the passing of a sentence wholly disproportionate to the offence. (How that came about is a mystery that I attempt to unravel.) And the convictions of Sir Roger Casement and Lord Haw-Haw proved on examination to be more justifiable than some critics contend. But it is to North America that we must turn for real controversy. Sacco and Vanzetti were two young Italian immigrants who went to the electric chair passionately denying their part in robbery and murder. Three decades later Julius and Ethel Rosenberg suffered the same fate for allegedly passing information about the atomic bomb to Russia. Heated debate still surrounds all four convictions, but I will not anticipate here my conclusions on their fascinating stories.

Anyone trying to understand what went on in the minds of men and women in generations long gone is faced with a question that has to be answered. When we have difficulty in judging the lives and morals of even our own grandparents, how can we expect to judge those who lived and died centuries ago? In fact, while outlooks and assumptions may change with the years, human nature seems to be remarkably consistent. For that reason I believe that we are justified in attempting to understand the lives – and deaths – of people condemned by courts now long forgotten, provided only that two criteria are satisfied: we must be in possession of a credible record of what took place and we must judge the past on its own terms, not ours.

To the student of history, one of the advantages of the courtroom is that its proceedings have long been recorded with care. Take, for example, the judicial murder of Joan of Arc. Without the careful account of a fifteenth-century notary public we would have only the barest outline of this exceptional young woman's story. And the unbelievably poignant tragedy of Admiral Byng comes down to us from the meticulous report made at the time by an attorney-at-law. I have stretched the 'credible record' criterion to its limits in the case of the Greek philosopher Socrates, as will be clear from the third note to that chapter. It has, however, ruled out any discussion of possibly the most intriguing trial of all, that of Jesus of Nazareth.

When it came down to it, I found that my decision to judge trials by the standards of their day and not by those of the twenty-first century was not as limiting as I had imagined. Most injustices proved not to turn on fine points of legal theory, but to be blatant attempts to subvert the court or the judicial process, a wrong that our ancestors had no difficulty at all in recognising, although sometimes quite a lot in preventing.

It is a curious fact that lawyers' concerns with injustice revolve almost exclusively around the question of whether a trial was conducted fairly or not. The consequence of this somewhat blinkered approach is that a trial can be considered 'fair' even though an innocent man has been convicted, and vice versa. The man in the street knows better; for him, a just trial is one that results in the conviction of the guilty or the acquittal of the innocent. Perhaps the time has come to pay more attention to this view?

Despite the great efforts that go into the preparation and conduct of criminal cases, the outcomes seldom satisfy everyone. This is because a trial is not a scientific experiment that can confirm or refute a hypothesis. Underneath the majesty of the law a trial is in fact nothing more than a mechanism – and a very imperfect one at that – designed to provide an agreed version of disputed facts. Viewed in the cold light of history, however, all facts are provisional. That is why I have felt no compunction in offering my own opinion on the guilt or innocence of those unhappy individuals who fill the starring roles in this book. I would be surprised, not to say disappointed, if all my conclusions prove to be acceptable to everyone. I ask only that readers should do what I have tried – no doubt imperfectly – to do: namely, to base their judgements, not on preconceptions and prejudices, but on a dispassionate review of the facts, wherever that might lead.

It is here that I must own up to a glaring omission. It is sometimes overlooked that an injustice occurs whenever a guilty person is acquitted. The verdict of the court is 'not guilty', rather than 'innocent', and convictions are upset on appeal only on the narrow grounds that they are unsafe or unsatisfactory, not that they were wrong – and that is how it should be. But the consequence of this is that, tabloid headlines notwithstanding, the courts do not 'clear' people of crimes; they are simply not equipped to do so. However, since the English law of libel has the capacity to draw blood, it would be a brave commentator who dared to suggest that a living person was guilty of a crime after he had been acquitted or his conviction quashed on appeal. No matter that wrongful acquittals are probably quite common even today, you will look in vain for any examples of them in this book.[1]

As a lawyer, I was first attracted to the topic of injustice by the legal questions it can pose, and I have certainly dealt with those whenever they have gone to the heart of the matter. Was Admiral Byng shot, for example, because of a misunderstanding of the Articles of War? Were the Tolpuddle Martyrs properly convicted under an Act of Parliament passed for an entirely different purpose? Should the Nazi leaders have been found guilty of offences that did not exist at the time they were committed? Intriguing though these questions are, when I came to examine the records I found that they were in every case overshadowed by the deeply moving human stories involved. I was particularly struck by the way in which even great men can bring about their own downfall. Socrates, for all his nobility of mind and spirit, seems almost to have invited the death sentence that was passed upon him; the misfortunes of the great Galileo were due as much to his own pride as to the machinations of his enemies; and Charles Stuart died, not merely for his belief in the divine right of kings, but also because of a series of bad decisions on his part.

Most of the cases in this book raise profound moral issues, many of which still resonate loudly in today's world. How far, for example, should society go in tolerating dissent? Can a burning belief in social justice ever justify terrorism? Is a charge of treason an appropriate response to someone who takes up arms to liberate his country? And, perhaps most topical of all, is a nation ever justified in attacking a tyrant who is not directly threatening it?

But the cases also raise a question deeper than any of these, a question that concerns the paradox that can sometimes be found at the heart of man: how can people devoted to humanity in general be so contemptuous of individuals in particular? John Wilkes Booth threw away his life in support of a bad cause already lost. Sacco and Vanzetti embraced a movement committed to indiscriminate murder in order to establish the just society. And the intelligent and socially conscious William Joyce walked to the gallows proclaiming his belief in a cause responsible for more misery than he could bring himself to believe possible. How is it that benevolence and malevolence, greatness and fallibility, bravery and wickedness, can sometimes all be combined in the same person? The stories in this book present a unique opportunity to study this enigma.

PART ONE

The Traitors

Introduction

There is always a temptation for those who come out on top at the end of a bitter conflict to use the courtroom to demonstrate their opponents' evil ways. These proceedings are usually so far removed from ordinary notions of justice that we describe them as show trials. But show trials sometimes backfire on those who set them up, as was the case with the trial of Charles Stuart.

When Parliament emerged victorious from the English Civil War, all that Oliver Cromwell wanted was for the defeated King to defer to Parliament in financial matters. Believing himself to rule by divine right, Charles did not feel he could concede this without abandoning his duty to God. Though the army fumed, Parliament might have borne even this obduracy had not the King, while ostensibly engaged in negotiations with his former enemies, secretly approached foreign powers with a view to recovering his throne by force. When his double-dealing came to light, the hard-headed, but hitherto tolerant, Cromwell finally snapped. He determined to bring about the King's death, but with as much of the trappings of legality as he could muster. It might be thought that a modern reader would have no difficulty in deciding where his sympathies lay as between a (more or less) democratically elected Parliament and a man who believed himself to be a divinely anointed ruler, but it is impossible not to admire the courage of the King before a court that he considered, probably correctly, to be lacking in any lawful authority. It was a trial in which legality and nobility inclined one way, brute force and the public will the other. Charles died nobly at the hands of an illegal tribunal, but which of them, ultimately, was in the right?

Ireland has long been a thorn in England's side, but the story of Sir Roger Casement's treachery is surely unique. A British consular official who had performed incalculable services for mankind, Casement came to believe that Irish independence justified supporting his country's

5

enemy in time of war. His feeble attempt at insurrection failed, but his controversial death probably did more for his cause than his life. To forestall any possibility of clemency for the convicted traitor, British Intelligence took a course for which it has since been widely vilified: it leaked to the press documents that appeared to show Casement as a man of depraved character. Nationalist opinion, buttressed perhaps by a degree of homophobia, became convinced that the documents were forged; it is only recently that the full story has come to light.

Casement at least believed in a noble cause. The same could not be said of William Joyce, who in the Second World War famously broadcast for Hitler under the sobriquet Lord Haw-Haw. His trademark, 'Germany calling, Germany calling', although threatening at first, came in time to be treated by his listeners with amused contempt. Nevertheless, there was a great deal of unease when at the end of the war he was sentenced to death on what many considered to be a technicality.

Of Casement's and Joyce's treasons there can be no doubt, but were the British justified in using Casement's diaries to blacken his name, and were they right in refusing clemency to Joyce, a man who had long become a figure of fun? Judge for yourself.

The last trial in this section took place in the 1950s when America was in the grip of the twin fears of Russian domination and atomic war. When Julius and Ethel Rosenberg were convicted of 'giving Russia the secret of the atom bomb', therefore, it is not surprising that many felt they should suffer the ultimate penalty. Their supporters – not all of them communists – sought to show the couple as the victims of an oppressive government and a corrupt legal system. The facts as they have finally emerged support neither scenario completely. Perhaps more than any other case in this book, that of the Rosenbergs exemplifies the conflicting issues and moral ambiguities that so often surround state trials.

CHAPTER ONE

The Divine Ruler

The Trial of Charles I, 1649

Relations between the English King and his Parliament were at breaking point. Charles I, having so long sidelined his most capable lieutenant, now brought Thomas Wentworth back from Ireland, which he had recently pacified, and made him Earl of Strafford and his chief adviser. He also gave him an assurance 'on the word of a King' that, whatever should befall, he would not suffer in life or fortune. But it was too late. Believing that he intended to use Irish troops against his own countrymen, the House of Commons threw Strafford into the Tower of London and began impeachment proceedings against him for treason. Strafford's formidable defence before his peers forced the Commons to resort to a bill of attainder, a procedure that dispensed with the need for proof of guilt. The bill passed both Houses of Parliament, but Strafford could not be put to death without the King's warrant. On Good Friday 1641, believing that he could still save his faithful servant, the King wrote to Strafford renewing his promise of protection; he had not reckoned with the strength of feeling in the country. The judges and the Church advised Charles that he had no option but to sign the warrant and Strafford generously released Charles from his promise. The King ruefully commented, 'My Lord of Strafford's condition is happier than mine' and on a sunny day in May 1641 the head of the King's first minister was struck from his body at Tower Hill. Eight years later Charles had occasion bitterly to regret his betrayal of the only man who, had he been called for earlier, might have saved him.

The English Civil War had many causes, chief among them religion and taxation. Puritanism – the idea that people did not need the clergy to mediate between them and their God – had taken firm hold in England during the fifteenth and sixteenth centuries, particularly among the 'lower' classes. It was anathema to England's religiously conservative King and his Catholic wife, Henrietta Maria, and the response was a series of increasingly repressive measures designed to secure conformity. It alienated large chunks of society. (In Scotland it even led to war.) But it was not only religion that led to unrest.

Charles had inherited from his father, James, a system under which the king had all the responsibilities of government without the power to raise the funds necessary to discharge them. Parliament held the purse strings and the king was forced to resort to various stratagems to circumvent its wishes. In 1628 Charles had reluctantly accepted a Petition of Right outlawing non-parliamentary taxes and arbitrary imprisonment, but it was not to last; the following year he dismissed Parliament and attempted to rule solely by virtue of the royal prerogative. The ensuing Eleven Years' Tyranny, as it came to be called, was a deep affront to a people accustomed to seeing their laws approved by their representatives from the shires.

In the end, lack of funds forced Charles to call another Parliament. It promptly declared the widely resented 'ship money' illegal,[1] abolished the unpopular court of Star Chamber and voted to support the Scots; everything, in other words, except provide the taxes necessary to run the country. A Catholic revolt in Ireland now prompted the parliamentary leader John Pym to organise what was known as the Grand Remonstrance. After listing Parliament's grievances, which it blamed on the King's popish advisers, the Remonstrance demanded that the King should employ only those whom Parliament 'may have cause to confide in'. Meanwhile, Pym and four other Members of Parliament were planning to impeach the Queen. Her crime? Attempting to enlist foreign aid against her own subjects.

Charles decided to make a stand. On 4 January 1642 he went to the Commons in an attempt to arrest the five awkward Members. As he entered the Chamber the door was left open so that Members could see his escort aiming their pistols at them. But firmness is effective only when it works and Charles had not laid his plans well. The five Members, who had had warning of his approach, had already left by the back door. Doffing his hat, Charles said, 'Mr Speaker, I must for a time make bold with your chair'. When he asked the assembly whether the five were present, the King was met with silence. When asked directly, Mr Speaker Lenthill memorably replied, 'Sire, I have neither eyes to see nor tongue to speak in this place but as the House is pleased to direct me.' As he left the Chamber empty-handed, the King wryly observed 'all my birds are flown'. From high drama his mission had turned into low farce. With popular opinion in London now firmly against him, the King felt compelled to leave town, first for Hampton Court and then for Windsor.

WAR

Rumours now began to circulate of a royal attack on London, and barricades were thrown up in the streets. Parliament issued an ordinance raising the militia; Charles's attempt to forbid it was ignored. Conflict was now inevitable, and on 22 August the King raised his standard at Nottingham. It was an inauspicious beginning to a military campaign: last-minute alterations to the text led to the proclamation being garbled by the herald, and the standard blew down in the wind.

The first major engagement was the inconclusive battle of Edgehill (23 October 1642). After that, fortunes swung from one side to the other until in 1645 the Parliamentarian generals Cromwell and Fairfax created the formidable New Model Army. Their efforts were to bear fruit in the decisive Parliamentary victory of Naseby (14 June 1645). The last Royalist force surrendered at Stow-on-the-Wold in March the following year. Charles, hoping to avoid falling into Parliamentary hands, disguised himself as a servant, fled to Newark and surrendered to the Scots. Although there were more battles, the King's cause was now lost. As with all civil wars, families had been split in their loyalties, with brother pitted against brother. The conflict was made all the more bitter by pamphleteering that graphically exaggerated the atrocities which violent hotheads on both sides sometimes perpetrated on their defeated opponents. All in all, nearly 800,000 people had died throughout the British Isles, directly or indirectly, as a result of the war, proportionately more than in the bloodbath that was to be the First World War of 1914–18.

The end of the war had not put an end to popular discontent, but this time it was combined with a new radicalism. The Parliamentary army, which had gone for many months without being paid, was concerned that all its sacrifices should not go in vain. Some regiments elected four of their number (known as 'agitators') to represent their views to the leadership, a system that was eventually embodied in the army structure. At the same time a loose populist movement called the Levellers was active among them. Its manifesto, *The Agreement of the People*, made a number of proposals well in advance of their time, including universal franchise and parliamentary constituencies based on population. (The movement proved to be an embarrassment to the generals and was put down by force in 1649.)

This new-found radicalism led to what was perhaps the most extraordinary political event of the war. From 28 October to 1 November 1647 in the chancel of St Mary the Virgin Church, Putney, Cromwell chaired a series of meetings between all strands of opinion in the army. To read the shorthand account of the Putney debates is to witness the first rehearsal of that great disputation between authority and the individual that the Western world has been engaged in ever since. It was during these discussions that Colonel Rainsborough, soon to be murdered by Royalists, memorably declared: 'I think that the poorest he that is in England has a life to live, as the greatest he; and therefore truly, sir, I think it's clear that every man that is to live under a government ought first by his own consent to put himself under that government.'[2] Ultimately, it proved impossible to reconcile all the conflicting opinions, and Cromwell dissolved the meeting before it got out of hand.

Meanwhile, the Scots, having sought unsuccessfully to persuade Charles to introduce Presbyterianism into England, effectively sold him to Parliament for £400,000 arrears of pay. The King's correspondence captured at Naseby had revealed how he had been plotting to offer concessions to Catholics in exchange for military aid. It was published within a month. Nothing could have upset the army more. One day, a troop of horse under the command of a cornet,[3] Joyce, arrived at Holdenby Hall in Northamptonshire, where the King was detained, for the purpose of removing him to a more secure place. Asked by what authority he was acting, Joyce indicated the soldiers behind him, saying: 'There is my commission.' Charles ruefully admitted: 'It is written in characters fair and legible enough.'[4] He was taken to Newmarket and thence to Hampton Court Palace in what was far from close confinement. Despite the fact that he was engaged in negotiations with Parliament, he foolishly escaped, as he claimed, 'for feare of being murder'd privatly [sic]'.[5] Without any clear plan of action, the King ended up in the Isle of Wight, whose Parliamentary governor he believed to be sympathetic to his cause.

WAR REIGNITES

Lodged comfortably at Carisbrooke Castle, the King resumed negotiations with Parliament. Behind their backs, however, he swallowed his pride and secretly agreed to introduce Presbyterianism into England in exchange for a Scottish army. With this agreement under his belt the King felt able to reject Parliament's terms, unaware that his duplicity had been revealed to Cromwell. As the Parliamentary commander Henry Ireton remarked, he 'sought to regain by art what he had lost in fight'. Matters now took a serious turn for the worse, provoked almost certainly by royal intrigue. In March 1648 uprisings took place in Wales that quickly spread to other parts of the country. In July the Scots invaded England. Order was swiftly restored, but only after a great expenditure in effort and blood. The Second Civil War, as it is called, was characterised by even greater acts of brutality on both sides, which only served to harden the resolve of those calling for extreme measures. But even at this late date Parliament still sought an accommodation with the King, the so-called Treaty of Newport. While these negotiations were going on, the now paroled Charles was secretly planning to escape.

The rift between Parliament, which wanted to continue talking with the King, and its impatient army now became wider. At the beginning of the war there had been no thought of deposing the King, let alone of his execution, but in November Parliament was presented with a 'Remonstrance of the Army' that called for the King to be put on trial. Even at this eleventh hour a council of officers sought an accommodation with the King. But Charles rejected their proposals and was removed to the more secure Hurst Castle on the Solent and thence to Windsor Castle, while London was garrisoned by the army. When Parliament voted to continue negotiations, 150 of its Members were forcibly turned away from its doors in an action that came to be known as Pride's Purge after the army colonel who undertook it.

Cromwell, who had not until then been directly involved in the discussions with the King, made one last effort to reach an agreement. He sought no more than what we would call a constitutional monarchy, but when the King refused even to see his representative Cromwell angrily commented: 'I tell you we will cut off his head with the crown on it.'[6] What manner of man was this king who could thus reject his only hope of survival?

CHARLES THE MAN

Charles was a second son, becoming heir to the throne only on the death of his charismatic elder brother, Henry, whom he had adored. Charles himself was short, suffered from a slight stammer and tended to keep his own company.

A loving husband and devoted father, Charles pursued interests in art and in the field. Disarmingly courteous even to the humblest, he did little to seek popularity. 'Princes', he once told the House of Lords, 'are not bound to give account of their actions but to God alone'. In the words of the historian C.V. Wedgwood, this slight, reserved man 'neither solicited nor gained the affection of his people from whom he expected neither more nor less than duty'.[7] Throughout his life the King had no doubts about the place of the monarch in God's plan. His father James had taught him that a good king had 'received from God a burden of government whereof he must be accountable'.[8] A king, in other words, ruled by divine right; his powers and duties were not temporal and could not be removed by man. In battle there was no question of the King's personal bravery, but he had little skill or interest in the art of government, which, combined with a dogmatic sense of divine mission and a naturally devious nature, was to prove his undoing.

Oliver Cromwell had his own understanding of the divine will and now turned all the force of his formidable personality to the task of bringing the King to trial. It was a narrow thing; the decision to set up a High Court of Justice to try the King scraped through the Commons by only 26 votes to 20. When the House of Lords refused its consent, the Commons decided to go ahead without it. Any attempt at impartiality was abandoned at the outset by the Act of Commons setting up the court, which charged that

Whereas it is notorious that Charles Stuart, the now King of England . . . not content with the many encroachments which his

11

predecessors had made upon the people in their rights and freedoms, hath had a wicked design totally to subvert the ancient and fundamental laws and liberties of this nation, and in their place introduce an arbitrary and tyrannical government, and that besides all other evil ways and means to bring this design to pass he hath prosecuted it with fire and sword . . .[9]

Well over a century before the American Declaration of Independence, the Act proclaimed the revolutionary doctrine that

the people are, under God, the original of all just power . . . That the Commons of England . . . representing the people have the supreme power in this nation . . . whatever is enacted, or declared for law, by the Commons . . . hath the force of law . . . although the consent and concurrence of King, or House of Peers, be not had thereunto.

There were 135 commissioners appointed to the court, including some of the chief officers of the army, landed gentry and City aldermen. The two chief justices (of the King's Bench and Common Pleas) and the lord chief baron refused to preside, ostensibly on the ground that the trial contravened the principle that all justice flowed from the king. In the end the presidency went to a reluctant Welsh judge, the little-known John Bradshaw. A barrister, John Cook, was appointed Solicitor-General and joint prosecutor, becoming sole prosecutor when his leader fell out.[10]

A Dutch scholar, Isaac Dorislaus, was brought in to assist in drafting the indictment, for which there was no precedent in England. It alleged that Charles

trusted with a limited power to govern by and according to the laws of the land, and not otherwise . . . out of a wicked design to erect and uphold in himself an unlimited and tyrannical power to rule according to his will, and to overthrow the rights and liberties of the people . . . he, the said Charles Stuart . . . hath traitorously and maliciously levied war against the present Parliament, and the people therein represented . . . [and] hath caused and procured many thousands of the free people of this nation to be slain . . .

All which wicked designs, wars, and evil practices of him, the said Charles Stuart, have been, and are carried on for the advancement and upholding of a personal interest of will, power, and pretended prerogative to himself and his family, against the public interest, common right, liberty, justice, and peace of the people of this nation, by and from whom he was entrusted as aforesaid.

By all which it appeareth that the said Charles Stuart hath been, and is the occasioner, author, and continuer of the said unnatural, cruel and bloody wars; and therein guilty of all the treasons, murders, rapines, burnings, spoils, desolations, damages and mischiefs to this nation, acted and committed in the said wars, or occasioned thereby.[11]

'NOT AN ORDINARY PRISONER'

The trial began on the afternoon of Saturday 20 January 1649 in the south end of a crowded Westminster Hall, where the law courts customarily sat.[12] In the event, only 68 of the 135 commissioners turned up. When the name of Fairfax was called, his wife shouted from an upstairs window: 'Not here. He has more wit than to be here.'

The judges sat at a table covered by a rich Turkey carpet, on which was placed the sword and mace. Lord President Bradshaw, flanked by two lawyers, sat in a chair raised above the rest wearing an iron-reinforced hat in fear of assassination. Armed men were stationed on the roofs and the cellars were searched.

The King was brought in by the Serjeant at Arms and took his seat on a chair upholstered in crimson velvet facing his judges. He was dressed in black and wore the silver Star of the Garter. Around his neck was the blue ribbon and jewelled George of the Order, a locket that contained a miniature portrait of his wife.[13] He refused to acknowledge the court, declining even to remove his broad-brimmed hat. His composure was disturbed, however, by a trivial incident at the outset of the proceedings. When the prosecutor Cook began to speak, Charles, seeking to interrupt, tapped him on the shoulder two or three times with his cane, causing its silver head to fall off. The King looked round but, finding no one willing to pick it up, did so himself. Some saw the incident as symbolic of his reduced circumstances.

The reading of the indictment was the first time that the King had been made aware of the accusations against him and he laughed at the reference to himself as 'tyrant' and 'traitor'. When asked to plead guilty or not guilty, Charles demanded to know

> by what power I am called hither . . . by what Authority, I mean, lawful; there are many unlawful Authorities in the world, Thieves and Robbers by the highways: but I would know by what Authority I was brought from thence, and carried from place to place, (and I know not what), and when I know what lawful Authority, I shall answer: Remember, I am your King, your lawful King and what sins you bring upon your heads and the judgement of God upon this land, think well upon it – I say think well upon it – before you go from one sin to a greater. Therefore let me know by what lawful Authority I am seated here and I shall not be unwilling to answer. In the meantime I shall not betray my trust. I have a trust committed to

me by God, by old and lawful descent. I will not betray it to answer to a new unlawful Authority.

This was not the answer that the judges wanted to hear. Bradshaw asked the King once more 'in the name of the people' to answer to the charge, adding inadvisably, 'of which you are elected King'. Charles promptly corrected him: 'England was never an elected kingdom, but a hereditary kingdom for these thousand years . . .'. He went on to challenge the court directly:

> I do stand as much for the privilege of the House of Commons, rightly understood, as any man here whatsoever. I see no House of Lords, here that may constitute a Parliament, and [the King too] should have been. Is this the bringing of the King to his Parliament? Is this the bringing an end to the Treaty in the public Faith of the world? Let me see a legal Authority warranted by the Word of God, the Scriptures, or warranted by the Constitutions of the Kingdom, and I will answer . . .

The King spoke confidently and without any sign of his usual slight speech impediment. The court, unsettled by his robust defence, retired to consider what to do. As they left the hall, the soldiers, seemingly acting under orders, shouted, 'Justice, Justice'. Nevertheless, the King had had the better of the first day's proceedings.

Next day, the commissioners met privately in the Painted Chamber of the Palace of Westminster to decide how to deal with the problem of the King's refusal to plead. Should he persist in it, they concluded, it should be treated as an admission of guilt. After they had filed back into court, Bradshaw announced that they were 'satisfied fully' with their authority and that the King was required to answer to the charge. Charles continued to challenge the authority of the court. 'A King cannot be tried by any superior jurisdiction on earth.' When Bradshaw insisted on a direct answer, the King replied,

> I do not know the forms of law; I do know law and reason, though I am no lawyer professed: but I know as much law as any gentleman in England, and therefore, under favour, I do plead for the liberties of the people of England more than you do; and therefore if I should impose a belief upon any man without reasons given for it, it were unreasonable.

He again required to know how the Commons, that is to say, the Commons alone without the Lords, had become a court of judicature. Told that it was not for prisoners to 'require', he responded bitterly: 'Sir, I am not an ordinary prisoner.'

The trial now went into its third day, still with no plea from the accused. When Bradshaw foolishly told the King that he was 'before a court of justice', Charles contemptuously replied: 'I find I am before a power.' Offered the opportunity to speak in return for a plea, the King replied,

> For the charge, I value it not a rush. It is the liberty of the People of England I stand for. For me to acknowledge a new court, that I never heard of before, I that am your King, that should be an example to all the people of England, to uphold justice, to maintain the old laws, indeed I do not know how to do it.

For the next two days the court sat in private and without the prisoner in order to hear the depositions of thirty-three witnesses concerning the behaviour of the Royalist forces in the field and the King's personal responsibility for it. By now, the commissioners' attendance had dropped to forty-six. At the end of this session the court ordered the preparation of a draft sentence, omitting only the form of execution. The omission was remedied the following day.

When the court met for the last time, on Saturday 27 January, cries of 'Justice' and 'Execution' were heard in the hall, no doubt as carefully orchestrated as those of the previous days. Charles asked to address the Parliament but was refused. At this point, Downey, one of the commissioners, publicly broke ranks and asked to speak against the sentence. The court promptly retired. After he had been reminded of his duty by Cromwell (one may imagine how forcibly), the hearing resumed. Bradshaw, dressed for the first time in scarlet robes, now began his address to the prisoner. As he started to speak, a masked woman cried out in objection: 'Cromwell is a traitor.' It was the indomitable Lady Fairfax once again. Bradshaw's peroration was a long one and after it was finished, the clerk of the court read out the sentence of death. The King was dismayed to realise that this had happened without his having been given another opportunity to address the court: 'I am not suffered to speak! Expect what justice other people will have!' As he was bustled out of the hall the soldiers scoffed at him and puffed smoke in his face; one even spat at him. Charles was heard to remark: 'Poor creatures. For a sixpence they would say as much of their own commanders.' The execution was to take place in three days' time.

Within forty-eight hours the warrant for Charles's execution was signed, but only by 59 of the 135 commissioners, 8 of them Cromwell's relatives. Some were later to claim that he had bullied them into submission. (Cromwell is said to have held the hand of one and forced him to sign.) Nevertheless, nine of those who had been present at the sentence failed to sign the warrant.

'THE BRIGHT EXECUTION AXE'

Charles, who had hitherto been lodged in a private house, was now taken to St James's Palace, perhaps in order to spare him the sound of the scaffold being built outside Inigo Jones's great Banqueting House in Whitehall, at where the execution was to take place. Two musketeers were stationed in his bedchamber all night and he got little sleep. (This indignity was removed after the first night.) Allowed to see his two youngest children, Charles commanded them to forgive his enemies but not to trust them. In an attempt to save his father's life, the Prince of Wales sent the Commons a blank sheet of paper with his signature at the foot. The Dutch ambassadors also sought to intervene. It was all in vain; the Commons now sent for 'the bright execution axe'.

It was a cold morning on the day of the execution and Charles asked for 'a shirt more than ordinary by reason the season is so sharp, which some will imagine proceeds from fear'.[14] He was attended by the Bishop of London, William Juxon, who read chapter 27 of St Matthew's Gospel, the trial and execution of Jesus. Asked by the King whether he had chosen this specially, Juxon explained that it was the reading prescribed for the day. At about ten o'clock the King was taken across the park accompanied by a guard of halberdiers marching to the beat of drums, but a delay in the arrangements meant that the execution could not take place until nearly two o'clock in the afternoon. When all was ready, the King, wearing the Star of the Garter, walked through the Banqueting Hall with its splendidly decorated Rubens ceiling and stepped out of a specially enlarged window onto the scaffold. The first people he must have seen there were two grotesquely disguised headsmen, ready, should the King resist, to fasten him to staples driven into the scaffold. (Their identities were to remain a closely guarded secret.)

Charles made a brief speech to the crowd, saying that he had 'forgiven all the world, and even those in particular that have been the chief causes of my death'.[15] He had made his confession and received absolution and was in a state of grace, but he could not resist protesting his innocence for the last time: Parliament had started the war, not him. He desired the liberty and freedom of the people, which even at the end he declared was his responsibility, not the people's. Referring to the fate of his faithful servant Strafford, he said: 'An unjust sentence that I suffered for to take effect is punished now by an unjust sentence upon me.' When the executioner inadvertently touched the axe with his foot, Charles broke off to remark, 'hurt not the axe, that may hurt me'. Almost his last words were: 'I go from a corruptible to an incorruptible crown; where no disturbance can be, no disturbance in the world.' (The language was from Corinthians via Bishop Juxon.) Few could have heard his words; the public had been kept well back behind a mass of soldiers.

Tidying his long hair under his cap, Charles arranged himself on the low block. When he stretched out his arms to indicate that he was ready, the executioner severed his head from his body with a single stroke. A young lad in the crowd later recalled that they gave 'such a groan as I have never heard before and desire I may never hear again'.[16]

A week later the monarchy was abolished and replaced by the Commonwealth, which in turn was replaced by the Protectorate in 1653. Though restored briefly following the death of Cromwell, the Commonwealth proved unable to survive. Two years later a commission was sent to Holland instructed to bring the late King's son back to his realm. With the Bill of Rights of 1689 England began to evolve into the constitutional monarchy that Charles I had refused to contemplate.

THE FATE OF THE REGICIDES

Charles II was wisely magnanimous towards his father's enemies, but about a hundred men who had been closely involved in the execution of the King were specifically exempted from the Act of Pardon. Of these, most were in fact pardoned, particularly if they had surrendered to justice. Twenty-nine were put on trial before a court set up for the purpose. They received more justice than the late King. In the end only ten were executed as traitors in the usual barbarous way (the prosecutor John Cook was one of them), and the rest were imprisoned for life. An equestrian statue of Charles now stands in Whitehall near the spot where they suffered their horrible deaths. Two years later three of the regicides who had fled abroad were extradited, tried and executed. Yet more were privily killed, the unfortunate lawyer Isaac Dorislaus among them.

Some were not to escape even after death. Cromwell, his son-in-law, Ireton, John Bradshaw, the president of the court, and Colonel Pride had all died before the Restoration. They were nevertheless tried posthumously for high treason, after which their bodies were exhumed and hung on the gallows at Tyburn (now Marble Arch). Time gives a better perspective, and a statue of Cromwell now stands outside Westminster Hall, the site of England's most famous trial.

But did Charles get a fair trial?

WHO WAS IN THE RIGHT?

The judgment of the court that Bradshaw had read out was a curious mixture of historical inaccuracies and legal truisms. In summary and stripped of the flowery language of the seventeenth century, it alleged that:

- the King is subject to the law;
- by his actions Charles had put himself above the law;
- the people of England had chosen their form of government;
- while 'the King had no equal within the realm', he was 'the lesser within the whole';
- the barons of old had stood up to King John for the people;
- today, the Parliament is doing the same;
- Parliaments were ordained to redress the grievances of the people;
- the King had refused to call a Parliament;
- kings have been called to account in the past (Edward II and Richard II were particularly mentioned);
- as 'protection entails subjection', so 'subjection entails protection';
- the King had been a 'tyrant, traitor, murderer and a public enemy'.

Charles's written defence,[17] which he had been denied the opportunity of reading out in court but which was published after his trial, argued that:

- a prosecution may be warranted only by God's laws or the municipal laws of the country (i.e. English law);
- the Old and New Testaments demand obedience to kings;
- English law states that the king can do no wrong;
- the House of Commons, acting alone and without the House of Lords, has no authority to set up a court;
- the authority of the Commons had been diminished by the forcible exclusion of so many of its Members;
- the Commons had no popular mandate (to use a modern expression) for trying the King;
- by doing so without authority the Commons was violating the privileges of both Houses of Parliament, as well as the liberties of the people;
- it was a breach of faith for the Commons to begin the trial while the King was negotiating a settlement with them.

The defence was legally correct in most of its particulars (though the last was a bit hypocritical when the King had been plotting war while negotiating peace). The Commons acting alone has never had power to act as a court. Even if it had, it was, following the *coup d'état* that was Pride's Purge, no longer a representative assembly. The law of treason had never contemplated the prosecution of a king. The worst criticism of the court that tried its king, however, was that it was not fair, either in its appointment, its composition or its procedures.

The court's verdict was implicit in the instrument by which it was set up ('Whereas it is notorious that . . .'). None of the judges was independent; in fact, all were enemies of the accused and for the most part determined on his death; any backsliding was met by the personal intervention of the most powerful man in the land. And the prosecutor John Cook's claim at his subsequent trial that his part was simply that of any lawyer dispassionately acting for a client was given the lie by a former pupil who had heard him declare: 'He must die and monarchy must die with him.'[18]

Charles was given no prior notice of the charges against him, charges that were of the utmost gravity. And the only evidence called affected the outcome not one whit. The trial was a procedural disaster. Throughout the proceedings the court permitted, indeed, probably arranged for, the prisoner to be publicly intimidated and humiliated by the soldiers. Today, though not then, his refusal to plead should have been treated as a plea of not guilty.

'CRUEL NECESSITY'

But none of this mattered to Parliament. The trial and execution of the King were political acts concealed only by a veneer of legality. As Charles rightly wrote in his defence, 'power reigns without rule or law'.[19] Rivers of blood had been spilt in the Civil War and the victors were determined to punish the person they saw as principally responsible for the tragedy.

For all its defects, the Civil War changed England for the better, perhaps the world. While Charles may have had the law on his side, the arguments deployed by Bradshaw probably represented the deeper feelings of the ordinary people. The king was not above the law; Parliament should not be merely an advisory body; sovereignty should lie, not with the king in person, but with 'the King in Parliament'. Without the victory of Parliament the Bill of Rights of 1689 might not have happened. Without the Instrument of Government of 1653 America might not have hit on the idea of a written constitution.

There is no record of the King ever having met his nemesis, Cromwell, in life, but a story told by Alexander Pope to Joseph Spence in the eighteenth century recounts that after the execution a muffled figure, suspected to be Cromwell, visited the King's corpse by night. Before turning away it was heard to mutter, 'Cruel necessity'.[20]

CHAPTER TWO

The Diarist

The Trial of Sir Roger Casement, 1916

The U-boat arrived off the Bay of Tralee at dawn; it was Good Friday 1916 and the war with Germany was at its height. Three men dressed in civilian clothes attempted to row ashore, but their collapsible boat overturned in the surf and the expected reception committee was nowhere to be seen. The leader was a tall (6 feet 4 inches), thin, bearded man with intense deep-set eyes. Soaked to the skin, having gone without sleep for twelve days and still recovering from a nervous breakdown, he decided to rest in an abandoned Iron Age fort, while his companions buried their kit in the sands and made for Tralee.

A local farmer called the police when he discovered his eight-year-old daughter playing with revolvers she had found on the beach. The leader of the three was soon arrested and taken to the police barracks, where he was searched. On him were found field glasses, maps, ammunition and a German bus ticket. He had also been seen trying to destroy a document that contained what appeared to be codes. He gave the police a false name but later, when examined alone by a doctor who was a nationalist sympathiser, identified himself as Sir Roger Casement and asked for help in calling off the planned uprising against the British. The doctor duly contacted the Irish Volunteers, but they were suspicious of his story and did nothing.

Later that morning not far off Tralee, the Royal Navy came upon the German MV Aud disguised as a timber ship and sailing under Norwegian colours. When stopped and taken to Queenstown harbour, the ship was scuttled by its crew. Divers were sent down and it was found to contain a cargo of 20,000 rifles and machine guns.

Casement now asked to see a Catholic priest on the pretence that he wished to make his confession. Through the priest he sent another message to the Volunteers. This time they took notice and orders went out accordingly; their only effect, however, was to confine the rebellion largely to the capital.

On Easter Monday some thousand armed members of the Irish Volunteers and the Irish Citizen Army seized the Post Office and other key buildings in Dublin and proclaimed a republic. The British army, caught by surprise and heavily outnumbered, brought in the artillery and swiftly reduced the buildings to rubble. Five days later the rebels surrendered; fifteen of their leaders were shot, one of them tied to a chair because of his wounds. A terrible beauty had been born.

After Ireland had lost its parliament in 1800, a combination of depressed living standards and a growing sense of nationalism led to a splutter of rebellions that had to be put down by force. Anti-English sentiment was fuelled by a disgraceful system of absentee landlords, a religious divide and London's inept handling of the food shortages resulting from the potato blight. Even at this stage, however, there was little talk of independence. Liberal opinion favoured its alternative, Home Rule, but progress was frustrated by a series of political blunders and private scandals. Eventually a Home Rule bill received the royal assent in 1912. It produced an instant reaction. In Ulster a 'Covenant of Resistance' attracted thousands of signatures and some 80,000 men flocked to join the paramilitary Ulster Volunteer Force. This in turn prompted the setting up of a rival organisation, the Irish National Volunteers, which quickly attracted some 12,000 recruits. Both sides brought in guns from abroad and all was set for bloodshed when an even greater catastrophe intervened: in September 1914 Britain declared war on Germany.

Reluctantly, the Home Rulers accepted suspension of the Act for the duration of the war, provided that the Unionists agreed to its ultimate implementation. They did, but only so long as Home Rule did not extend to Ulster. This did not satisfy extreme nationalist opinion, and, on the basis of the old adage that 'England's difficulties are Ireland's opportunity', plans were laid for an uprising in Ireland while England was otherwise engaged. Even at this stage only a minority supported violence; it took the combination of a hopelessly romantic insurrection and its bloody repression for this to become a popular movement. Few were more responsible for this deadly metamorphosis than an honoured servant of the British Crown, Sir Roger Casement.

Roger David Casement was born in Kingstown, now Dun Laoghaire, County Dublin, on 1 September 1864, the son of a captain in the Antrim militia. He was the youngest of four, three brothers and a sister. Roger's Catholic mother died in childbirth when he was nine, but not before she had had him secretly baptised as a Catholic. Roger's Protestant father died when he was thirteen and the four children were made wards of an uncle, John Casement, in County Antrim, where they were brought up as Protestants.

With the help of family influence, the young Casement obtained a job with the Elder–Dempster Shipping Line, first as a clerk and then as a purser on a West Africa steamer. His name, however, was to be made in the Congo, which at that time was ruled by the Belgian king Leopold. At the age of twenty Casement began working for the American adventurer Henry Morton Stanley in the AIC (Association Internationale du Congo, a front organisation for Leopold). After working in a trading post and as a surveyor, Casement secured a job in an Anglican mission, where he underwent some sort of religious experience. This also seems to have been the time at which he began to demonstrate what was to become a lifelong predilection for young men. Two years later he found himself working once again for Leopold, this time in the construction of a railway being built by forced labour procured for the project by Stanley. His employers were pleased with Casement, describing him as an *agent exceptionelle*; however, when after a year his contract expired, he did not renew it, later professing to have become disillusioned with the enterprise. He was now twenty-eight years of age. It is a curious irony that Casement should have begun his career working for the very organisation whose brutalities he was in later years so famously to expose.

In 1892 Casement joined the British consular service in the Niger region of Africa; it was to be the turning point in his career. After undertaking a number of exploratory expeditions that opened up large tracts of the country, he settled down to the more prosaic work of the customs and excise. Despite a lack of formal education since the age of fifteen, Casement found himself in 1895 appointed HM Consul in Lorenço Marques, Portuguese East Africa (now Mozambique). The climate and the hard work took their toll, but after a period of recuperation in England he was promoted to be Consul in Portuguese West Africa (now Angola) with responsibility for British interests in both the French and Belgian Congos.

The administration of the vast Congo region of Central Africa had been entrusted to King Leopold by the Congress of Berlin. He had declared it a free state, but, as the writer Martin Booth comments: 'It was in effect neither free, nor a state, but a private estate belonging to the King of the Belgians, who owned and exploited it.'[1] After expelling the slave traders, Leopold had granted concessions to various companies that had no compunction about treating their native employees as slaves. In 1900 a separate British consulate was formed for this area and Casement was put in charge. There had been persistent rumours of atrocities against the natives, and in 1903 the Foreign Office instructed Casement to look into them. He held meetings with the King, who assured him that the 'well-being and good government of the natives' was his chief desire. This did not satisfy Casement, who resolved to see for himself. His subsequent report to the Foreign Office was in such damning terms that it was at first quietly filed away. But Casement was not alone: Edmund Morel, a former clerk in the Elder–Dempster Line but now a journalist, had also become concerned and managed to secure a debate on the subject in the House of Commons. It led to Casement being instructed to make further enquiries.

'THE HORROR! THE HORROR!'

For over three months Casement travelled through the Congo on a chartered riverboat, becoming increasingly disturbed at what he found.

He reported to the Foreign Office that swingeing – and unlawful – fines were imposed on the natives, but there was worse. In the words of an informant:

> Men, he said, still came to him whose hands had been cut off by the government soldiers during those evil days, and he said there were still many victims of this species of mutilation in the surrounding country. Two cases of the kind came to my actual notice while I was on the lake. One, a young man, both of whose hands had been beaten off with the butt-ends of rifles against a tree, the other a young lad of eleven or twelve years of age, whose right hand was cut off at the wrist . . . In both these cases the government soldiers had been accompanied by white officers whose names were given to me.[2]

Casement also reported a sinister relationship between guns and rubber. A witness told him:

> 'The [contractor known as the] S.A.B. on the *Bussira*, with 150 guns, get only ten tons [rubber] a month; we, the State, at Momboyo, with 130 guns, get thirteen tons per month.'
>   'So you count by guns?' I asked him.
>   'Partout,' M.P. said. 'Each time the corporal goes out to get rubber, cartridges are given to him. He must bring back all not used; and for every one used, he must bring back a right hand.'

Belgian interests worked hard to suppress the report, but the press had got wind of its contents and public pressure mounted for its publication. When the report finally appeared in February 1904, the Belgians sought to explain away Casement's evidence: it was, they said, unreliable hearsay. Britain's pro-Leopold minister to Brussels claimed that the soldiers were only 'sentries' who were there to protect the workers and that the missing hands had been amputated to prevent the spread of cancer. Casement, too, was unhappy with his report's content, but for a different reason; he had agreed to the names of minor officials being concealed. But the report had been abridged even further to exclude the large body of additional evidence that the Foreign Office had received over the years. (To have revealed this would have led to embarrassing enquiries as to why the British government had not acted sooner.)

Although Casement's report did not at first generate the interest he had hoped for, public indignation, whipped up by the Congo Reform Association that Morel had set up with Casement's assistance, eventually forced the Belgian King to appoint his own commission of inquiry. Despite the fact that it had been set up for the purpose of a whitewash, the report's conclusions were so damning that the governor of the territory committed suicide on reading it. In 1908 the flag of the Congo

Free State was lowered for the last time, though the atrocities appear to have continued, if less blatantly than before.

IRELAND REDISCOVERED

The Congo report was Casement's first major service for humanity, and he paid for it with his health. In 1905 he had undergone an operation for a fistula. Now broken mentally as well as physically, he was allowed leave of absence for the next three years. During this period of turmoil, when he felt bitterly let down by the British government, Casement rediscovered the land of his birth. An initial involvement with Irish cultural, historical and language societies gradually developed into a passionate nationalism. Ironically, it was at this point that the British government decided to recognise his work in the Congo. When, in 1905, a now disillusioned Casement was made a Companion of the Order of St Michael and St George, he declined to accept the honour in person, using the state of his health as an excuse.

It is not known exactly how or at what point this diligent servant of the British Crown became seriously disaffected, but his extended stay in Ireland must have been a critical period. Casement began to draw parallels between the Congo and Ireland. (He referred in correspondence to 'the white natives of Connemara' and to the Irish as 'another race of people once hunted themselves'.) He saw similarities between the two countries. There had been no ownership of land in either prior to colonisation, in each the colonising power had appropriated land to itself and in each, as he saw it, the people were oppressed. So the man who in 1902 had organised a collection for Queen Victoria's commemoration fund now contributed to the drafting of a leaflet stigmatising as a traitor any Irishman who joined the armed forces or police of the Crown. But Casement's work for Britain and for humanity was not yet finished.

PERU

In 1906, at the age of forty-four, Casement was appointed British Consul General in Rio de Janeiro. Four years later he was summoned to the Foreign Office and instructed to investigate allegations concerning the ill-treatment of native workers employed in the rubber empire of Julio Cesar Arana in the 12,000-square-mile Putumayo region of the Upper Amazon Basin in Peru. The situation there was curiously similar to that which Casement had discovered in the Congo, perhaps worse, and Casement's task was not made easier by threats from the murderous thugs who were exploiting the natives. Nevertheless, he found that in the first twelve years of the century some 30,000 natives had been murdered or starved in pursuit of rubber. Tortures and mutilations, which had begun as a means of ensuring greater production, had over the years turned into sadism for its own sake. The natives had not merely been overworked; section chiefs admitted to having beaten Indians to death, to having crushed their testicles and to having baked them alive.

Casement reported his conclusions to the Foreign Office in January 1911, but they were not published until the following year. This time Casement had taken the precaution of leaking his report to the Anti-Slavery Society. The result was another public outcry. A parliamentary select committee sat to hear evidence from Casement, Arana and others. It found that, while the principal blame for the atrocities lay with Arana, the British directors of the company had failed properly to investigate the allegations. The outbreak of war in 1914 prevented any proper follow-up action and in the short term the situation of the natives hardly improved at all.

In July 1911 Casement, who had not up to then made his anti-British sentiments public, was again honoured by the Crown, this time by the conferment of a knighthood. Two years later illness forced him to retire from the consular service and he went back to live in Ireland. Here, his disaffection with his former masters turned to detestation. Casement toured the country recruiting for the Irish Volunteers and, at a time of growing tensions between Britain and Germany, wrote to a friend: 'I pray for the salvation of Germany night and day. And "God save Ireland" is another form of "God save Germany".'[3] But paramilitary forces are useless without arms, and arms cannot be acquired without money. Casement knew where the money was to be found.

THE 'IRISH BRIGADE'

Only weeks after Britain had declared war, the ex-Consul set sail for the United States on a false passport and with his beard shaved off. After obtaining $3,000 from the Fenian Clan na Gael, he continued on to Germany, now Britain's enemy, via Norway. He travelled with a perfumed and painted 'manservant' who was, eventually, to betray him to the British.

In Berlin, Casement met the German Under Secretary of State, Count Artur Zimmerman, and told him of his wish to recruit Irish prisoners of war to serve in what he confidently described as an Irish brigade. (He was so far out of touch with his countrymen as to believe that it was only financial necessity that could drive Irishmen to serve in the British army.) The Germans expressed their support for Irish independence and allowed Casement to conduct a recruiting tour of the camps holding Irish prisoners of war. In view of what was to happen later it is interesting to read the justification for treason that Casement offered to his prospective volunteers:

Your Oath binds you to serve your king and country. Now a man has only one country and he cannot have a divided allegiance. The only country that can claim an Irishman's allegiance is Ireland. The king you agreed to serve is, in law, King of Great Britain and Ireland. There is no such person as the King of England in law. How have these sovereigns discharged their duty to their Irish subjects? For remember these obligations are mutual. Our Kings, whose sole title to our allegiance is that they are Kings of Ireland, as well as Kings of Great Britain, have not once in all these centuries performed their duties to their Irish people or fulfilled any of the sacred obligations laid upon them by the title and the allegiance they claim from their subjects.[4]

To his surprise and dismay, Casement found himself jeered and insulted by the Irish soldiers, ending up with only fifty-two recruits, mostly men in search of nothing more than better rations.

Now disillusioned with the German government ('swine and cads of the first order') and realising the hopelessness of any military action in Ireland without the assistance of his 'Brigade', Casement sought to call off the planned uprising; his pleas went unregarded. At this critical juncture Casement's health gave way once again and he was forced to enter a sanatorium suffering from severe depression. While there, he learnt that the arms the Germans intended to send to Ireland were only one-tenth of the number he considered necessary. Determined to warn his nationalist friends, he dragged himself out of bed and demanded to be taken back to Ireland, but travelling separately from the arms in order to get there first. A U-boat was accordingly provided for him. Accompanying Casement in the submarine were Robert Monteith, a former sergeant in the British army and now a captain in the Irish Republican Army (IRA), and Daniel Bailey, a former private. (Bailey appears to have had no nationalist sympathies and saw the venture only as a means of escaping the privations of a prisoner-of-war camp.)

What Casement did not know was that the German government had given instructions that he should not be allowed to land in Ireland in time to stop the insurrection. And neither of them was aware that British Naval Intelligence had for over a year been intercepting coded radio traffic between the German Foreign Office and their agents in the United States and knew exactly what was being planned. His mission, in other words, was doomed from the start.

IN THE TOWER

After his arrest in Tralee Bay, Casement was taken to England, where he was confined in the Tower of London. He was still suffering from depression, which, coupled with the appalling conditions under which he was detained, caused him to attempt to take his own life with a poison that he had concealed about his person. After that episode, two soldiers were posted permanently in his cell, which only made his plight worse. From the Tower, Casement was taken daily to New Scotland Yard to be questioned by the head of the CID, Basil Thomson. He proved totally forthcoming.

> Some Irishmen are afraid to act, but I was not afraid to commit high treason. I am not endeavouring to shield myself at all. I face all the consequences. All I ask is you to believe that I have done nothing dishonourable, which you will one day learn. I have done nothing treacherous to my country. I have committed many follies in endeavouring to help my country according to what I thought was best, and in this last act of mine in going back to Ireland I came with my eyes wide open, knowing that you were bound to catch me. Knowing all the circumstances, I came from a sense of duty, in which if I dared to tell you the fact you would be the first to agree with me.[5]

Casement complained that the Germans could not understand him: 'They called me a dreamer.' He had been kept in the dark until the last moment about the date of the planned revolt. Realising all too late that it had no hope of success, he had wanted to call it off. If the first submarine provided for him had not broken down, he would have been in time to postpone the insurrection.

During these interrogations Casement acknowledged ownership of several diaries and account books that had come into the possession of the police. Three of these (for 1903, 1910 and 1911) came to be known after the colour of their binding and, inevitably, the scandalous nature of their content, as the Black Diaries. The remaining diary, also for the year 1910, came to be called the White Diary. While the contents of the White Diary were innocuous, the Black Diaries painted an extraordinary picture of a man who spent much of his days cruising the streets in search of sexual satisfaction from young men.

Following his interrogation, which took place at the same time as the Easter Rising in Dublin, Casement was transferred to civil custody and lodged in the slightly less insalubrious conditions of Brixton Prison. On 15 May he was brought before the Chief Metropolitan Stipendiary Magistrate and, after a brief hearing, committed to stand trial at the Old Bailey.

A number of sympathisers, notably his friend the author Sir Arthur Conan Doyle, contributed to Casement's legal costs. But money alone will not secure a defence. A leading nationalist solicitor, Gavan Duffy, offered to act for Casement; it was to cost him his partnership. But it is to the eternal discredit of the English Bar that no leading counsel would accept

Casement's brief. In the end, Duffy's brother-in-law, the Irish barrister Serjeant A.M. Sullivan, was prevailed upon to represent him. (Sullivan was the last person to hold the ancient title of Serjeant-at-law, the highest rank of barrister.) Sullivan's junior was Thomas Artemus Jones, already immortalised as the plaintiff in a famous libel case.[6] And a Professor J.H. Morgan was permitted to address the court as amicus curiae (or friend of the court) on the legal issues. But what defence could possibly be made to the charge of treason when the case against the prisoner seemed so open and shut?

Sullivan advised his client to make his stand on the ground that his conduct did not fall within the statutory definition of treason. Casement, unwisely judging that the British government were not 'men enough'[7] to hang him, was convinced that any death sentence would be commuted to life imprisonment. Possibly as a result of this miscalculation, he was determined to 'admit one's full responsibility and accept all the consequences'.[8] His letters give a clear picture of his state of mind. His achievement, he claimed, was to get the Germans to commit themselves to supporting the cause of Irish independence. Had he got to Dublin, the loss of life would have been much less. Such attitudes, however, would get him nowhere and Casement was eventually brought round to take his counsel's advice.

THE OLD BAILEY

Casement's trial began at the Old Bailey on 26 June 1916.[9] It took the unusual form of a trial at Bar, that is to say, a trial before a full bench (a bench of three judges) and a jury. In the chair was the Lord Chief Justice, the recently ennobled Viscount Reading, sitting with Mr Justice Avory and Mr Justice Horridge. The prosecution was led by the Attorney General, Sir Frederick Edwin Smith KC, MP, supported by the Solicitor-General and a strong legal team. (This was the same F.E. Smith who before the war had been involved in gun-running for the Ulster Volunteers in their resistance to Home Rule!) Smith's appointment gave rise to a curious professional dilemma. Though a King's Counsel in Ireland, Sullivan did not enjoy this status in England; in other words, he was of lower rank than his opponent, F.E. Smith. Smith asked the Lord Chancellor as a matter of professional courtesy to elevate his opponent to KC in order to redress the balance. Somewhat churlishly, the request was refused.

After Casement had pleaded 'not guilty', the Attorney General opened the case for the prosecution by referring to the 'very grave charge' against Casement; 'the law knows no graver'. He outlined the prisoner's career, not omitting credit for his work in Africa and Peru, and then turned to Casement's 'inexplicable' change of allegiance. He told the jury of the defendant's recruiting activities in Germany and the incriminating material, such as the military code, found upon him in Tralee Bay and poured scorn on someone who could help the King's enemy in such a manner while being the recent recipient of his country's honours. Smith concluded with a dramatic flourish: 'The prisoner, blinded by a hatred for this country, as malignant in quality as it was sudden in origin, has played a desperate hazard. He has played it and he has lost. Today the forfeit is claimed.' The prosecution had no need to call much in the way of evidence; Casement's activities in Germany were amply confirmed by a number of Irish prisoners of war whom the Germans had conveniently repatriated. It was now the turn of the defence.

'TO HANG A MAN UPON A COMMA'

Casement's defence depended upon a close reading of an ancient Act of Parliament that codified the law of treason. Translated from the original Norman French, an Act of 1351 declared it to be treason, 'if a man do levy war against our said Lord the King in his realm or be adherent to the enemies of our Lord the King in his realm giving to them aid and comfort in the realm or elsewhere . . .'.

The kernel of Sullivan's argument concerned the words 'or elsewhere'. What did they refer back to? Sullivan contended that they qualified the giving of aid and comfort to the King's enemies. If this reading was correct, it was not an offence under the Act to adhere to the King's enemies *outside* the realm, and the case against his client fell away. The prosecution on the other hand argued that the provision should be read as if it contained parentheses, thus: 'if a man do levy war against our said Lord the King in his realm or be adherent to the enemies of our Lord the King in his realm (giving to them aid and comfort in the realm) or elsewhere . . .'. If this was correct, the words in parentheses were simply an explanation of what 'adherence' consisted of. All would have been clear with punctuation, but fourteenth-century statutes did not have punctuation. Whatever the merits of the syntactical argument, there was a vast body of precedent and legal authority against Sullivan's interpretation of the law and, after extensive argument, the court ruled in accordance with authority.

But Sullivan had a second string to his bow. Until the reign of Henry VIII there had been no procedure that would have allowed a charge of adhering to the King's enemies outside the realm to be heard in an English court. It was unlikely, he argued, that the statute intended to create an offence for which no procedure existed. (In the early days of the law procedure was everything.) The court ruled against him on this too. The motion to quash the indictment having failed, Sullivan called no witnesses but instead invited his client to make an unsworn statement from the dock. (The advantage of such a statement is that it cannot be the subject of cross-examination. Sullivan was later to explain that he saw no evidence that his client could have given that would not have confirmed and enlarged the evidence against him.) Casement did not use the opportunity well.

Shortly after he had begun his closing speech for the defence, Sullivan collapsed in court from the strain of the case and his address had to be completed the following day by Artemus Jones. Essentially, the defence contended that the purpose of Casement's 'Irish Brigade' was to help the National Volunteer movement resist the Ulster Volunteers, not to assist the Germans in their war against the British.

This being a treason trial, the prosecutor had the right to the last word, and the Attorney General took full advantage of it. When he was finished, the Lord Chief Justice summed up for the jury. They should, he said, 'understand that if the prisoner knew or believed that the Irish Brigade was to be sent to Ireland during the war with a view to securing the national freedom of Ireland, that is, to engage in a civil war which would necessarily weaken and embarrass this country, then he was contriving and intending to assist the enemy'. Given the court's ruling on the law, there was really very little for the jury to decide, and it took them under an hour to return a verdict of guilty. Casement now had the right to address the court before the inevitable sentence was passed. He used it well.

THE SPEECH FROM THE DOCK

After reviewing the controversial record of the English in Ireland, Casement, now addressing a wider audience than those in court, said:

> The condemnation of English rule, of English-made law, of English government in Ireland is that it dare not rest on the will of the Irish people, but it exists in defiance of their will; that it is a rule derived not from right, but from conquest. But conquest, my lord, gives no title, and if it exists over the body, it fails over the mind. It can exert no empire over men's reason and judgement and affections; and it is from this law of conquest that I appeal . . .
>
> We had seen the working of the Irish constitution in the refusal of the army of occupation at the Curragh to obey the orders of the Crown.[10] And now we were told the first duty of an Irishman was to enter that army, in return for a promissory note payable after death – a scrap of paper that might or might not be redeemed – I felt over there in America that my first duty was to keep Irishmen at home in the only army that could safeguard our national existence . . . I saw

no reason why Ireland should shed her blood in any cause but her own, and if that be treason beyond the seas I am not ashamed to avow it or to answer it here with my life.

In a pointed reference to the Attorney General, he continued:

The difference between us was that the Unionist champions chose a path they felt would lead to the woolsack;[11] while I went down a road I knew must lead to the dock. And the event proves that we were both right. The difference between us was that my treason was based on a ruthless sincerity that forced me to attempt in time and season to carry out in action what I said in word, whereas their treason lay in verbal incitements that they knew need never be made good. And so I am prouder to stand here today in the traitor's dock to answer this impeachment than to fill the place of my right honourable accusers.

At this point, F.E. Smith got up and walked out of court with his hands in his pockets. Casement went on:

In Ireland alone in this twentieth century is loyalty held to be a crime. If loyalty be something less than love and more than law, then we have had enough of such loyalty for Ireland or Irishmen. If we are to be indicted as criminals, to be shot as murderers, to be imprisoned as convicts because our offence is that we love Ireland more than we value our lives, then I know not what virtue resides in any offer of self-government held out to brave men on such terms. Self-government is our right, a thing born in us at birth; a thing no more to be doled out to us or withheld from us by another people than the right to life itself – than the right to feel the sun or smell the flowers, or to love our kind. It is only from the convict these things are withheld for crimes committed and proven – and Ireland, that has wronged no man, that has injured no land, that has sought no dominion over others – Ireland is treated today among the nations of the world as if she was a convicted criminal.

If it be treason to fight against such an unnatural fate as this, then I am proud to be a rebel, and shall cling to my 'rebellion' with the last drop of my blood. If there be no right of rebellion against a state of things that no savage tribe would endure without resistance, then I am sure that it is better for men to fight and die without right than to live in such a state of right as this. Where all your rights become only an accumulated wrong; where men must beg with bated breath for leave to subsist in their own land, to think their own thoughts, to sing their own songs, to garner the fruits of their own labours – and, even while they beg, to see things inexorably withdrawn from them then, surely, it is braver, a saner and a truer thing, to be a rebel in act and deed against such circumstances as these than tamely to accept it as the natural lot of men . . .

This speech was later to be described by the English poet Wilfred Blunt as 'the finest document in patriotic history'. But no amount of eloquence can alter a mandatory sentence. The black caps were placed on the heads of the judges and the ancient formula of the death sentence pronounced, Mr Justice Avory adding, 'Amen'. The trial was over; minutes later, Casement's place in the dock was taken by Private Bailey. No evidence being offered against him, he was duly discharged.

APPEAL

Casement's appeal against conviction was heard by the Court of Criminal Appeal on 17 July. It was a strong court chaired by the redoubtable Mr Justice Darling.

Sullivan rehearsed once again the arguments he had deployed in the Old Bailey and added fresh ones based on the history and development of the law, but, to his client's annoyance, he failed to argue the wider political issues that Casement desperately wanted to ventilate. (Though he has been criticised for this omission, such arguments would have carried no weight in court.) It was all in vain. After indicating to the Attorney General that he need not bother to reply, Darling ruled against the prisoner. Giving the judgment of the court, Darling confirmed that the words 'giving aid and comfort to the King's enemies' in the old statute simply explained what was meant by being 'adherent to'. A subject, the Court held, 'is the King's liege wherever he may be'.

Earlier in the course of argument the judges had revealed that two of them had inspected the original statute rolls at the Public Record Office and were persuaded that the Act of 1351 could not bear the interpretation that the defence had placed upon it. The break in the roll at a critical point was the result of a fold and not the mark of a pen. Casement was later to write to a friend that it was as if 'to hang a man's life upon a comma, and throttle him with a semi-colon',[12] but this was a distortion of the truth; it was the prisoner's defence that sought to place a fanciful significance on a well-understood text.

There was one final avenue open to Casement. A convicted man could appeal from the Court of Criminal Appeal to the House of Lords, but only if it could be shown that a point of law of general public importance was involved. This required the fiat (approval) of the Attorney General; it was refused. The defence immediately obtained the opinion of two constitutional lawyers, one of them the respected Sir William Holdsworth, author of the classic *History of English Law*, to the effect that the defence arguments were anything but trivial. Refusing to change his mind, Smith is said to have remarked with characteristic lack of modesty: 'I am well acquainted with the legal attainments of Sir William Holdsworth. He was, after all, runner up to me in the Vinerian prize when we were at Oxford.'[13]

CLEMENCY REFUSED

Powerful voices were raised in favour of clemency for Casement, including that of the Foreign Secretary Sir Edward Grey. A petition organised by Conan Doyle was signed, among others, by John Galsworthy, G.K. Chesterton and Arnold Bennett. (Conrad refused to sign.) With his usual insight into Irish affairs, George Bernard Shaw argued that hanging would only create a martyr.

The Cabinet now asked the Home Office legal adviser, Sir Ernley Blackwell, to provide it with a memorandum on the question of Casement's sanity. It was not the first time that this issue had arisen. Casement was known to have a history of mental breakdowns, and two of his three siblings were of a fragile temperament. In 1914 Conan Doyle, who, it will be recalled, was a doctor as well as a writer, had written of his friend: 'His actions for the last two years can only be explained on the ground of insanity.' He described Casement as 'a sick man . . . worn by tropical hardships, [who] complained of pains in his head'. And in his autobiography he was to paint him as 'a fine man afflicted with mania'.[14]

Casement's state of mind had also been discussed among counsel at his trial. At the beginning of June 1916 Travers Humphreys, one of the junior counsel for the Crown, had handed a typed copy of the Black Diaries to Artemus Jones, together with a message to the effect that it had occurred to F.E. Smith that they might support a plea of 'guilty but insane'. Serjeant Sullivan had refused even to read the documents on the ground that the defendant would not be pleading insanity. He was later to explain why he had taken the ethically dubious course of giving his client no choice in this matter: 'I finally decided that death was better than besmirching and dishonour.' Immediately after the trial Sullivan wrote to Smith thanking him for having put the diaries at his disposal. 'In view of our defence it was right that they should be available for any information.' He was later to describe his client as a megalomaniac.

It is difficult to understand how any lawyer could have believed that the defence of insanity had any chance of success in Casement's case. Under the law at the time, a plea of insanity could succeed only if the prisoner could be shown to have been 'labouring under such a defect of reason, from disease of the mind, as not to know the nature and quality of the act he was doing, or, if he did know it, that he did not know that what he was doing was wrong'. It would have been difficult, with or without the diaries, to argue that Casement had suffered from either of these mental states. Others took a different view. The content of the diaries was beyond their experience or comprehension; the nature and frequency of the sexual encounters described seemed to them incredible, something that could only come from the pen of a mind lost in fantasy. The Home Office legal adviser thought otherwise. He observed that the entries in the Black Diary had been made at the same time as Casement's competent reports to the Foreign Office and that his lucid performance in court had not been that of a disturbed man.

The Cabinet discussed the issue of clemency three times. The Permanent Under Secretary at the Home Office pointed to the anomaly that would arise if Casement, 'a Protestant, an ex-official and a member of the "ascendancy class"' were to be let off the extreme penalty while Catholic nationalists were executed out of hand. The Secretary to the Cabinet wrote: 'So far as I can judge, it would be far wiser from every point of view to allow the law to take its course, and by judicious means to use these diaries to prevent Casement attaining martyrdom.'[15] And this is what appears to have been done, though whether with the Cabinet's approval or not we do not know. Extracts from the diaries were now touted around among influential people. At a time when homosexuality was considered, not merely unlawful but degenerate, the picture that the diaries painted of a particularly predatory homosexual did away with any last vestiges of sympathy for Casement. Many, even those who had campaigned for Congo reform, now abandoned him; which was exactly the effect the government had hoped for.

The government's official reasons for refusing clemency were set out in an official statement put out after the execution. It read:

> The Irish rebellion resulted in much loss of life, both among soldiers and civilians; Casement invoked and organized German assistance to the insurrection. In addition, though himself for many years a British official, he undertook the task of trying to induce soldiers of the British Army, prisoners in the hands of Germany, to forswear their oath of allegiance and join their country's enemies. Conclusive evidence has come into the hands of the Government since the trial that he had entered into an agreement with the German Government which explicitly provided that the brigade, which he was trying to raise from among the Irish soldier prisoners, might be employed in Egypt against the British Crown. Those among the Irish soldiers, prisoners in Germany, who resisted Casement's solicitations of disloyalty were subjected to treatment of exceptional cruelty by the Germans; some of them have since been exchanged as invalids and have died in this country, regarding Casement as their murderer.[16]

The reference to 'conclusive evidence' referred to the fact that at the end of the trial Casement had inadvertently left in court a bundle of papers that had found its way into the hands of the authorities. One of these was a copy of an agreement of December 1914 between Casement and the German government by which his 'Irish Brigade' could have been used to support a revolt against British rule in Egypt. Worse, the file contained a note in Casement's handwriting that read: 'There is enough in these papers to hang me ten times over. If I had been thirty-three instead of fifty-three, the arms would have been landed, the code would not have been found, and I should have freed Ireland, or died fighting at the head of my men.'

The final argument for letting the law take its course, however, may have been none of these, but the execution by the Germans only days before the date set for Casement's execution of the captain of a British ferry that had attempted to ram a German submarine.

THE FIRST COMMUNION

At the end, Casement, now stripped of all earthly honours, converted to Catholicism and received his first – and last – communion in the condemned cell at Pentonville Prison. On 3 August 1916 he was hanged, the last of the Easter Rising leaders to be executed. The executioner, Albert Ellis, was to recall that he 'appeared to me the bravest man it fell to my unhappy lot to execute'.[17] In 1965 the then British Prime Minister, Harold Wilson, returned what were believed to be Casement's remains to Ireland. After a state funeral attended by well over half a million people they were reinterred in Glasnevin Cemetery in Dublin.

WAS JUSTICE DONE?

A strong Court of Criminal Appeal found nothing to criticise in Lord Reading's conduct of the trial. The defence counsel, Professor Morgan, while criticising the release of the diaries, described the court proceedings as 'worthy of the best traditions of English justice'. The Lord Chancellor's refusal to make Sullivan an English silk is the sort of nicety that keeps barristers awake at night, but it had absolutely no effect on the trial. The same was true of the shameful failure of the English Bar to provide a suitable leader for Casement's defence.

The poet Alfred Noyes complained that the Attorney General 'hated Casement as his political enemy'. Smith, he suggested, had 'appointed himself prosecutor' and by refusing leave to appeal had 'personally pronounced sentence of death upon a man more chivalrous than himself'.

That may be so, but no one has proved that F.E. Smith conducted the prosecution with anything but scrupulous propriety. He has been criticised for walking out of court during Casement's speech from the dock, but this gesture, which amounted to no more than a discourtesy, was made in reaction to a personal attack by the prisoner from the dock. More seriously, he has been criticised as someone whose gun running was in no way different from Casement's. But, however reprehensible Smith's conduct, it was not designed to give support to the King's enemies. In any event, the Attorney's actions in Ireland had absolutely no effect on the trial. There were, however, two matters that cast a shadow over the proceedings, both of them involving F.E. Smith.

We would find it inconceivable today that a leader of the Ulster Volunteer Force could ever be deemed a suitable person to prosecute a leader of the Irish Republican Army, yet this would be almost exactly what happened in Casement's case. While it was the practice for the Attorney General to undertake personally the prosecution of the most significant criminal cases, there was no legal requirement for him to do so, and in a case such as this the Attorney should have stood down. Smith could easily have requested another law officer, or indeed any other member of the Bar, to prosecute the case on his behalf. Although he was no doubt sure in his own mind that he could do the job impartially, Smith's character was such that standing down for the sake of appearances would never have occurred to him. But the fact that he did not abuse his position does not detract from the unease with which many people then, and since, regarded his dual role.

And there is the question of the Attorney's fiat. It is quite unacceptable that the power to deny the accused the right to a final appeal should reside in the lawyer who also happens to be the prosecutor, as subsequent changes in the law have recognised. It has been suggested that Smith should have granted his fiat whatever he thought of the merits of the case, but to have done so would have been the easy way out, and someone like Smith would never have adopted the easy way out, whatever the world might have thought. Legal opinion has not seriously questioned the correctness of the Court of Criminal Appeal's decision; the fault in this respect lay, not with the actual decision taken, but in the conflict of roles with which the office of Attorney was then encumbered.

THE LEAKING OF THE DIARIES

The most contentious act associated with this case, however, was undoubtedly the leaking of the Black Diaries. After Casement's death *The Times* newspaper, while endorsing the decision to let the sentence take its course, protested against the 'irrelevant, improper and un-English campaign of inspired innuendo' that had followed him to the gallows.

What appears to have happened was that a Captain 'Blinker' Hall, head of Naval intelligence, who had assisted Basil Thomson in Casement's interrogations, summoned a number of English and American journalists to the Admiralty, at about the time of the committal hearing, where he showed them photographic copies of extracts from the Black Diaries. It is possible that he did so on his own initiative and without the knowledge of the prosecution. On the last day of the trial F.E. Smith wrote to the Foreign Secretary saying:

> I am told that the FO [Foreign Office] is photographing or proposes to photograph portions of Casement's diary with a view to showing them to various persons so as to influence opinion. It is I think rather a ghoulish proposal and without expressing a final opinion on it I should be glad if you would see me before sanctioning it.

Grey replied that he had not heard of such a proposal, did not approve it and certainly would not sanction it without the authorisation of the Cabinet, which he considered improbable. If disclosure did take place prior to Casement's conviction, it is difficult to see what the authorities would have hoped to gain from it. The act would have been a serious contempt of court, putting the discloser at risk of a stiff prison term. It could even have resulted in a mistrial, thus frustrating the object of the exercise. Whatever happened, there is no reason to believe that any juror was influenced by – or even became aware of – the contents of the diaries before the conviction.

The Cabinet decision to use the diaries *after* the trial to block a possible reprieve was an altogether different matter; it was an act of state for which any country fighting for its existence might be forgiven. In any event, it could not have interfered with a trial that had already been concluded. Naval intelligence no doubt had its reasons for doing what it did, and they are not hard to guess. England was engaged in the bloodiest war of its history. Two days after Casement was sentenced to death the British army suffered some 60,000 casualties on the first day of the battle of the Somme, 20,000 of them fatalities. Many of the soldiers were Irishmen.

In summary, therefore, while there were features of Casement's trial that were unsatisfactory, none of them seems to have affected the result. It would have been unrealistic to expect anyone committing Casement's undeniably treasonable acts at the height of Britain's bloodiest war to have got away unscathed. For all his talk of lawyers' disputes about words, Casement was guilty of the most blatant treason, and he knew it. In the end, justice was done.

The 'revelation' of Casement's homosexuality had come as no surprise to those in the know; for years, rumours had been circulating about him. In those days, homosexuality was tolerated among polite society so long as it was neither flagrant nor acknowledged. Where these rules were broken, the consequences were dire. In the year that Casement took up his first consular appointment, the poet and dramatist Oscar Wilde was sentenced to two years' hard labour for acts of gross indecency (which is how the law describes homosexual acts short of buggery). And, when Casement began his investigations in the Congo, the British military hero Major-General Sir Hector Macdonald chose to shoot himself in a Paris hotel room rather than undergo a court martial for similar conduct. Casement's diaries testify to the fact that Macdonald's tragedy weighed heavily on his mind. He could have had no illusions as to what was likely to happen to him if his own sexual inclinations were exposed.

When the Black Diaries first came to light no one had any doubts about their authenticity. John Harris was a friend of Casement's in the Anti-Slavery Society who was at first suspicious. When the diaries were shown to him he was shaken to discover facts known only to Casement and himself. Following the Irish settlement discussions in 1921, F.E. Smith showed one of the diaries to the Sinn Fein delegates Michael Collins and Eamonn Duggan. Senator Duggan later recorded that 'Michael Collins and I saw the Casement Diary by arrangement with Birkenhead. We read it. I did not know Casement's handwriting. Collins did. He said it was his . . . It was disgusting . . . Collins was satisfied that it was Casement's.'[18]

After Casement's death an examination of the body by the medical officer at Pentonville Prison revealed dilation of the anus and the lower bowel. Nevertheless, there were among Casement's friends and supporters many who refused to believe that a man who had done so much good for mankind could at the same time have been a homosexual, and a promiscuous homosexual at that. The diaries were a put-up job, a diabolical name-blackening by the British establishment. These suspicions were strengthened by the fact that Basil Thomson had at different times given differing accounts as to how the diaries had come into his possession. (In fact, what appears to have happened is that Casement deposited the diaries with a Mr Germain of Ebury Street in May 1914, and in April 1916 Germain had brought them voluntarily to New Scotland Yard, where they had lain unexamined in Special Branch.) The conspiracy theorists' suspicions were strengthened by the fact that the Black Diaries were kept under wraps in the Public Record Office until 1959. The reason for this, however, was more likely to have been English prudery than any desire to conceal a dark and sinister secret.

The first direct assault on the integrity of the Black Diaries was made by an American, William J. Maloney, MD in his 1936 book *The Forged Casement Black Diaries* – a title that rather takes the surprise out of the book's conclusions. In it he argued that the diaries were created by the British government from a (heterosexual) diary kept by one of the section chiefs in Putamayo. The author's case, if it can be dignified with that term, was not helped by the fact that he had neither read nor even seen the diaries. George Bernard Shaw pertinently wrote of the book that it 'takes more trouble to put the British government in the wrong than to put Roger in the right'. Nevertheless, others were to jump on the bandwagon.

In 1957, shortly before his death, Alfred Noyes, who had originally denounced Casement on the basis of the Black Diaries, was moved to change his views. The outcome was his book *The Accusing Ghost, or Justice for Roger Casement*, which accepted the diaries as genuine except for the homosexual entries. These, he suggested, had been inserted by the police and the Attorney General, though he failed to explain how such a masterly and extensive forgery could have been made in the time available.

The following year the Home Secretary, R.A. ('Rab') Butler, set up a working party under Dr Wilson Harrison of the South Wales Forensic Science Laboratory to look into the authenticity of the diaries. On the basis of handwriting comparisons, Dr Harrison concluded that the diaries were in Casement's hand, but that some of the material had been interpolated by the author at a later date. In 1994 Dr David Baxendale was asked to examine the diaries for the BBC and came to a similar conclusion. But the controversy would not go away and in 1997 Angus Mitchell, an Amazonian expert and editor for publication of Casement's White Diary, advanced the view that the Black Diaries were 'riddled with inaccuracies and inconsistencies'.[19]

Most recently, Professor Bill McCormack of Goldsmiths College, London, with financial backing from RTE (the Irish television service), the BBC and the Irish government, commissioned an examination of the diaries by Dr Audrey Giles, formerly of the Questioned Documents Section of New Scotland Yard.[20] In March 2002 it was announced that

> The unequivocal and confident conclusion which the Giles Document Laboratory has reached is that each of the five documents collectively known as the Black Diaries is exclusively the work of Roger Casement's hand, without any reason to suspect either forgery or interpolation by any other hand. The Diaries are genuine throughout and in each instance. This investigation, based on impartial scientific analysis, should bring to an end more than 80 years of controversy.

If only it were that simple. Whatever the truth about the Black Diaries, it is a sad commentary on public opinion that so many even today refuse to believe that a such a noble humanitarian and patriot could at the same time be a homosexual.

CASEMENT THE MAN

Sexuality apart, how did it come about that a man who had ruined his health in the service of mankind came to betray the country to which he owed allegiance? Sir Arthur Conan Doyle, a long-time friend and admirer, once described Casement as 'a man of the highest character, truthful, unselfish – one who is deeply respected by all who know him'. A similar view was recorded in 1890 by another famous author, Joseph Conrad, with whom Casement had shared rooms: 'Thinks well, speaks well, most intelligent and sympathetic.' Seven years later he was to shade this assessment somewhat:

> He was a good companion; but already in Africa I judged that he was a man, properly speaking, of no mind at all. I don't mean stupid. I mean that he was all emotion. By emotional force (Congo report, Putumayo, etc.) he made his way, and sheer temperament – a truly tragic personality: all but the greatness of which he had not a trace. Only vanity. But in the Congo it was not visible yet.

F.E. Smith was right to draw attention to Casement's apparent hypocrisy in the matter of honours. Explaining his position to Basil Thomson, Casement said:

> I went abroad and what morally and intellectually brought me back here to Ireland were two things – the Boer war in which I took part, and the Congo. I started in the Boer war feeling that I was doing the right thing, but I felt shame on myself afterwards going against those people. I have a medal for the Boer war but I never wore it. I refused to be invested with the CMG that you offered me for my work in the Congo.[21]

Thomson interrupted to say, 'You could have refused the decorations altogether.' Casement replied, 'Only by retiring from the Service altogether, and that I could not afford to do.' He was to give an altogether different explanation as to why, some six years later, he had accepted his knighthood in terms that can only be described as courtier-like. In a letter to Sir Edward Grey Casement had written that he was 'grateful for this signal assurance of your personal esteem and support' and that he was 'deeply sensible of the honour done to [him] by His Majesty': the honour was deeply appreciated.

Much later Casement was to excuse himself to his solicitor as follows:

> Had I been asked beforehand I would certainly have refused. Once I was publicly announced as a knight it was impossible without giving *great offence* to King, Grey, the public etc., etc., to refuse the honour thrust unsolicited on me [emphasis in the original]. Had I done so I should have been forced to resign my post also, and at the same time to abandon the cause of the Putumayo natives. This last weighed with me too. So I was bound to swallow the knighthood, and that being a

necessity the terms in which I acknowledged it are really beside the question.

It is nevertheless difficult to understand why someone who would shortly be plotting treason with the King's enemies should be so sensitive about the feelings of the British establishment that he should feel compelled to accept in such fulsome terms an honour that he so shortly after professed to scorn.

It has frequently been observed that Casement was emotionally riven in more ways than most. Brought up a Protestant, he was secretly baptised a Catholic; an out and out homosexual, he had to hide his sexual proclivities in an age in which the only acceptable alternative to heterosexuality was celibacy; a diligent servant of the Crown, he had secretly turned to treason. None of this, of course, explains Casement's promiscuous attitude towards young men and boys.

However hotheaded and vainglorious he may have been, Casement was deeply affected by human suffering, of which he had seen more than most. In his middle years he had formed a connection in his mind between colonial exploitation, of which Britain had not been guiltless, and British rule in Ireland, which he came to see as the principal cause of Irish suffering. Elements deep within his character and life experience, which we may never fully understand, led him to opt for a violent rather than a constitutional solution.

AND THE CONSEQUENCES?

Contrary to nationalist myth, the Easter Rising did not have wide support in Ireland; when they surrendered, some of the rebels actually had to be protected from hostile crowds by the British army. As a military operation the rising was a botched job that had no realistic prospect of success. But the way the British dealt with it in the execution sheds of Dublin and London was a terrible blunder that changed the course of history. Home Rule was no longer enough; only independence would do. And so it came to pass; instead of a self-governing Province that could have evolved peacefully into an independent state, we were left with a divided Ireland and a truncated Province that remains to this day a hotbed of religious and political hatreds that may or may not only now be dying down. Casement must bear a part of the blame for this. What might he have achieved if, instead of supporting violence, he had used his great name to promote peaceful reform?

CHAPTER THREE

The Broadcaster

The Trial of William Joyce, 1946

All German armed forces in Northern Europe surrendered to Field Marshal Montgomery on 4 May 1945. A fortnight later Captain Lickorish of the British Reconnaissance Regiment and Lieutenant Perry, an interpreter, were gathering wood on a hill outside Flensburg near the Danish–German border when they overtook a limping man. The man pointed to some wood and said, first in French and then in English, 'Here are a few more good pieces.' Perry and the stranger spoke for a few minutes 'about coniferous and deciduous trees'. Thinking that he recognised the man's voice, Perry said, 'You wouldn't happen to be William Joyce, would you?' Joyce reached into his pocket for his passport, but before he could get it out Perry, thinking he was about to produce a weapon, drew and fired his revolver. The bullet went through Joyce's right thigh and left leg. As he fell to the ground he cried out, 'My name is Fritz Hansen.' When searched, Joyce was found to be carrying two documents, one identifying him as a teacher, Wilhelm (sic) Hansen, and the other as William Joyce. The wounded man was brought to England on a stretcher and on 18 June appeared at Bow Street magistrates' court charged with high treason.

So ended the controversial career of the most famous of the Nazi apologists, popularly known as Lord Haw-Haw. His trial was to prove every bit as controversial as his life.

Perhaps the most surprising fact about the quintessentially English traitor William Joyce is that he was an American. His father was Michael Francis Joyce, an Irishman from County Mayo at a time when that territory was part of the United Kingdom. Michael had emigrated to America and in 1894 had been naturalised as an American citizen, renouncing his British nationality. In 1905 he married an Englishwoman, Gertrude Emily Brooke. Their first child, William, was born on 24 April 1906 in Brooklyn, New York, making him an American citizen. Three years later the family moved back to Ireland, settling first in County Mayo and then in Galway. (It has been suggested that they may have felt themselves driven out of New York by the more recent Jewish immigrants.)[1] William was enrolled in a convent school and, later, at a Jesuit college, where he proved to be a bright, if somewhat odd, pupil. He was asked to leave, however, when, at the age of fifteen, he threatened a fellow pupil with a gun.

The Joyce family, though American by nationality, were fierce supporters of the British Crown at a time when Irishmen were increasingly resentful of its suzerainty over their island. With the creation in 1921 of the Irish Free State, the Joyces found themselves living under what they would have regarded as foreign occupation. Michael had owned a house that he let to the Black and Tans, an auxiliary British force with a fearsome reputation for brutality. It was not a popular move; the house was burned down by the nationalists and Michael's business was attacked. The young William was later to claim that during this period he had helped the police in counter-terrorist activities, but it seems likely that this consisted of little more than hanging around the soldiers. A threat by the Irish Republican Army (IRA) to William's life was enough for his father to send the boy out of the country. At the age of fifteen he left for England on his own, staying with relatives in the depressed northern town of Oldham.

The following year the rest of his family came to Britain, his father eventually setting up a small grocery shop in Clapham, south London. As an alien, Michael should have registered with the police; instead, he tore up his American passport and encouraged his family to pose as English. It has been speculated that this may have been due to something in Michael's Irish past; we will probably never know the truth. However that may be, the father's deception was to play a significant part in his son's tragedy.

Just under average height and strongly built, William excelled at boxing, swimming and fencing. These interests and a fascination with the military led him in 1921 to join the Royal Worcester Regiment, but he was swiftly discharged when discovered to be under age. The following year he applied to join the University of London Officer Training Corps (OTC), membership of which was restricted to British subjects of pure European descent. Joyce's father wrote to the War Office: '[My son] was born in America. I was born in Ireland. His mother was born in England,' adding untruthfully, 'We are all British and not American citizens.' Explaining his wish to obtain a regular commission, William grandiloquently declared, 'I am prepared to draw the sword in British interests.' He was duly enrolled in the OTC, in which he served until 1926.

Strange as it may seem for someone who was later to espouse one of the most vacuous political philosophies of his age, William Joyce was no slouch academically. After matriculating in 1922 he enrolled at Battersea Polytechnic to study science. The following year he transferred to Birkbeck College to read English and History, graduating in 1927 with first-class honours. The following year he took a one-year postgraduate course in philology and from 1931 to 1933 he studied educational psychology at King's College, London. But all this was in the future.

NOT THE ENGLAND OF HIS DREAMS

The England that William Joyce discovered in the 1920s did not live up to the image he had formed of it in Ireland. The British Empire was in decline abroad and at home the poor lived in slums. Conventional politics seemed to offer no solution and the postwar years saw many of the liveliest minds turn to extreme solutions, notably communism and fascism. In 1923 at the age of seventeen William was attracted to the British Fascisti, a 'King and country' movement modelled on an Italian counterpart, though he never actually became a member of the organisation. Later, in what appear to have been attempts at acquiring respectability in his chosen country, Joyce joined the Conservative Party and applied to join the Foreign Office; he was rejected by both. Despite being a powerful speaker, William proved unpopular among the Conservatives and was forced to resign, ostensibly on the ground of his affair with a young woman. And the Foreign Office rejected him as 'not being one of us'. Both experiences left deep marks on William, one of them physical. While acting as a steward at a Conservative Party meeting in Lambeth he was attacked and received a razor cut that left him with a lifelong scar running from his right ear to the corner of his mouth. Joyce blamed the assault on 'Jewish Communists', despite the fact that the Tory candidate he was defending was a Jew.

In 1933 the now disillusioned Joyce turned to the recently formed British Union of Fascists (BUF) led by the former Labour Cabinet minister Sir Oswald Mosley. He quickly established himself as a witty and powerful, if vitriolic, public speaker. (On one occasion when heckled by a middle-aged woman who shouted, 'You bastard!' he shouted back, 'Hello, mother!') After his appointment to the paid post of BUF Director of Propaganda, Joyce gave up his postgraduate studies. In December 1934 he was charged at Worthing with riotous assembly along with Mosley and others, but acquitted. Other charges followed in 1938 and 1939, but Joyce eventually broke with Mosley on the subject of the Jews.

Anti-Semitism had always been endemic throughout Europe and the disease was rampant in 1930s Germany. In England discrimination took a less overt form, but Jews were widely regarded with distrust. The more paranoid suspected them of being part of a worldwide capitalist conspiracy, but also of financing international Bolshevism (a paradox that does not seem to have bothered them unduly). There was even a suggestion that the Jews were behind the Irish rebellion. But, as anti-German sentiment grew, the BUF began to turn its (official) policies away from anti-Semitism towards opposition to what was now seen by many as the coming war. However, and for reasons that are not entirely clear, by 1937 Joyce had developed an implacable hatred for the Jews that did not fit with the new party line. Declining support for the BUF and the consequent loss of income gave their leader an excuse to dismiss his

Director of Propaganda. Along with some sixty former members of the BUF, Joyce now formed his own political organisation, the British National Socialist League, whose name clearly echoed that of the German Nazi Party.

Joyce's love life was seldom stable for long. As soon as he came of age in 1927 he married his first wife, Hazel Kathleen Barr, by whom he was to have two daughters. They were divorced in 1936 on the grounds of his adultery, Hazel taking the children with her. Three days after the divorce was finalised he remarried. His new wife, Margaret Cairns White, an extrovert Lancashire girl and former nightclub dancer, became Assistant Treasurer to the League. Joyce, now funded it seems from Berlin, moved to an expensive flat in South Kensington from where he set up a fascist news sheet called the *Helmsman*. At his party's often violent street-corner meetings Joyce did not conceal his admiration for Adolf Hitler; it was not a popular stance. Support fell away, the party ran into debt and Joyce began to drink heavily. There seemed to be only one place to which he could turn.

THE FLIGHT TO GERMANY

In 1933 Joyce had applied for a British passport 'for the purpose of holiday touring' in Europe, describing himself on the application form – untruthfully – as a British subject by birth, 'having been born at Rutledge Terrace, Galway, Ireland'. He was granted a five-year passport, but the proposed trip never took place. In 1938 at the height of the Sudeten crisis Joyce applied for renewal of the passport, repeating the untruth: 'I declare that I am a British subject by birth, and I have not lost that national status and that the whole of the particulars given by me in respect of this application are true.' On 24 August 1939 with war imminent he took the fateful step of renewing his passport for a further year and at the same time dissolved the British National Socialist League.

Two days later Joyce and his wife fled to Berlin. His sister claimed to have received a tip-off from someone in MI5 (the British counter-intelligence agency) that in the event of war he would be interned for the duration. It is likely this was true, because Joyce was known to have passed information about communists to the security service. Friends in Germany put Joyce in contact with the Foreign Ministry, which in turn passed him on to the *Reichsrundfunk* (German Broadcasting Service) with a view to finding a job. Joyce read his first news bulletin for them on 6 September 1939, only three days after Britain had declared war on Germany. On the 18th he received a formal contract as editor and speaker for the German transmitters for Europe in Charlottenburg, Berlin. Later, he was given an editorial slot of his own entitled 'Views on the News'. It was through these broadcasts that Joyce's name, or at least his sobriquet 'Lord Haw-Haw', became notorious in England.

'GERMANY CALLING'

Joyce was not the original 'Lord Haw-Haw', but he was by far the most successful. Before Joyce, German radio had broadcast fictitious dialogues between an 'Englishman', Smith (played by Wolff Mitler, a German national) and a 'German', Schmidt. Their 'conversations' were cringingly unconvincing to British listeners because of 'Smith's' caricature of an upper-class English accent. An academic had once criticised BBC announcers for being too 'haw, haw' in their diction; the term came to be applied to Mitler and, later, to Joyce. In fact, Joyce's accent was far from upper class. He spoke in a slightly nasal monotone, caused by a nose broken in a school fight with a boy who had called him an Orangeman (a Protestant supporter of the union with Britain).

It was not until August 1940 that the BBC Monitoring Service definitely identified Joyce as the English-speaking voice of German radio. The content of his broadcasts was by no means as contemptible as the British press liked to make out. He cleverly played on his listeners' fears of a militarily superior Germany – all too real in 1940 – and of anti-profiteering sentiment, which was in part anti-Semitic in origin. He often scooped the cautious and somewhat stuffy BBC by being the first to report war news, at least news favourable to the Germans, of which at that time there was a great deal. He was sometimes even able to inform his English listeners that their soldier sons were not dead but prisoners of the Germans. Many of the stories about Lord Haw-Haw have proved apocryphal – such as his having reported that the town clock in Darlington was two minutes slow – but the fact that they were in circulation in England is testimony to the influence of his broadcasts. The following extract from one of them gives a taste of his style.

> There are times when it is unchivalrous to disparage an opponent, and there are times when it is definitely unwise, but it is not possible to view otherwise than with contempt the conceptions of fighting that Britain has shown in this war . . .
>
> First of all it was expected that after all the mighty threats and all the angry gestures of her politicians, real and instant action would be taken to help Poland. Downing Street gave her a few drums of mustard gas, and the false assurance that 1,500 planes were on the way to help her. And there the British contribution ended.
>
> Then the Norwegian government received every assurance, holy and unholy, that Norway would be defended to the last British Tommy, and, relying on this assurance, committed its country to a

very foolish course of action. Three weeks sufficed to chase the British Expeditionary Force out of Norway into the sea . . .

Next came the campaign in Holland and Belgium . . . Of these two states that were to be used as a base of attack against the Ruhr, one surrendered in five days, and the other in eighteen. What was England's contribution? An expeditionary force that carried out a glorious retreat, leaving all its equipment and arms behind, a force whose survivors arrived back in Britain, as *The Times* admits, practically naked.

There was enough truth in broadcasts like this to make the British government uneasy. But Joyce's broadcasts were not confined to military matters. He struck a chord with many listeners when he compared the slums and beggars of England with the full employment and sophisticated health services of Germany. Such comments were not merely propaganda but also manifestations of the idealism, however misplaced, that had driven Joyce into politics.

Early in 1940, at the request of the German Foreign Office, Joyce wrote a short book entitled *Twilight over England.* It consisted largely of a diatribe against Jewish influence in Britain and of its consequential decadence and decline. When Hitler called off his planned invasion of England, the book's only circulation was to British prisoners of war; they gave it short shrift. In September of that year Joyce and his wife were granted German citizenship. This had the effect of making Joyce someone entitled to both German and American nationality (but not, of course, British). In April 1941, following the German invasion of Russia, Joyce dropped his anonymity and began broadcasting under his own name, including himself for the first time in the phrase 'We Germans'.

Joyce's father died in London in 1941. At what must have been a time of great stress Margaret began sleeping around and the couple divorced. To the surprise of their friends, however, they got together again almost immediately and in February 1942 remarried. A few months later Joyce was appointed chief commentator in the English editorial department of German Broadcasting Stations for Europe at a monthly salary of 1,200 Reichsmarks. Was he worth it to the Germans?

It is difficult to know exactly what influence Joyce and his fellow broadcasters had on British opinion. According to a BBC survey conducted at the beginning of 1940, about one in six adults in Britain, or six million people, listened regularly to German radio, and many more did so occasionally. They tended to be people interested in public affairs, and a thirst for news may have been as important a reason for tuning in as curiosity. Listening 'shrank to insignificant proportions' as soon as the phoney war period was over and the shooting war began. The British reaction now became one of mocking amusement. From that time on, though he continued to work hard for his employers, Lord Haw-Haw's glory days were over.

THE LAST BROADCAST

With the war patently drawing to a close in September 1944, Joyce was awarded the War Service Cross, 1st Class, by his Führer. By this date, Paris had been lost to the Allies and a second front had opened in southern France. As the military situation deteriorated Joyce volunteered for the *Volkssturm*, a form of German Home Guard, swearing to fight to the death. In November he was issued with another German passport, this time in the name of Wilhelm Hansen, a member of the *Volkssturm* born in Galway. Once again, he began drinking heavily.

With the Red Army approaching Berlin, Dr Goebbels, the Nazi propaganda chief, ordered that the Joyces 'should at all cost be kept out of Allied hands'. William Joyce burned his *Volkssturm* uniform and moved to Hamburg, where on 30 April 1945 he made what proved to be his final broadcast, warning his listeners, not entirely without justification, of the Red menace. Audibly affected by drink, Joyce ended his transmission with the words: 'You may not hear from me again for a few months. I say, *Es lebe Deutschland!* [Long live Germany!] *Heil Hitler*, and farewell.' The following month saw his fateful encounter with the British officers at Flensburg.

THE OLD BAILEY

Joyce's trial opened at the Old Bailey in July 1945 before Mr Justice Tucker.[2] It was immediately postponed at the request of the defence in order to allow evidence of Joyce's nationality to be obtained from America. The court reconvened in mid-September.

As was usual in such cases, the Attorney General, Sir Hartley Shawcross KC, acted for the Crown. G.O. Slade KC and Derek Curtis-Bennett KC were for the accused. The author Rebecca West, who was present at the trial, left this impression of Joyce's appearance in court:

His voice had suggested large and flashy handsomeness, but he was a tiny little creature and not handsome at all. His hair was mouse-coloured and sparse, particularly above the ears, and his pinched and misshapen nose was joined to his face at an odd angle. His eyes were hard and shiny and above them his thick eyebrows were pale and irregular. His neck was long, his shoulders narrow and sloping, his arms very short and thick. His body looked flimsy and coarse.[3]

The enquiries in America had revealed that Joyce had never been a British subject, and the judge directed that he should be acquitted upon the first two charges (which alleged that he had committed treason while a British subject). The remaining count, upon which he was ultimately convicted, alleged that Joyce,

> not being a British subject but being a person owing allegiance to the Crown, was guilty of high treason by adhering to the King's enemies elsewhere than in the King's realm, namely in Germany, between 18 September 1939, and 2 July 1940,[4] by broadcasting to the King's subjects propaganda on behalf of the enemies, contrary to the Treason Act, 1351.

There was no disputing that Joyce had broadcast for the enemy; the only issue was whether, when he did so, he was a person owing allegiance to the Crown. The Attorney General rested his case on the principle that allegiance was based on the protection of the Crown. Citing the opinion of the noted eighteenth-century jurist Blackstone, as well as precedent in cases going back as far as the seventeenth century, the Attorney summed up his position thus:

> It is unthinkable that a person who has apparently been domiciled in this country, who has the whole of his family living in this country, and who leaves the whole of his family, his relatives, his father and mother and sister and brothers, with the exception of his wife, in this country, who has secured from this country the substantial matter of protection that the issue of a passport involves, who has secured the right to return to this country at any time as a British subject, who has declared himself to be a British subject, who uses the passport and travels on it as a British subject, even perhaps, in this case, secures employment on it – it is in my submission, unthinkable that such a person should not at the corresponding date owe allegiance to the Crown.

The defence made two quite separate submissions. First, that there was no jurisdiction to try an alien for a crime committed abroad; secondly, that an alien owed allegiance to the Crown only so long as he was resident within the realm. A passport, it was claimed, did not confer status; it was merely evidence of status, evidence that could be rebutted.

Mr Justice Tucker then gave his controversial direction to the jury, that, if they found the facts that had been proved in the case without having been denied, then, as a matter of law, Joyce owed allegiance to the Crown. Lest the jury should think the protection of a British passport to have been specious in Nazi Germany, he reminded them that even enemy aliens had rights under international law. The jury took just 23 minutes to find Joyce guilty and the judge passed the mandatory sentence of death. Joyce bowed to the court and left, giving the Nazi salute to a follower in court.

The Court of Criminal Appeal dismissed his appeal unanimously.

THE LAST THROW

The Attorney General having certified that the case involved a point of law of general public importance, Joyce was able to appeal for the second time, and to the highest court in the land. The Judicial Committee of the House of Lords sat to hear the appeal in the Robing Room of the House, the Commons still occupying the chamber because their own had been bombed. The tribunal that heard the appeal was a strong one chaired by Lord Jowitt, the Lord Chancellor. Joyce was present to hear the case and Rebecca West memorably saw him as 'looking at us from a territory whose clocks kept another time, and listening to the striking of an hour that had not yet struck for us'.[5]

After four days' legal argument the appeal was dismissed, with only one dissentient. The Law Lords did not give the reasons for their decision until a month after Joyce had been hanged, a fact that was to attract some criticism on the ground that the Home Secretary had been deprived of the judges' reasons when considering the issue of clemency.

The majority opinion was delivered by Lord Jowitt. Treason, he said, could be committed only by someone in dependence to the Crown. The law recognised the need of the man for protection and of the Crown for service. Joyce had done nothing that could be regarded as a surrender of that protection.

> The possession of a passport by one who is not a British subject gives him rights and imposes upon the Sovereign obligations which would otherwise not be given or imposed. It is immaterial that he has obtained it by misrepresentation and that he is not in law a British subject . . . By his own act he has maintained the bond which, while he was within the realm, bound him to his Sovereign . . .

The special value to the enemy of the appellant's services as a broadcaster was that he could be represented as speaking as a British subject, and his German work-book confirmed that it was in this character that he was employed. The Lord Chancellor gave short shrift to the argument that the crime could be committed only within the realm. 'No principle of comity demands that a State should ignore the crime of treason committed against it outside its territory.'

Lord Porter was the only Law Lord to dissent. Interestingly, he held that whether an alien had withdrawn his allegiance was a question of fact that the judge should not have ruled on but left to the jury. '[A] reasonable jury properly directed might have considered that the allegiance had been terminated.' If this view had prevailed at the trial, the outcome might have been totally different.

A CONTROVERSIAL DECISION

One authority described the Lords' decision as 'judicial legislation at its best'. Others were less charitable.

The barrister, J.W. Hall, for example, pointed to the anomalous situation that would have arisen had 'Joyce, instead of being American . . . been German by birth, but had lived here and honestly believed himself to be British. On the outbreak of war he is claimed as a German subject, liable to military service for that country. If he obeys he is (under this decision) liable to be hanged by the British; if he refuses he will certainly be shot by the Germans.'[6] The problem with this argument was that, since Joyce chose not to give evidence at his trial, we simply don't know whether he 'honestly believed' that he was British. It seems unlikely.

But it was in the pages of the *Cambridge Law Journal* that the forensic battle was to be fought out between two leviathans of the law. First, the views of the Law Lords were championed by the eminent Professor Lauterpacht.[7] Next, they were made subject to a wrecking job by the equally distinguished Dr Glanville Williams.[8] Where two such giants of jurisprudence could not agree, the only firm conclusion that can safely be drawn is that the point was a difficult one.

Even if the House of Lords were right, however – and there is seldom an absolute 'right' in difficult questions of law, merely a well- or less-well-argued case – the human argument is probably the stronger. As Glanville Williams put it:

> Despite the unanimity of the Bench in Joyce's case, the great body of contemporaneous opinion at the Bar, so far as one could gather it from private conversations, was against the decision. As soon as it became generally known that Joyce was not a British subject, and that the continuation of the charge against him was made possible only by the fact that he possessed a British passport, there was a remarkable revulsion of feeling even in lay circles against a conviction. To many men in the street, notwithstanding the odious character of Joyce's activities in Germany, a conviction seemed undesirable when it could be gained only by what was regarded as a legal device.

Whatever the law may have said, Joyce seemed to many to have been hanged for simply making a false statement in a passport application form, a crime that normally results in nothing more serious than a fine. Others who had broadcast for Germany, such as Norman Baillie-Stewart, the ex-Seaforth Highlander, had been sentenced to relatively short terms of imprisonment for the lesser crime of committing 'acts likely to aid the enemy'.

Ironically, Joyce himself had no doubt about his guilt. In *Twilight over England*, he had written:

> The preface is usually that part of a book which can most safely be omitted . . . When, however, the author is a daily perpetrator of High Treason, his introductory remarks may command from the English public that kind of awful veneration with which £5,000 confessions are pursued in the Sunday newspapers.[9]

Later in the war, in conversation with the American war correspondent William L. Schirer and a Norwegian Quisling, Joyce appeared to accept with equanimity the likely consequences of his conduct. Nor did he seem to take his defence seriously at his trial, remarking privately to a prison official, 'It will be amusing to see if they get away with it.'

Joyce was no fair-weather Nazi. Confronted with evidence of the concentration camp atrocities, he blamed the deaths on starvation and disease caused by Allied bombing. In his last letter to his wife he wrote:

> In death, as in this life, I defy the Jews who caused this last war: and I defy the power of Darkness which they represent. I warn the British people against the aggressive Imperialism of the Soviet Union. May Britain be great once again; and, in the hour of greatest danger to the West, may the standard of the *Hakenkreuz* [Swastika] be raised from the dust, crowned with the historic words! *'Ihr habt doch gesiegt.'* ['You have nevertheless triumphed.'] I am proud to die for my ideals; and I am sorry for the sons of Britain who have died without knowing why.

A few minutes past 9 a.m. on 3 January 1946, and five days after the execution of his fellow prisoner, John Amery, William Joyce was hanged in Wandsworth Prison; he was not yet forty. It was said that on the way to the scaffold he looked at his shaking knees and smiled. After a post-mortem and inquest in the afternoon, his remains were buried within the prison grounds. Thirty years later they were to be exhumed and sent for reinterment to Ireland.

Margaret Joyce, who like her husband had made no effort to renounce her British citizenship, had made weekly broadcasts from Germany to Great Britain, mainly about women's economic issues. Explaining why no proceedings had been taken against her, Captain W.J. Skardon, her MI5 interrogator, commented: 'There is no lack of evidence implicating her in the treasonable activities of her late husband, but the authorities do not think that she need be punished further.' Margaret died in London in 1972.

THE GENESIS OF HATE

Literary psychoanalysis is seldom enlightening, but it is impossible not to notice the number of times that William Joyce had been rejected: from school, from Ireland, from the British army to which he aspired so ardently to belong, from the Conservative Party, from the Foreign Office and from the BUF. He had even been divorced by the mother of his children.

After allowing for exaggeration of his youthful exploits, William Joyce had, in the words of MI5, 'seen battle, murder and death at a very early age'. There can be no doubt about the sincerity of his political views. He had a well-developed sense of social injustice and when he gave his allegiance he did so without reserve. During his 'British patriot' phase William was known to stand and sing the national anthem with friends at home. Having transferred his allegiance to another country, he would in moments of crisis likewise stand and give the Nazi salute, even in private.

In a statement made to British Intelligence after the war Joyce wrote that he 'was brought up as an extreme Conservative with strong Imperialist ideas, but very early in my career, namely in 1923, became attracted to Fascism, at times as a Conservative but mainly as a Fascist or National Socialist'. Joyce's complex character may perhaps best be understood in the context of the Unionist bigotry in which he had been brought up. To be a British patriot in 1920s Ireland was to feel constantly threatened by the 'traitors' within, people of a different religion who seemed to hate the country that he loved. On moving to England as a child, he discovered there another religious group that, according to its home-grown bigots, threatened the security not merely of his chosen country but of all countries, the Jews. To Joyce, the flight to Germany in 1939 must have seemed not so much an escape as a redeployment to where he could continue the struggle under a leader whose views he shared. Among his possessions when he was admitted to Wandsworth Prison was a copy of *Dr Faustus*, the story of a man who sells his soul to the devil.

Intelligent, brave and not without personal charm, Joyce was destroyed by his own xenophobia. But if few Englishmen were proud of his execution, even fewer mourned his death.

CHAPTER FOUR

The Atom Spies

The Trial of the Rosenbergs, 1951

This is a story of love and betrayal, of a devoted husband and wife who elected to suffer an appalling death rather than betray a cause they believed to be just; of a man forced to choose between betraying his sister or his wife; of lying witnesses; of a seriously flawed legal process; and of the use of these events for its own ends by the most cynical political philosophy of modern times.

Shortly after 8 a.m. on Friday 16 June 1950 agents from the Federal Bureau of Investigation (FBI) arrived at the New York City apartment of an unsuccessful businessman, Julius Rosenberg. They wanted to question him in connection with his brother-in-law's work some years earlier at the atomic energy research establishment at Los Alamos. Julius agreed to go with them, but insisted on shaving, and on dressing his two children first; he refused, however, to allow his apartment to be searched. Later, at the FBI office, he was asked, 'What would you say if we told you that your brother-in-law said you asked him to supply information to the Russians?' Julius replied, 'Bring him here. I'll call him a liar to his face.'[1] Almost a month later he was arrested on suspicion of espionage, his apartment was searched and papers, books and jewellery were seized.

Next morning, Julius's wife, Ethel, held a press conference in their apartment at which she claimed to be bewildered at the accusations that had been made against her husband. With a dishtowel in her hand she asserted, 'Neither my husband or I have ever been communists and we don't know any communists. The whole thing is ridiculous.'[2] Three weeks later she herself was arrested. Offered bail in the same sum as her husband, she was taken to prison when, like him, she was unable to post it. Thus became public one of the most extraordinary episodes in the history of espionage in America.

On 6 August 1945 an American bomber had dropped the first atomic bomb, on Hiroshima. It took only one more to ensure Japan's surrender: the Second World War was over. As the West began to disarm, its erstwhile ally, the Soviet Union, strengthened its grip over Eastern Europe and made it clear that its aim was nothing less than the spread of socialism throughout the world, by force if necessary. The secret of the atomic bomb now assumed immense significance to Americans as the only thing standing between them and Soviet domination. Imagine their dismay, therefore, when in 1949 the Soviet Union detonated its own atomic bomb. Since few in the West believed the Soviets to be capable of developing the bomb on their own, it was assumed that the secret of its construction could have been obtained only by treachery. This seemed to be confirmed when in 1950 a senior State Department official, Alger Hiss, was sent to prison for falsely denying on oath that he had passed secret documents to a Soviet agent. The following month Senator Joseph McCarthy made his place in the history books by claiming, 'I have in my hand a list of 205 cases of [members of the State Department] who appear to be either card-carrying members or certainly loyal to the Communist Party.' Although this figure had been picked out of the air by the self-promoting Senator, it led to a witch-hunt of unparalleled ferocity against suspected communists in all branches of public life, in the course of which the careers and even lives of many innocent people were sacrificed on the altar of security.

The irony is that McCarthy was right; there had been a massive penetration of the West by the Soviet Union. We now know that in the United States alone some 350 communist agents and sources occupied strategic positions in government and the armed forces. One of these, it was now discovered, had provided the Soviet Union with a report on the Manhattan Project, the top-secret mission to develop the atomic bomb. The spy was a man who was later to become the head of the physics department of the British nuclear research centre at Harwell, Klaus Fuchs. Dr Fuchs had entered Britain as a refugee from Nazi Germany and had been cleared to work on the bomb. (His known communist sympathies were assumed to have been nothing more than a reaction to Nazism.) Uncovered by a Soviet defector, he admitted, under interrogation, to having spied for Russia and named various members of his spy ring in America, including his courier, known to him only as 'Raymond'. Intelligence sources identified 'Raymond' as an industrial chemist, Harry Gold.

Like so many others involved in this affair, Gold was the son of a poor Jewish family that had emigrated from Europe to America before the war. After a week's questioning by the FBI, Gold confessed to having spied for Russia since 1934. His Soviet controller, known to him as 'John', was in fact Anatoli Yakovlev, a former Vice Consul and head of the Russian delegation to the UN. Gold's confession led in turn to David Greenglass, a former US army sergeant who had once worked at the Manhattan Project. Greenglass admitted passing secret information to Gold and another Soviet agent, his brother-in-law, Julius Rosenberg. The information had included notes and sketches concerning something called a lens mould, an arrangement of shaped charges used to create an implosion shock wave; it was nothing less than the detonation device for the atomic bomb.

THE YOUNG FRIENDS

Julius Rosenberg was born in 1918, the son of a Polish tailor in the Lower East Side of New York. At the age of fourteen he joined the Young Communist League and was later to become its secretary. In 1935 he met and fell in love with the slightly older Ethel Greenglass. Ethel too was the child of a poor Jewish family consisting of a Russian father and an Austrian mother. She had two younger brothers, Bernard and David. Her ambition to be an actress and singer was frustrated by her domineering mother, so she took a secretarial job with a shipping company, but was fired for organising a strike. Julius and Ethel soon discovered a common interest in radical politics every bit as strong as the mutual passion that was to remain with them for the rest of their lives. They married as soon as Julius graduated in 1939, and two sons, Michael and Robert, were born to them in 1943 and 1947 respectively.

After leaving high school Julius studied engineering at the City College of New York (CCNY), where he met many of those who were to play a part in his tragedy. In 1942 he obtained a job as a civilian engineer with the Army Signal Corps, rapidly rising to inspector. His interest in the Communist Party grew, and in 1943 he became chairman of a branch of its Industrial Division; party meetings were held in his apartment. Shortly after, both husband and wife severed all public links with the Party for reasons that were to become clear only much later.

In late 1942 Ethel's brother David Greenglass had married his childhood friend Ruth Printz; they too were both members of the Young Communist League. David failed at every college course he undertook, but when in 1943 he was inducted into the army he was trained as a machinist and sent to work at the Manhattan Project in Oak Ridge, Tennessee, where he became assistant foreman in the high-explosives unit. (How he got this job with his political background is still a mystery.) Ruth came out to join him, and they rented an apartment in Albuquerque, New Mexico. Discovery of Julius's party membership card led to his dismissal from the Signal Corps. After the war he opened a small machine shop in Manhattan along with David and his brother Bernard, but they did not get on, and by 1947 the business had collapsed.

Another of the friends at CCNY with leftist leanings was Morton Sobell, the son of Russian-born immigrants. After obtaining a master's degree in electrical engineering he shared a room in Washington DC with Max Elitcher (also of CCNY), whom he recruited to the Communist Party. Together, they obtained jobs as electrical engineers at the Bureau of Naval Ordnance. Sobell married in 1945 and by 1948 was living with his wife next door to the Elitchers in New York City.

Shortly after the arrest of Klaus Fuchs a number of people began disappearing from their homes and places of work. One of them was Morton Sobell, who, on the pretext of needing time off work owing to exhaustion, had flown to Mexico along with his wife, son and stepdaughter. When the arrest of Julius Rosenberg became public, Sobell cashed in his return tickets and tried to book a passage to Europe. This proved difficult, since the family had entered Mexico on tourist visas and none of them had passports. Two months later armed police burst into Sobell's flat in Mexico City, seized Morton and drove him and his family to the American border, where he was handed over to the FBI. Max Elitcher was the bird that did not fly. Fearing that he might be prosecuted for having lied on oath about his membership of the Communist Party, he agreed to cooperate with the FBI.

On 31 January 1951 a grand jury indicted Julius and Ethel Rosenberg, David Greenglass, Yakovlev and Sobell. The charge was conspiring between 1944 and 1950 to communicate to the Soviet Union documents, writings, sketches, notes and information relating to the national defence of the United States, with intent and reason to believe that they would be used to the advantage of the Soviet Union. The Greenglasses were named in the charges as conspirators, but not as defendants; this was because they had both agreed to give evidence for the prosecution. Yakovlev was later removed from the list of defendants because he had been in the United States on a Russian diplomatic passport. (The point was academic; he and his wife and children had already left for Russia.)

The Rosenbergs, unable to post the necessary bail, were committed to custody, where the prison guards reported that they sang to each other. (Ethel sang 'One Fine Day' from *Madame Butterfly*, and 'Good Night, Irene'. Julius sang 'The Battle Hymn of the Republic'.) Their young sons were taken to a temporary shelter in the Bronx.

THE TRIAL

The trial of the Rosenbergs, Sobell and David Greenglass began on 6 March 1951 in the New York Federal Courthouse, Judge Irving R. Kaufman presiding. The diminutive Kaufman was a formidable figure despite standing only 5 feet 4 inches in his socks. Known for his scholarly opinions and civil libertarian views, Kaufman seems privately to have assumed the defendants' guilt, and it is difficult to resist the conclusion that he saw the Rosenberg trial as a stepping-stone to judicial advancement. Critics have pointed to the fact that the jury did not contain a single Jew, despite the fact that all the defendants and most of the lawyers, like nearly a third of New Yorkers, were Jews. This was probably more unfortunate than sinister since there were a number of Jews called to the jury panel who had excused themselves.[3]

The Rosenbergs were represented by Emanuel ('Manny') Bloch. A well-known civil-rights lawyer, Bloch had little experience of the criminal courts, and it showed in the way he conducted his case. His assistant counsel was his elderly father, Alexander Bloch, an attorney specialising in the buying and selling of bakeries. Whatever Manny's shortcomings, his devotion to the Rosenbergs was total. (He was to deliver the eulogy at their funeral and was appointed guardian of their two sons.)

The Chief Prosecuting Attorney was the able and relentless Irving H. Saypol, formerly Sapolsky, the US Attorney for the Southern District of New York, already well known as the prosecutor of Alger Hiss.[4] Another rising young attorney, Roy Cohen, was brought into his team at a late stage to assist him. In his opening statement Saypol claimed that the defendants had engaged in a 'deliberate, carefully planned conspiracy to deliver to the Soviet Union the information and the weapons the Soviet Union could use to destroy us'. They had, he said, 'committed the most serious crime which can be committed against the people of this country'. His first witness was Max Elitcher.

RECRUITMENT

Elitcher gave evidence of Julius Rosenberg's attempt to recruit him as a spy. He described how in 1944 Julius had

> called me and reminded me of our school friendship and came to my home. After a while, he asked if my wife would leave the room, that he wanted to talk to me in private. She did. Then he began talking about the job that the Soviet Union was doing in the war effort and how at present a good deal of military information was being denied them by some interests in the United States, and because of that their effort was being impeded. He . . . asked whether in my capacity at the Bureau of Ordnance working on anti-aircraft devices and computer control of firing missiles, would I turn information over to him? He told me that any information I gave him would be taken to New York, processed photographically and would be returned overnight – so it would not be missed. The process would be safe as far as I am concerned.

Elitcher's evidence was that of a deeply conflicted person who wished to deny any involvement in espionage, while at the same time conceding that 'I didn't reject [Rosenberg's overtures]. I went along.' He claimed that Julius had asked him at the end of the war to go on working at the Bureau of Ordnance. He told the court of an occasion when he had driven in a car, along with Morton Sobell, to somewhere near the Rosenberg apartment. Although they believed that they were being followed, Sobell had left the car and later told Elitcher that he had delivered a can of 35mm film to the Rosenbergs.

David Greenglass had agreed to give evidence for the prosecution in exchange for immunity for his wife, Ruth. Together, they testified how they were recruited at about the same time as Elitcher. In Ruth's words:

> Julius said that I might have noticed that for some time he and Ethel had not been actively pursuing any Communist Party activities, that they didn't buy the *Daily Worker* at the usual newsstand; that for two years he had been trying to get in touch with people who would assist him to be able to help the Russian people more directly other than just his membership in the Communist Party . . . He said that his friends had told him that David was working on the atomic bomb, and he went on to tell me that the atomic bomb was the most destructive weapon used so far, that it had dangerous radiation effects, that the United States and Britain were working on this project jointly and that he felt that the information should be shared with Russia, who was our ally at the time, because if all nations had the information then one nation couldn't use the bomb as a threat against another. He said that he wanted me to tell my husband, David, that he should give information to Julius to be passed on to the Russians.

David, reluctant at first, eventually agreed to cooperate in Julius's plans. Two months later, on furlough in New York, David provided Julius with a sketch of the lens mould and a list of potential spies. Ethel, he said, had typed it out, while Ruth and Julius had corrected the grammar. Afterwards, Julius had burned the handwritten notes in a frying pan and flushed them down the drain.

'I COME FROM JULIUS'

David Greenglass told the court how Julius had told him that someone might be sent to collect information from him at Los Alamos. They would bear the torn half of the top of a box of jello,[5] while Ruth kept the other half. (In court, at Roy Cohen's request, David demonstrated how the jello packet had been cut up.) Later, a man had arrived at the door of his apartment in Albuquerque with the torn half of the jello box and spoken the agreed recognition phrase, 'I come from Julius.' David had then given the man, whom he subsequently identified as Harry Gold, information about people working on the project who might be recruited for espionage. He also provided another sketch of the lens mould. In return, Gold gave David an envelope containing $500 in cash. Gold, who before the trial had been sentenced to thirty years' imprisonment for spying for Russia, confirmed David's account of the Albuquerque meeting.

David then went on to tell of an encounter arranged by Julius between himself and an unknown Russian in a car. David had described the lens to the Russian and answered questions about his work at Los Alamos. Finally, in December 1945, David, again in New York on furlough, had drawn a cross-section of the lens mould, together with a twelve-page explanation of the atomic bomb, which he gave to Julius. At that meeting, he claimed, Julius had admitted stealing a proximity fuse and other material for Russia.

THE CONSOLE TABLE

A key piece of evidence in the case that was never produced to the court was a console table that was said to have been in the Rosenbergs' apartment. David told the court, 'I believe they told me they received a console table from the Russians.' Ruth added that Ethel had told her it was a special table. A lamp could fit underneath it so that the table could be used for photographic purposes; the table was used to take 'pictures on microfilm of the typewritten notes'. Despite having been told that it had been altered for this purpose, the FBI had inexplicably failed to seize the table from the apartment. It was not to come to light until much later.

REWARDS AND FLIGHT

According to David, Julius told him that after the war he had received a citation as a reward for his services to the Soviet Union and that both he and Ethel had each received watches. When Fuchs was arrested in 1950, Julius told David to leave the country immediately; he, Julius, would supply the money and make the arrangements. A month later, following the arrest of Harry Gold, Julius repeated his warning and gave David $1,000 and passwords with which to make contact with sympathisers in Mexico City who would help him escape to Europe. Julius added that he and his family also intended to leave the country. Later, he gave David another $4,000 for the trip. After her husband's arrest, Ethel had asked Ruth to warn David to keep quiet about Julius and to take the blame alone. A photographer later gave evidence of a family posing for three dozen passport photos needed for a visit to France. He identified Julius as having been among them.

The prosecution called other witnesses, including a former spy, popularly known as the Red Spy Queen, who gave evidence of receiving telephone calls for the Russians from someone who gave his name as Julius. None of this added much to what had gone before.

The Rosenbergs' defence amounted to a complete denial of the prosecution case. They had never asked the Greenglasses for atomic information or taken part in any kind of espionage work. Julius denied having stolen a proximity fuse. He did not know Harry Gold, he had never seen Yakovlev, had never sat with a Russian in a car and it was not he who had telephoned the Red Spy Queen. After college, Julius had looked up Elitcher only once when he was in Washington, but it was a social visit and espionage was not discussed.

The Rosenbergs denied that the console table had come from the Russians or that it had been used for photography. It had been bought at Macy's, the New York department store, for $20 or $21, 'a really good buy'. (The Rosenbergs' part-time maid was later called to give rebutting evidence. Ethel, she said, had told her that a friend of her husband had given the table to him as a gift. 'It was a sort of a wedding present.')

Julius denied having had passport photographs taken. He had visited his family doctor, but in order to find out for David what kind of injections were necessary for entry into Mexico. He had given David $1,000, not $4,000, and not to help his brother-in-law's escape but because he believed him to be in trouble. (The prosecution later called the secretary to the Greenglass's lawyer to refute this. She testified to having received the suspiciously close figure of $3,900.)

'TAKING THE FIFTH'

Neither Julius nor Ethel was an impressive witness; he appeared nervous and pedantic, she cold and unbending. But it was probably their decision to 'take the Fifth' that finally sealed their fate. ('Taking the Fifth' is what the exercise of the right to silence is known as in America, 'the Fifth' referring to the Fifth Amendment to the Constitution, which guarantees this right.)

It began when Judge Kaufman intervened to question Julius about his political beliefs. Asked, 'Did you ever belong to any group that discussed the [political] system of Russia?' Julius replied: 'Well, Your Honour, I feel at this time that I refuse to answer a question that might tend to incriminate me.' When Saypol's cross-examination got round to Elitcher and his political views, Julius said: 'I don't intend to waive any part of my right of self-incrimination, and if Mr Saypol is referring to the Young Communist League or the Communist Party, I will not answer any question on it.' And when questioned about conversations he might have had 'in any communist unit', Julius again said, 'I refuse to answer that question on the ground that it may incriminate me.' The attorney Louis Nizer summed up Julius's response to questioning: 'Instead of forthrightness, there was furtiveness. Instead of uninhibited truth, there was legalism. Instead of courage which he had exhibited by praising what he liked in Russia, there was fear.'[6]

Ethel took the same line. Asked whether her husband had been dismissed from government employment on the grounds of his membership of the Communist Party, she at first refused to answer, on the ground that it might incriminate her. She also refused to answer questions concerning Julius's response to the threat of dismissal and whether she had helped her brother join the Communist Party; she even refused to say whether she had discussed the case with him.

Judge Kaufman directed the jury not to draw any inferences from these refusals to answer, but human nature does not always observe the legal proprieties and the harm had been done.

VERDICT AND SENTENCE

Manny Bloch began his summing-up ('summation' in American usage) with a curiously effusive expression of thanks to the jury with which he coupled his thanks to the court, the prosecutor and even the FBI – which rather cut the ground from his later criticisms. He tried to portray the trial as 'the Greenglasses against the Rosenbergs', and the Greenglasses' evidence as being due to bitterness arising out of the failed business venture. But he laid plain the paucity of his case by his virulent attacks on the couple. He described David Greenglass as 'the lowest of the lowest animals that I have ever seen', and Ruth as 'the embodiment of evil'.

Saypol then calmly recapitulated the evidence against the Rosenbergs, going out of his way to paint their crimes in the worst possible light:

> These defendants stand before you in the face of overwhelming proof of this terrible disloyalty, proof which transcends any emotional consideration and must eliminate any consideration of sympathy. No defendants ever stood before the bar of American justice less deserving of sympathy than these three.

Finally, Judge Kaufman warned the jury against relying on the uncorroborated evidence of accomplices and against considering Communist Party membership as relevant to anything except the question of intent. They then retired, returning to the courtroom later to ask to know the judge's views on sentence. Kaufman explained that the question of sentence was for him alone; the jury retired again and continued deliberating until after midnight. The next morning, 5 April, at 11 a.m. the jury returned verdicts of guilty on all the charges. They made no recommendation for mercy despite having been advised by the judge that they could do so.

Judge Kaufman sentenced each of the Rosenbergs to death and Morton Sobell to thirty years' imprisonment. The next day, he sentenced David Greenglass to fifteen years.

THE ROSENBERGS IN PRISON

Ethel and Julius were then taken to separate prisons, but after a while they were reunited in Sing Sing. There, they continued to write to each other in terms that proclaimed their misery, their love and their political convictions. Some have read the letters for what they appear to be on the surface; others believe that they were written for publication. Ethel's style was certainly inclined to the dramatic:

> Wait, wait and tremble, ye mad masters, this barbarism, this infamy you practice upon us and with which you regale yourselves presently, will not go unanswered, unavenged, forever! The whirlwind gathers before which you must fly like chaff.[7]

They were permitted to see each other once a week, but separated by a screen. Only once were they allowed any physical contact. Louis Nizer described the distressing scene that took place when Julius arrived:

> 'Ethel!' he cried. They rushed at each other and embraced tightly, covering each other's faces with fierce kisses. Before anyone knew what was happening, they began pawing one another with wild abandon. They lost all control and wrestled passionately. The witnesses to the scene were stunned by the suddenness and violence of the outburst. They looked on in amazement at the writhing, groaning figures. Finally, the guards and matron recovered. They pounced on them, pulling them apart. Julius was lifted bodily and plumped hard into a chair. Ethel was dragged none too gently. They were still panting . . . Julius's face was so smeared with lipstick, it looked as if he were bleeding. He laced his hair back with his fingers; Ethel pulled her shirt together in a modest gesture which seemed ludicrous under the circumstances. She pulled her skirt down and demurely patted her disheveled hair. She could not see the red blotches on her face from her own lipstick smudged off from Julius'. When Bloch's face came into focus, she felt humiliated and began to cry.[8]

The two were never allowed to touch each other again.

APPELLATE TWISTS AND TURNS

Nothing was left undone in the desperate attempts to overturn the Rosenbergs' convictions and sentences.

The day after the trial ended, appeals were filed that had the effect of automatically blocking the sentences of death. The grounds of appeal covered most of the objections that were to be rehearsed endlessly in subsequent legal manœuvrings over the next two years. All were examined thoroughly and dismissed unanimously by the US Court of Appeal, Second Circuit, in an opinion written by the distinguished jurist Judge Jerome Frank, a known 'liberal'. The Rosenbergs, his judgment commented, claimed that they had been sentenced for political unorthodoxy in giving secrets to a friendly power, but 'the conspiracy did not end in 1945, while Russia was still a "friend", but . . . continued during a period when it was apparent to everybody that we were dealing with a hostile nation'. The United States Supreme Court refused to review this decision.[9]

A further appeal was then made on various grounds including the prejudicial atmosphere in which the trial had been held. (The press had not been kind to the Rosenbergs during the trial, and Saypol had inexcusably issued a press release promising further evidence that did not materialise.) This too was dismissed by a federal judge, and the Court of Appeal upheld his decision. In February the following year President Eisenhower denied a petition for clemency, commenting, 'these two individuals . . . have . . . betrayed the cause of freedom for which free men are fighting and dying at this very hour' (a reference to the war in Korea).

By April 1953 the notorious console table had seemingly turned up in the apartment of Julius's mother. Unable by reason of illiteracy to follow the press reports, she claimed not to have realised its significance. Macy's furniture buyer made an affidavit to the effect that: 'It is possible that Macy's handled and sold the particular table shown in these photographs during the years 1944 and 1945.' Armed with this information, Bloch appealed to Judge Kaufman, but without success. The Court of Appeal affirmed the judge's decision.

A Committee to Secure Justice in the Rosenberg Case had been set up after the trial, but it was not until a year later that the Communist Party began seriously to agitate on their behalf. (Their uncharacteristic silence may have had something to do with the unsavoury spy trials then going on in Eastern Europe.) A vigil was held outside the White House and mass meetings were arranged around the world. It was at this point that two new lawyers, Fyke Farmer and Daniel Marshall, entered the arena with a wholly novel point of law: the Court, they argued, simply did not have power to impose the death penalty. Bloch was not impressed by their arguments but nevertheless presented them, somewhat reluctantly, to Judge Kaufman. It got him nowhere. Discarding the Farmer/Marshall point, Bloch now made an application for a stay of execution to Justice Jackson of the US Supreme Court, who referred it to the full Court with a recommendation that Bloch should be allowed to argue his case in full. Although four of the justices would have allowed the application, a majority refused.

Next day, 16 June and with time rapidly running out, Farmer and Marshall boldly put their novel ground of appeal to another Justice of the US Supreme Court, William O. Douglas.[10] They were financed by and acting for a wealthy supporter of radical causes, Irwin Edelman, who, in an attempt to circumvent his lack of status in the case, had taken the dubious step of appointing himself as the appellants' 'next friend'. Douglas, who had only recently voted against granting a stay on Bloch's grounds, professed to be impressed by the Farmer/Marshall argument and granted a stay of execution to allow it to be put before the District Court.

Douglas's colleagues on the Supreme Court were horrified that he was considering the application and even before it had been granted had moved to frustrate it. Concerned that 'Farmer's motion was ridiculous and that Douglas should turn it down . . .', Justice Jackson arranged a meeting between the Chief Justice and the Attorney General that resulted in an unprecedented decision to reconvene the Court. After hearing legal argument, the full Court vacated (or reversed) Douglas's stay and refused to hear further argument.

On the same day as the Court's final rejection of the Rosenberg appeal President Eisenhower denied a second petition for clemency, commenting,

> There is no question in my mind that their original trial and the long series of appeals constitute the fullest measure of justice and due process of law. Throughout the innumerable complications and technicalities of this case, no judge has ever expressed any doubt that they committed most serious acts of espionage.

The latter statement was not correct; as Justice Hugo Black was to observe in his dissenting opinion: 'It is not amiss to point out that this court has never received [the] record [of the trial] and has never affirmed the fairness of the trial. Without [that] . . . there may always be questions as to whether these executions were legally and rightfully carried out.'

This was effectively the Rosenbergs' last throw and it had failed. They were to die that very day.

THE DEATH CHAMBER

A last-minute appeal was now made for the execution to be rescheduled, on the ground that it was to take place at 11 p.m. on a Friday, that is to say, after the commencement of the Jewish Sabbath, which begins at sundown that day. Judge Kaufman agreed, but instead of putting the execution back, moved it forward to before sundown.

Julius went to the execution chamber first, apparently oblivious of the ten official witnesses in the tiny room. He sat quietly as he was strapped into the electric chair. After three jolts of electricity, one long and two short, the physicians examined the body and declared him dead. Ten minutes later his wife was brought into the room. The Associated Press report describes how

Ethel, a short, plumpish woman of 37, stood before the electric chair in a shapeless green patterned dress and slippers, her small mouth seemed twisted, though none could say if it was a smile or a sneer. She took one step, then turned suddenly toward Mrs Helen Evans, prison matron, who had walked to the chamber with her. Mrs Rosenberg pulled Mrs Evans to her and they kissed. Visibly affected, the matron quickly left the room with Mrs Lucy Many, a telephone operator who had also accompanied Mrs Rosenberg. Mrs Rosenberg sat down calmly and her arms dropped limply on the chair sides. She winced slightly as the electrode helmet was attached to her clipped head and the restraining thongs were fitted in place. The other electrode was connected to her bare right leg. Then a long moment, followed by a low rasping rattle as the execution switch was thrown. Her hands clenched and her body surged against the straps as three jolts were sent through her. Two physicians examined her in murmured consultation. They signalled, and again Joseph Francell, the executioner, threw the switch a fourth and fifth time. The body moved again. Then it was over.

It was their fourteenth wedding anniversary.

Two questions remain, and they are big ones: were the Rosenbergs given a fair trial and did they spy for Russia? Let us look first at the Farmer/Marshall point, the legality of the death sentences.

WERE THE DEATH SENTENCES LAWFUL?

The point was a simple one. The Rosenbergs had been convicted under an Act of Congress (the Espionage Act of 1917) for which the penalty was death. However, a later Act (the Atomic Energy Act of 1946) created a different offence – to which the Rosenbergs' conduct could be said to have amounted – that was also punishable by death, *but only if that sentence had been recommended by the jury.* Farmer and Marshall argued that the requirement in the later Act for a jury recommendation for death applied to the passing of sentence for convictions under the earlier Act and that, since there was no such jury recommendation, the sentences were illegal.

After the point had been argued before the full Court,[11] Justice Douglas, a 'liberal' but no great legal theorist, declared himself convinced that he had been right to be 'deeply troubled' about the issue raised. 'It is law too elemental for citation of authority that where two penal statutes may apply – one carrying death, the other imprisonment – the court has no choice but to impose the less hard sentence.' Justice Hugo Black agreed that the argument 'presented a substantial and serious issue' which the Court had not had sufficient time to consider. The much respected but quirky Justice Frankfurter was even more supportive, saying, 'it cannot be left within the discretion of a prosecutor whether the judge may impose the death sentence wholly on his own authority or whether he may do so only upon recommendation of the jury'. But it was all to no avail; by a six to three majority, the Court held that there was no need for the involvement of the District Court: the problems were purely legal and could be decided by the Supreme Court, which is exactly what they proceeded to do.

'[T]he Atomic Energy Act', the Court held, 'does not, by text or intention, supersede the earlier Espionage Act. It does not purport to repeal the earlier Act, nor afford any grounds for spelling out a repeal by implication. Each Act is complete in itself and each has its own reason for existence and field of operation . . . It is obvious that an attempt to prosecute under the later Act would in all probability fail.' Furthermore, the Atomic Energy Act contained a provision that it should 'not exclude the applicable provisions of any other laws . . .', which the Court described as 'an unmistakable reference' to the 1917 Espionage Act. For what it is worth and with great respect to Felix Frankfurter, the arguments of the majority seem to the present writer to have the edge over those of the dissenters.

Commentators have wondered why, when there had already been so many stays, an issue that three Supreme Court Justices, including the great Felix Frankfurter, considered to be worthy of extended argument should have been dismissed so summarily. The Court's explanation was that it had a 'duty to see that . . . the laws are enforced with a reasonable degree of promptness and certainty. The stay which had been issued promised many more months of litigation in a case which had otherwise run its full course.' Perhaps. There could, of course, have been another explanation of the rush to judgment. Behind the scenes there had been deep divisions within the Court. Frankfurter and Vinson were incensed at Douglas's seemingly erratic and, in their view, cynical conduct throughout the Rosenberg hearings. While there was force in the majority's argument that they could decide a legal issue as well as an inferior court, it was certainly not the Supreme Court's finest hour.[12]

It might all have been very different if the Justices had been aware of what had gone on behind the scenes at Judge Kaufman's court.

Despite the claims of his detractors, Kaufman's conduct of the trial in court could not be faulted; the Court of Appeal had examined and rejected all complaints against him on this score. It was his conduct out of court that gave cause for concern.

Gordon Dean was the chairman of the Atomic Energy Commission and a former Justice Department attorney. His office diary of a month before the trial began records that an official of the Department of Justice had 'talked to the judge and he is prepared to impose [a death sentence] if the evidence warrants it'. Such a statement – which is confirmed by FBI records – is, of course, unimpeachable in itself; a judge should be prepared to impose whatever sentence is warranted by the evidence. What was wrong here is that there should have been any discussion of sentence between a Justice Department official and a judge prior to the hearing of a case.

But worse was to follow. The Judge had consulted the prosecution secretly after conviction. Unlike the practice in the English courts, it was common form for federal judges to seek the views of the prosecutor before passing sentence, but this had to be done in open court so that the defence could be aware of the representations and be able to respond to them. Many years after the trial, Irving Saypol wrote to the then Director of the FBI revealing that he had been summoned to Judge Kaufman's chambers and asked for his views on the sentences to be imposed the next day and those of the Justice Department. Saypol recommended death for both the Rosenbergs and thirty years for Sobell, exactly the sentences that Kaufman was to pass. Interestingly, neither the Justice Department nor its autocratic director, J. Edgar Hoover would support him in calling for the death sentence; indeed, Hoover sagely pointed out that execution would make a martyr out of Ethel.

Kaufman went out of his way to cover up his indiscretion. After having consulted the prosecutor privately, he asked Saypol not to make any recommendation on sentence in open court. And he compounded this deception when in court the following day he untruthfully said, 'Because of the seriousness of this case and the lack of precedents I have refrained from asking the government for a recommendation.' Even after the trial was over, Kaufman maintained an unusual interest in the case. As the *New York Times* reporter Sam Roberts remarked, 'he appeared to be taking the repeated delays personally'. In consulting the prosecutor privately and in subsequently denying that he had done so Judge Kaufman had clearly acted improperly, but were the sentences themselves justified on the facts of the case?

HOW GRAVE WERE THEIR CRIMES?

Critics have rightly pointed to Kaufman's verbal gaffe when in passing sentence he referred to the defendants' 'treason', a crime with which they had not been charged. This was probably little more than a slip of the tongue, though perhaps a revealing one. What is clear from his remarks is that the Rosenbergs were sentenced to death rather than imprisonment because of a complete misconception of the gravity of their offence. This is what he said:

> I believe your conduct in putting into the hands of the Russians the A-bomb years before our best scientists predicted Russia would perfect the bomb has already caused, in my opinion, the Communist aggression in Korea, with the resultant casualties exceeding 50,000 and who knows but that millions more of innocent people may pay the price of your treason. Indeed, by your betrayal you undoubtedly have altered the course of history to the disadvantage of our country.

The problem with these assumptions is that they were just not true. The Rosenbergs did not give the Russians the secret of the atomic bomb and there was not the slightest reason for thinking that their activities had in any way contributed to the outbreak of the Korean War. Just how important, then, was the information provided by the Rosenberg network to the Russians?

Bloch had sought to show at the trial that someone with Greenglass's limited education could not have grasped the principle of the atomic bomb, let alone make a useful description of it. But a Los Alamos official called by the prosecution gave evidence that an 'expert, interested in finding out what was going on at Los Alamos, could get enough from [the sketches] to reveal what was going on at Los Alamos'. And no one at the time had gainsaid him. After the trial, however, a number of scientific experts came forward to challenge this view. General Leslie Groves, the Director of the Manhattan Project, summed up their view when he told the Atomic Energy Commission in secret session in 1954, 'I think that the data that went out in the case of the Rosenbergs was of minor value.'[13] Whatever the value of the sketch, it is a fact that Klaus Fuchs had already provided the Russians with a detailed description of the atomic bomb. It is now generally agreed that Greenglass's contribution could be described at best only as corroboration of what the Russians already knew.

Why, then, did Kaufman consider the information that the Rosenbergs had passed to Russia to be so damaging? The answer is to be found partly in the climate of fear prevailing in America at the time of the trial and partly in a curiously misjudged intervention by Emanuel Bloch. Just as the prosecution were about to introduce the Greenglass sketch into evidence, Bloch rose and objected, saying that it would threaten national security to make the material public. His object in doing so, he said, was to preserve 'the secret of the atom bomb'. Judge Kaufman remarked that this was a rather strange request coming from the defendants, to which Bloch rejoined, 'even at this late day this information may be of advantage to a foreign power'. Kaufman accordingly directed that the sketch be sealed after it had been shown to the jury. In this way, and no doubt unwittingly, it seems that the Rosenbergs' attorney may have confirmed in the Judge's mind the vital importance of the sketch to the nation's security.

THE REAL INJUSTICE

Regardless of the seriousness of the information passed to Russia, it is difficult to see how death sentences could have been warranted. There was no justification or precedent for them. Tokyo Rose, the American who in the Second World War broadcast for Japan, had received a sentence of only ten years. And in England, Allen Nunn May and Klaus Fuchs, who passed on far more useful information to Russia, had been given only ten and fourteen years respectively. As Judge Kaufman well knew, the prosecution had sought the death sentences for the Rosenbergs solely as a means of applying pressure to the accused to reveal their confederates. The argument for the death sentence was particularly weak in the case of Ethel, whose proved culpability was appreciably less than her husband's. Whatever may have come to light since, the evidence at the trial revealed little more than a willingness on Ethel's part to go along with what her husband was doing. The idea that that alone could justify the execution of this mother of two young children simply beggars belief.

But all this, of course, is predicated upon the evidence as it stood at the time of the trial. Since then, information has come to light that gives reason to doubt the credibility of one of the key witnesses for the prosecution, while another has frankly admitted that he lied in the witness box.

THE LYING WITNESSES

Perhaps the most damaging part of Harry Gold's testimony concerned the password phrase, 'I come from Julius', which he said he had used when visiting David Greenglass in Albuquerque. What the court was not told – and what was disclosed only years later – is that this was not the phrase he had first given to the FBI. In fact, he had first recollected the name as Ben, not Julius. What happened then was that in an attempt to jog his memory, the FBI had brought Gold and Greenglass together. The notes of that meeting state:

> Greenglass says that he had no recollection of [the phrase, 'I come from Ben'] a statement by Gold, pointing out further that the name Ben would mean nothing to him. Greenglass proposed that possibly Gold had said 'greetings from Julius' which would of course make

sense to Greenglass. Gold's spontaneous comment to this was that possibly Greenglass was right and that he had mentioned the name of Julius rather than Ben. Gold, however, is not at all clear on this point.[14]

There was nothing wrong in law with what the FBI did, but it should have been disclosed to the defence, with what consequences we can only guess. But Gold was not the only liar who gave evidence against the Rosenbergs.

Nearly half a century after the trial, Sam Roberts managed to trace and interview the eighty-year-old David Greenglass, now living in anonymity. After much difficulty he got him to speak frankly about the case. Greenglass comes across in the Roberts interviews as someone who did not have the slightest respect for the truth. A key part of his testimony at the trial concerned Ethel's supposed role as a typist of secret information. In speaking to Roberts he told a very different story. The idea that it was Ethel who had done the typing, he said, had come from the prosecutor, Roy Cohen, who had claimed that this was what Ruth had said. Greenglass had replied, 'If she says so . . .'. He told CBS News: 'I don't know who typed it, frankly. And to this day, I can't even remember that the typing took place, see. But somebody typed it. Now I'm not sure who it was. And I don't even think it was done while we were there.'[15] He also admitted lying when testifying to having seen the console table in the Rosenberg apartment. So why did he perjure himself at the trial of his sister and brother-in-law? According to him, it was in order to protect his wife, Ruth. The transcript of the television programme in which he appeared reads:

> He says he had a deal with the prosecution. The deal: 'My wife was not gonna be indicted. She's never gonna be prosecuted and she wouldn't have any problem at all from the government. And I said, "OK, now I'll tell you what I have to know." And I told them.' For Greenglass, the deal was a simple matter of priorities. 'I would not sacrifice my wife and my children for my sister. How do you like that? And that's what I told the FBI. I said if you indict my wife, you can forget it. I'll never say a word about anybody.'

This was exactly what he had denied in cross-examination under oath.[16]

Worse even than their witnesses' lies was the malpractice on the part of the prosecution.

PROSECUTION MALPRACTICE

There is no doubt that the prosecution in the Rosenberg case, seemingly at the behest of the FBI, used the threat to prosecute Ruth Greenglass as a means of getting her husband to agree to give evidence against his sister and brother-in-law and used the threat of a death sentence on Ethel as a means of securing the cooperation of Julius.

It is difficult to criticise the threat against Ruth; in cases of criminal conspiracy particularly, the prosecution is under great difficulties in securing evidence. Where, as here, the security of the country seemed to be at stake and the prosecution believed it had evidence of Ruth's guilt, it is easy to understand why this threat should have been made. Ethel was another case altogether. Not only were the government and the judge well aware of the paucity of evidence pointing to anything but a minimal involvement in her husband's spying activities; they were prepared to take their threat all the way to the electric chair, even when it could no longer serve any purpose. Such conduct was both unethical and immoral.

But there was more. Just before he died in the early 1970s, Roy Cohen boasted to the noted attorney Alan M. Dershowitz that the government had 'manufactured' evidence against both of the Rosenbergs because their guilt had been confirmed to them from secret intelligence.[17] If this statement was true, this would have been a most serious interference with the course of justice that, if proved, would have called for prison sentences for all concerned.

There were, then, many elements of the Rosenbergs' trial that were profoundly unsatisfactory and that, had they been known at the time, would almost certainly have resulted in the acquittal of both Ethel and Julius. (Indeed, this was the outcome of a mock retrial conducted by the American Bar Association in 1993 on the basis of the information known at that date.) But whether the Rosenbergs should have been convicted or not, we are still justified in asking, were they in fact guilty as charged?

TRUTH WILL OUT

The Rosenberg trial has long been held up by their supporters as the act of a corrupt government assisted by a 'contaminated' judiciary prepared to frame and put to death an innocent couple as a means of diverting public attention from its reactionary policies. As we have seen, the conduct of the government and the judge certainly fell well short of the standards expected of them. But this does not mean that the Rosenbergs were innocent.

The first insight into what really happened came in 1975, when, as a result of an application by the Rosenbergs' sons under the American Freedom of Information Act, the FBI and various other government agencies released a mass of information that they held on the case. The first person to take advantage of this and conduct a proper critical examination of the evidence was the leftist historian and former executive committee member of the National Committee to Re-open the Rosenberg Case, Ronald Radosh.

After studying the documents and interviewing over forty of those involved, many of whom opened their files for the first time, Radosh and his collaborator Joyce Milton concluded that, 'while some of the arguments of the Rosenberg case critics were well taken, Julius and Ethel were not, as they claimed, executed as part of a giant Cold War conspiracy orchestrated by the FBI'. Instead, they found that Julius had 'managed over a period of years to become the coordinator of an extensive espionage operation whose contacts were well placed to pass on information on top-secret military projects in the fields of radar and aeronautics', and that 'Ethel Rosenberg probably knew of and supported her husband's endeavors, and it seems almost certain that she acted as an accessory'.[18] Their conclusions were soon to be dramatically confirmed from an unexpected source.

FEKLISOV

Two years after publication of the Radosh book the Rosenbergs' Soviet controller, the former Colonel Alexander Feklisov, emerged from obscurity to tell the world that 'Julius was a true revolutionary, who was willing to sacrifice himself for his beliefs'. Of Ethel, he said, 'She had nothing to do with this – she was completely innocent. I think she knew, but for that you don't kill people.'

In a book published two years later, the still unreconstructed communist Feklisov explained how Julius was first approached by the Soviets in 1942 and agreed to 'fight the common enemy', Nazi Germany. The engineer was provided with a Leica camera and taught how to microfilm secret documents.[19] Feklisov described how Julius had stolen the proximity fuse and handed it over to the Russians disguised as a Christmas present. (The principle of the fuse was later to be used to shoot down the American U2 spy plane flown by Garry Powers.) Finally, he described how Julius went on to recruit a ring of spies, including Sobell and Greenglass. Feklisov described Julius's collaboration with Soviet Intelligence as a 'kind of religious calling'. He sought no financial reward and only accepted money at a late stage in order to assist the escape of his comrades. Overall, Feklisov assessed Julius's contribution to Soviet Intelligence as 'extremely valuable', but he considered the information concerning the atomic bomb to be 'very minor'.[20]

Incredible as it might seem, even more disclosures concerning the Rosenbergs were about to emerge from the secret world of espionage.

VENONA

Before the end of the Second World War the US Army Signals Service set up a project, known by the codename 'Venona', for the purpose of deciphering the diplomatic code of America's then ally, the Soviet Union. When this code was finally broken in about 1946 it became possible for the Americans to read the secret cable traffic between the Soviet consulate in America and KGB headquarters in Moscow. At the time of the Rosenbergs' trial the Venona decrypts were still a closely guarded secret (and, of course, were not used in the trial), but with the end of the Cold War and the normalisation of relations with Russia the need for secrecy gradually disappeared. Beginning in 1995 almost 3,000 decrypted cables were released into the public domain.

They were revealing. Take, for example, the text of a Venona intercept dated 21 September 1944. (The words in square brackets give the meanings of the Soviet code words.)[21]

Lately the development of new people has been in progress. LIBERAL [Julius Rosenberg] recommended the wife of his wife's brother, Ruth GREENGLASS, with a safe flat in view. She is 21 years old, a TOWNSWOMAN [American], a GYMNAST [member of the Young Communist League] since 1942. She lives on Stanton Street. LIBERAL and his wife recommend her as an intelligent and clever girl. Ruth learned that her husband was called up by the army but was not sent to the front. He is a mechanical engineer and is now working at the ENORMOZ [Manhattan project] plant in SANTA FE, New Mexico . . .

And on 14 November another intercept read:

LIBERAL [Julius Rosenberg] has safely carried through the contracting of HUGHES. HUGHES is a good friend of METER. We propose to pair them off and get them to photograph their own materials having given a camera for this purpose. HUGHES is a good photographer, has a large darkroom and all the equipment but he does not have a Leica. LIBERAL will receive the films from METER for passing on. Direction of the PROBATIONERS [agents] will be continued through LIBERAL, this will ease the load on him.

(HUGHES and METER were engineers recruited by Julius Rosenberg to his spy ring. They subsequently fled to Russia, where they became important figures in Soviet electronics research.)

On 29 November yet another intercept included the following,

Information on LIBERAL's wife. Surname that of her husband, first name ETHEL, 29 years old. Married five years. Finished secondary school. A FELLOWCOUNTRYMAN [Communist Party member] since 1938. Sufficiently well developed politically. Knows about her husband's work and the role of METER and NIL. In view of delicate health does not work and as [sic] a devoted person.

Other cables concerned the provision of a German camera for Julius. The complicity of the Rosenbergs had finally been confirmed beyond any doubt.

'GREATER LOVE'

So Julius and Ethel were a couple of no-good commies after all? Commies, certainly, but no-good? In seeking to control the untidy world of leftist politics in America, the Soviet Union acted at all times only in pursuit of its own naked self-interest, but that was not true of the mass of its supporters. It is easy to forget that most people who joined the Party in the 1930s and 1940s and later spied for Russia did so, not for personal gain but out of a feeling that this was the best way to improve the lot of the poor, to stamp out inequality and injustice, to make a better world; much the same motivations in other words as good people of every party, if perhaps a bit more fervently held. Julius and Ethel can be accused of naivety, of stupidity, of gross disloyalty, but they probably had at least as much feeling for their fellow men as any others, perhaps more if compared with the McCarthys and the Roy Cohens of their time. And they were prepared to pay for their beliefs with their lives.

Julius was unlucky in many ways; he had become an idealistic young communist at a time when the Soviet Union was America's ally, but by the time his spying came to light American boys were fighting communists in Korea. He would not have died if he had been prosecuted under another Act; he would not have died if he had been convicted in a different country. He might not have died if his counsel had not thought fit to ask for the bomb sketch to be kept secret 'for reasons of national security'. Ethel was a different matter.

Even now we don't know the true extent of Ethel's involvement in her husband's spying activities. Her prison friend Miriam Moskovicz, a fellow radical, described her as 'a good soldier. She followed the Party line uncritically, unquestionably, and aggressively. It wasn't only that she followed the Party line, but she argued for it and justified it with a lot of voluminous verbosity. She was absolutely uncritical.'[22] Common sense suggests that a wife who passionately shared her husband's political interests was likely to be involved in them up to the hilt, but common sense alone was not a good enough reason for Judge Kaufman so much to have misjudged Ethel's involvement.

At the end, both Ethel and Julius were prepared to accept a frightful death rather than betray their principles. Perhaps they believed that a martyred communist would be of more use to the cause than one who had saved his life by cooperating with the authorities. It was a high price to pay, particularly when much of it fell on their young sons, who were given no option in the matter. The fallible Judge Kaufman may have got it right after all when he said:

> The evidence indicated quite clearly that Julius Rosenberg was the prime mover in this conspiracy. However, let no mistake be made about the role which his wife, Ethel Rosenberg, played in this conspiracy. Instead of deterring him from pursuing his ignoble cause, she encouraged and assisted the cause. She was a mature woman – almost three years older that her husband and almost seven years older than her younger brother. She was a full-fledged partner in this crime. Indeed, the defendants Julius and Ethel Rosenberg placed their devotion to their cause above their own personal safety and were conscious that they were sacrificing their own children, should their misdeeds be detected – all of which did not deter them from pursuing their course. Love for their cause dominated their lives – it was even greater than their love for their children.

IN LATER YEARS

Because of bad feeling over the Rosenberg case, Irving Kaufman had to wait until 1961 before he was elevated to the Court of Appeal, Second Circuit, and he never achieved his ambition of becoming a member of the US Supreme Court. Shortly after the trial, Irving Saypol received the judicial appointment that he deserved. Roy Cohen went on to become chief counsel to the McCarthy witch-hunts and then enjoyed a lucrative career at the Bar, despite being tried on (and acquitted of) charges of conspiracy, bribery and fraud. Two months before his death from AIDS in 1986 he was disbarred for misappropriation of clients' funds, pressuring a client to amend his will and lying on a Bar application.

Manny Bloch continued to protest his clients' innocence after their execution, describing them as 'victims of a military dictatorship dressed up in civilian garb'. These and other wild remarks led to an investigation with a view to disbarment. Perhaps it all hastened his death by a heart attack some seven months after the execution of his last clients, the Rosenbergs.

The publicly reviled David Greenglass served ten of his fifteen-year prison sentence before disappearing into an obscurity that was to be breached only in the 1990s, when he still believed himself justified in betraying his sister and lying to the court. Morton Sobell was not conclusively identified in the Venona cables and never admitted to having spied for Russia (though Feklisov claimed him as a former spy). Harry Gold was released from prison in 1966 and died six years later.

Robert and Michael Rosenberg were adopted by Abe Meeropol (the writer of the anti-lynching song 'Strange Fruit') and his wife, Anne. They proved to be loving parents. The boys still defend their natural parents' memory, and Robert has founded an organisation devoted to assisting the children of parents who have suffered for their progressive activities.

AN EXECUTION VIGNETTE

Robert Lamphere, the FBI liaison to the Venona project, left this description of the night of the Rosenbergs' deaths:

the judge went ahead with the death sentence, but made it clear to the attorneys for the defendants that if they would co-operate with the government, he would reduce both death sentences to some other sentence. But only if they talked, and if only they told the authorities the truth. So on the night of the executions, the scheduling of the executions, I was sitting next to the desk of the number-three man in the FBI, Mickey Ladd, and we had an assistant director of the FBI at Sing Sing. I sat there hoping and hoping and hoping that they would decide to talk, but instead they chose to die for their belief in support of a man like Joseph Stalin.

PART TWO

The Ungodly

Introduction

It is a sad comment on the human race that the more we concern ourselves with godliness the more cruelly some of us behave towards each other. Nothing demonstrates this more than the activities of the tribunal that forms the subject of the two trials in this section, the Congregation for the Doctrine of the Faith or, as it is better known, the Inquisition.

The Inquisition most familiar to us today, from Edgar Allen Poe to Monty Python, is the Spanish Inquisition; it has not always had a good press. Set up in the fifteenth century as a means of keeping Jewish converts within the faith, the Spanish Inquisition, under its leader, Tomás de Torquemada, earned a fearsome reputation for its use of torture and its autos-da-fé. However, it is not the Spanish Inquisition that we are concerned with here but an altogether different creature that, though less oppressive, was not without its faults.

Even in its earliest days it would be wrong to imagine the Inquisition that tried Joan of Arc (the medieval Inquisition) as a body without rules. It had its own strict procedures and kept a careful record of its proceedings – which is how we know so much about Joan's fate. What went wrong in her case was something that no amount of rules can prevent: the principal inquisitor was in the pay of the prisoner's enemies and was prepared to do whatever was necessary to secure her death. In this respect at least history can redress the balance.

Joan was an extraordinary young woman. She was courageous, wise beyond her years, spiritual and, some say, possessed of the gift of prophecy. Today, her belief that she could hear the voices of angels would probably be enough to have her locked up; fortunately for France, this was not so in the fifteenth century. Her military successes, though not as remarkable as they are sometimes depicted, were nevertheless extensive and certainly important enough to incur the wrath of her enemies, the English – so much so, that as soon as they had her in their power they were determined to make her pay. The appalling injustices of Joan's trial and tragic death were later to be laid bare, but not before her ashes had long since blown away.

A century after Joan's death the Inquisition was thoroughly reformed, and show trials like Joan's became impossible. Those accused before the Roman Inquisition, as the new body came to be known, were given the right to give evidence on their own behalf (a privilege refused to them in Britain until the nineteenth century), to call witnesses, to be told in detail the nature of the charge against them and to have legal representation, even, if they could not afford to pay for it, at the expense of the court. Interrogation under torture – still common in lay courts at the time – was permitted only in very restricted circumstances and was rarely used in practice.

Unquestionably the most famous person to appear before the Roman Inquisition was the astronomer Galileo Galilei; his crime, suggesting that the earth went round the sun. The proceedings were a disaster for the Church and have been held up ever since as an example of the worst sort of clerical narrow-mindedness, which was not entirely just. But there was worse. Recent discoveries have revealed that Galileo's fate, like Joan's, was almost certainly brought about by corrupt practice. Every conclusion of the Inquisition that tried him now appears to have been defective. The irony is that the whole sorry episode need never have happened had Galileo displayed even a modicum of prudence.

CHAPTER FIVE

The Maid

The Trial of Joan of Arc, 1431

It took the threat of burning at the stake for the Inquisition to force a 'confession' from the nineteen-year-old girl. But this was not enough for her enemies; a carefully stage-managed 'relapse' gave them the excuse they needed. Her end was horrific; whether from accident or design, the stake had been built in such a way that the executioner could not take the usual steps to hasten the prisoner's release. The Maid died in agony invoking the names of Jesus and all the saints. Thus ended the life of a devout and innocent young woman who had inflicted such military setbacks on her country's enemies as they would never recover from. How did all this come about?

England had been at war with France for nearly a century when hostilities were brought to a close, albeit briefly, by the treaty of Troyes (1420). Under this it was agreed that Henry V of England would immediately become 'Regent and heir' of France and on the death of the French King, Charles VI would assume the throne. One of the benefits of this arrangement was that it would disinherit Charles's son, the heir to the throne (the Dauphin) who was believed to have been implicated in the murder of the Duke of Burgundy. Mortality spoiled this tidy arrangement when Henry died before Charles. The Dauphin assumed the title of Charles VII, and war with England broke out afresh. The English controlled large chunks of France, including everything north of the Loire. The French forces were deeply divided between the Orléanists (who supported their king) and the Burgundians (who supported the English). As ever in such wars, the land between the two warring factions suffered greatly. The little village of Domrémy near Lorraine in the Vosges region was a case in point. It supported the Dauphin, but bordered land owned by his enemies and was marched over by the armies of both sides. In the year 1425, when the village was partially burnt by the marauding armies, one of its young women experienced visions for the first time.

Jeannette Darc, also known as Jeanne d'Arc, was born in about 1412, the child of a prosperous farmer and his wife. Jeanne, or Joan as we know her, was the youngest of a family of five. At about the age of thirteen this quiet, religiously inclined child, while fasting in her father's garden, had an epiphany. In her words:

I heard a voice from God for my help and guidance. The first time I heard this voice, I was very much frightened. I heard this voice to my right towards the Church. Rarely do I hear it without its being accompanied by a light . . . I believe it was sent to me from God. When I heard it for the third time, I recognized that it was the voice of an Angel.[1]

By 'voice' Joan seems to have meant speaking apparition.

Today, the hearing of non-corporeal voices is seen as a sign of mental disturbance (such as temporal lobe epilepsy); it was not so in the late Middle Ages. Nor was it surprising that such an ecstatic experience should have occurred to a serious-minded, but illiterate adolescent brought up in the heady atmosphere of religious piety, patriotism and insecurity that was Domrémy. Nevertheless, had she not strayed from the family farm, few would have heard of Joan; her glory – and her tragedy – was that she became caught up in the murderous politics of her day.

'NOTHING EVIL, ONLY GOOD'

Joan first came to public notice when her voices told her to go to Robert de Baudricourt, captain of the nearby town of Vaucouleurs, with a view to relieving the French-held city of Orléans, then under siege by the English. At first she was rudely rebuffed, but Joan's persistence and the fact that she was able accurately to predict another French victory finally won over de Baudricourt, who sent her through enemy lines under military escort with a letter for the King at Chinon. It was on this journey that she first dressed, for practical reasons probably, in male attire. At about this time she also began calling herself La Pucelle (the Maid).

At court, the Dauphin is said to have stood among his attendants in order to see whether Joan would recognise him. She passed the test, claiming afterwards that she knew him 'among many others by the counsel of her voice, which revealed him to her'. Joan is said to have produced a 'secret sign' that she had promised to disclose to no one except her king. (She later described it as a golden crown brought to her by an angel, but her accounts on this point are inconsistent.) At the time, Charles, known unflatteringly as the Bastard of Orléans, had serious doubts about his legitimacy, and it is more likely that it was the assurance offered by Joan's heavenly voices rather than any magical crown that convinced the King. Before giving her any tangible help, however, he first sent Joan to the Archbishop of Rheims at Poitiers, asking him to appoint a commission to discover if Joan's mission was 'contrary to the faith'. After three weeks' questioning and prayer, this learned body declared that 'in her has been found nothing evil; only good, humility, virginity, devotion, honesty, simplicity; and of her birth and of her life several marvellous things are told as true'. The King, it concluded, 'must not prevent her from going to Orléans with his soldiers, but must have her conducted honourably, trusting in God'. For good measure, Joan's status as a virgin was certified by the Queen of Sicily.

Confident of her probity and virtue, the Dauphin now furnished Joan with an armed escort, the exact size of which is unclear, and a confessor with whom she went to Blois to take command of an army preparing to march on Orléans. (The idea of soldiers being led by an untrained adolescent girl sounds odd to modern ears, but it was not unknown in medieval times.) She was given a *harnois blanc*, an all-in-one suit of armour, but rejected the offer of a sword in favour of one that was found, as she had prophesied, in a trunk behind a church altar. The sword, which had probably been left there as a votive offering, was engraved with the words 'Jesus Maria'. She ordered the words to be sewn on her banner. Her quest had begun.

WAR AND PEACE

One of the most extraordinary aspects of Joan is her apparent prophetic ability. For example, in a letter from Sire de Rotslaer dated 22 April 1429 and franked as having been received well before the events it forecast, the writer reported that Joan had claimed

> that she would save Orléans and would compel the English to raise the siege, that she herself in a battle before Orléans would be wounded by a shaft but would not die of it, and that the King, in the course of the coming summer, would be crowned at Rheims . . .

The following month, after the English had rejected her offers of an honourable retreat, Joan's forces marched to relieve the besieged city of Orléans, where the Maid did in fact receive an arrow wound and had to retire briefly from the battle. When she resumed the fight, the English are said to have 'trembled with terror' and the city was relieved. Within a month they had been driven from the Loire Valley by a series of successful French assaults, and Charles was crowned, once again as Joan had prophesied, at Rheims. The Maid was there with her banner: 'as it had shared in the toil,' she announced, 'it was just that it should share in the victory'.[2] Joan now made an offer of peace to the English, but it was rejected.

But it was not a story of unmitigated success. An attempt to retake Paris was a costly failure at which Joan suffered a wound in the thigh from a crossbow bolt. The army was forced to withdraw to the Loire for the winter. The King refused Joan's request to be allowed to return home; instead, he ennobled her with the title Du Lis. (The fleur de lys was the ancient heraldic device of the French kings.) It is difficult to say just what contribution Joan had made to the earlier victories. Her bravery and élan must have had considerable effect, but she displayed no outstanding qualities as a military leader and she disclaimed the title *chef de guerre*.

CAPTURE AND BETRAYAL

Hostilities were resumed in 1430, and on 23 May, while returning from a sortie out of Compiègne, Joan was captured by the Burgundians when the gates of the city were closed in her face – whether by treachery or accident we do not know. Joan was later to claim that her voices had warned her that she would be captured 'before St John's Day' (24 June).[3]

Joan's worst fear was that she would be handed over to the English. At one point she even leapt in desperation from a tower of the castle in which she was imprisoned. After three months in captivity Joan's nightmare was to be fulfilled: she was sold to the English for 10,000 livres. Although the Dauphin had English captives who could have been offered in exchange for Joan, he does not appear to have lifted a finger to secure her freedom. But what were the English to do with her? They could not kill her out of hand and they could not themselves try the young woman who had beaten them. But they knew someone who could.

Henry now wrote to his 'beloved and loyal counsellor', Pierre Cauchon, Bishop of Beauvais, 'inviting' the Holy Inquisition to try Joan for the crime of dressing as a man, for 'murder' and for her scandalously false claim to have been sent by God. Cauchon, knowing where his best interests lay, readily agreed, and Joan was sent to Rouen, where she was imprisoned in the castle to await her trial. (Paris, the obvious choice of venue, was considered too insecure.) A small iron cage was built to contain her, but in the end it seems that she was kept shackled in her cell. This was no nominal security measure; the irons were removed only for her appearances in court.

The unpleasant Jean d'Estivet, a canon of Beauvais, was appointed promoter (or prosecutor) of the court. Like Cauchon, he was in the pay of the English. Assisting the court were some sixty assessors, many of them theologians and clerics of the University of Paris, where Cauchon had formerly been rector. A letter from Henry referred to this compliant body as men whom 'we had summoned to this aforesaid town [Rouen] in order to conduct the trial'. The court, in other words, was far from impartial, as it was soon to demonstrate. Before the trial began Cauchon caused enquiries to be made about Joan's past at Domrémy; nothing was discovered to her discredit. A bodily examination of Joan found her still to be a virgin (and thus not a witch). None of this was reported to the tribunal. Nor was it informed of her earlier examination at Poitiers by Cauchon's superior and of his commission's commendatory conclusions.

Not everyone was happy with the proceedings. The boundary of the bishopric was the river, and some objected that Joan's capture had taken place on the wrong side of it. The court knew better than to accede to such pedantry. Others took objection to Joan being held, contrary to canon law, in a secular prison instead of in a convent; they were overruled by Cauchon. Jean de Saint-Avit, Bishop of Avranches, reminded Cauchon of the rule that 'in matters of faith which are in doubt reference should always be made to the Pope or to the General Council'.[4] This obstacle Cauchon dealt with simply by removing the objector from the list of assessors. Lesser personages who voiced doubts were thrown into prison or threatened with drowning.

After eight months in close confinement guarded by English soldiers who seem to have treated her disgracefully, Joan was brought before the court. We are fortunate in having a careful and complete record of the proceedings that was made at the time by a notary public, Guillaume Manchon. It is a convincing and seemingly impartial document.[5] The English hid two further note-takers in the courtroom, but Manchon claims (apparently with justification) to have resisted their attempts to influence his account.

THE INVESTIGATION

The trial was held under the rules of the French Inquisition. It began with an interrogation of the prisoner, from which charges, called Articles, could be brought. Once the accused had had the opportunity of responding to those Articles, the court would proceed to judgment. There is no reason why such a procedure should not produce a just result, but it was not justice that was being offered to Joan.

The preliminary investigation began on 9 January 1431 in the great hall of the castle at Rouen. Sixty assessors attended at first, but throughout the trial their numbers varied from day to day. Some were present at every hearing; some at hardly any. After initial objections, Joan agreed to take the oath, but made it clear that there were certain matters that her conscience would not allow her to disclose, notably her private discussions with the King. She also refused at first to answer detailed questions about her visions.

After some initial questions about her background and how she came to be in command of the Dauphin's armies, Joan was asked about her voices. She told the court that she believed that they were those of the Archangel St Michael and other angels, including Sts Margaret and Catherine. They were not merely internal visions: 'I saw them with these very eyes, as well as I see you.' She had 'asked three things of her voices: one concerning her deliverance; secondly that God should help the French and watch over the towns which were in their possession; and lastly the salvation of her own soul'. Joan's jump from the castle tower was a natural subject for enquiry. Was she attempting the crime of suicide or was she relying on the well-known ability of witches to fly? Joan replied that she had acted only out of fear of falling into the hands of the English. She regretted the attempt, which had been against the advice of her voices. The interrogator then tried to show that Joan had made superstitious use of her ring and her banners and that she had used magical powers to find lost objects; he got nowhere.

The questioning, which lasted for three or four hours a day over twelve days, began in public but, once it was plain that Joan could give as well as she got, was removed to a smaller room, where those present could be restricted to a carefully selected few chosen by Cauchon.

No one reading the official transcript of Joan's trial can fail to be impressed at the way this unlettered young woman stood up for herself despite the absence of friends, the intimidating circumstances of her confinement and the physical weakness she was experiencing while fasting for Lent. The questioning by skilled and learned interrogators was subtle, persistent and moved rapidly from topic to topic, but Joan proved to be a clear, intelligent and brave witness well able to handle the inquisitors' tricks. When asked a question she had already answered, she would reply brusquely, 'That does not concern your trial' or 'Move on to the next question'. If the inquisitor asked about matters she was reluctant to talk about, she would undertake to respond the following day. On one occasion she tartly told the interrogator that he would find the answer to his question in the minutes of the previous session.

At one point Joan said that her voices had assured her that in the end she would come to the kingdom of heaven. The questioner jumped in immediately to ask whether this meant that Joan believed that she could not commit mortal sin. She confounded him by replying, 'As to this I know nothing; but commit myself in all things to Our Lord.' Asked whether she knew she was in a state of grace, Joan deftly replied, 'If I am not, may God bring me into it; if I am, may God keep me in it.' Asked whether she approved of the Dauphin's murder of the former Duke of Burgundy, she once again played a straight bat by saying that it was a great tragedy for the kingdom but that, whatever occurred between them, she had been sent to help the King.

All the skills of experienced interrogators were used to trip Joan up. She was, for example, asked which of the three claimants to the papacy should be obeyed. She said the Pope at Rome. She was asked why she had fought at Orléans when her voices had warned her that she would be injured there. She replied that she had told the King of the warning but could not give up her work. Referring to the root of the mandrake plant, which was believed to possess magical powers, the interrogator tried one of the oldest tricks in the book. Instead of asking whether she had one, Joan was asked where her root was. She denied having one. Another 'trap' question was whether God hated the English. Joan answered that she did not know but she did know that God would drive all the English out of France except those who died there.

The wearing of male dress was a serious offence in those days. When questioned about it, Joan's answers were inconsistent. She did, however, remark, pertinently, that neither man's nor woman's dress made any difference in receiving her Saviour. As for undertaking womanly duties, Joan wryly observed that there were enough other women to do them. In a moment of inspired prophecy she claimed – the words are recorded plainly in the transcript – that 'within seven years' space the English would have to forfeit a bigger prize than Orléans'.[6] In fact, Paris fell to the French on 12 November 1437, some six years and eight months later.

THE 'KINDLY AND MERCIFUL' MEN

The trial proper (the trial in Ordinary as it was called, as distinct from the preliminary investigation) began on 27 March before the bishop, the vice-inquisitor and the assessors. Seventy Articles had been prepared against Joan, many of them of a fanciful nature. They included, for example, references to sorcery, fairies, magic trees, mandrake roots, Joan's 'immoral life', placing spells and melting wax on children's heads.

Cauchon began by telling Joan that the court was composed of 'kindly and merciful' men who desired only to proceed 'with gentleness and pity, without demanding vengeance or bodily punishment, but wishing to teach her and lead her into the way of truth and salvation'. Nice words from a man determined on her death.

Joan denied all the charges as they were read out, one by one. Her only concession was to having once claimed in a letter that everything she did was by the advice of God. She should, she said, have written everything *good* that she did. Accused of having made false prophecies, she replied, 'By their fruits ye shall know them.' Asked whether she was subject to the Church on earth she answered, 'Yes, Our Lord being first served.' If all defendants were as adept in standing up to questioning, few would be convicted.

The accusations against Joan were then pruned drastically, the more fanciful being struck out. The remaining charges alleged in summary:

1. Joan's visions were 'lies, untrue, pernicious and evil . . .' proceeding from 'evil and devilish spirits'.
2. The sign given by Joan to the King was 'a presumptuous lie, seductive and pernicious and a pretence that is derogatory of both ecclesiastical and angelic dignity'.
3. Joan had believed in the angels and saints 'too lightly' and affirmed her belief 'too rashly'.

4. Her prophecies were 'superstition and divination, presumptuous assertion and vain boasting'.

5. Joan's male dress blasphemed God in His sacraments and transgressed divine law, the Holy Scriptures and canon law.

6. Joan was 'cruel and a murderess, desirous of the shedding of human blood, seditious, provoking to tyranny and blaspheming God'.

7. In leaving her parents Joan had transgressed the commandment to honour her father and mother and in promising the King to drive his enemies out of France she had been 'presumptuous and rash'.

8. Her leap from the tower was 'cowardice tending to despair and suicide'. In saying that she had been forgiven Joan had misunderstood the doctrine of free will.

9. It was 'rash and presumptuous' for Joan to have claimed that the angels had promised to bring her to heaven if she remained a virgin.

10. It was 'rash presumption' for Joan to assert that God loved others more than herself.

11. In claiming that she had made reverence to the angels and saints she was an idolater and invoker of demons and a wanderer from the faith.

12. In defying the Church Joan was schismatic and in pernicious error.

Most of these accusations had little or no basis in fact. Since the court had hardly any evidence before it other than Joan's own testimony, the indictment, as we would call it, can in no way be said to have been forensically justified. In any event, there were answers to the two principal accusations. The charge concerning her visions ignored the fact that the voices had urged Joan to go to church. And the charge concerning male dress failed to acknowledge the teaching of St Thomas Aquinas that women were allowed to wear men's dress out of necessity. These imperfect Articles were nevertheless sent to the assessors for comment, together with a carefully edited summary of the interrogation. They were then submitted to the University of Paris to be examined by sixteen doctors of theology and six licentiates.

By now, the middle of April, the weakened Joan had fallen ill with food poisoning. Admonished once more to confess, she again asked to be taken before the Pope for judgment. (Jean de la Fontaine, the *examinateur de la cause*, was later to resign when he discovered that Joan's professions of willingness to submit herself to Rome had been suppressed from the court record.) Faced with her 'intransigence', Joan was taken to the great dungeon of the castle, shown the instruments of torture and asked to recant. Her response was: 'Truly, if you were to tear me limb from limb and make my soul leave my body, I would not say to you anything else. And if you force me to do so, then afterwards I shall say that you made me say so by force.' The master executioner later observed that 'she answered with such prudence that all present marvelled'.

The report from the English-dominated University of Paris was finally received. It agreed with all the charges with only minor reservations. The assessors now decided that one final 'charitable warning' should be put to Joan. Peter Maurice, a canon from Rouen, came to her cell and, after reading out the University's lengthy condemnation, asked Joan to submit to the Church. She replied bravely, 'if I were to be condemned and saw the fire lit and the wood prepared and the executioner who was to burn me ready to cast me into the fire, still in the fire would I not say anything other than I have said. And I will maintain what I have said unto death.' Her courage was to fail her all too shortly.

THE MOCK EXECUTION

The following day Joan was taken to the cemetery of Saint-Ouen, where a scaffold and stake had been erected. A sermon was read to her in the presence of the executioner, followed by a reading of the charges. 'Jeanne, my very good friend' was once again 'charitably admonished' and asked to submit to the Church for the salvation of her soul and body. Once more, she discomfited her accusers by expressing her willingness to appeal to the Pope. This was not the response the tribunal wanted to hear; the court was competent, she was told, and the Holy Father was far away. As the horrifying sentence of death by burning began to be read out, Joan's spirits finally broke and she called out that she was willing to do all that the Church and the judges desired. What followed can come as no surprise to anyone aware of the depths of Cauchon's depravity.

A written declaration was produced to the court by the secretary to the English King and thrust before the illiterate Joan with a demand that she should sign it without it having even been read to her. It is said that Joan laughed when she made her mark. (The writer, Pernoud, has speculated that this was because Joan used the same sign of a cross in her correspondence to indicate secretly to the reader that a statement was not intended, but it could just as easily have been nervousness.[7]) The document read,

> I, Jeanne, called The Pucelle, a miserable sinner, after I recognized the snare of error in which I was held, and now that I have by God's grace returned to our mother Holy Church, in order that it may be apparent that not feignedly but with good heart I have returned her, I do confess that I have grievously sinned, in falsely pretending that I have had revelations from God and his angels, St Catherine, and St Margaret etc. And all my words and deeds which are contrary to

the Church I do revoke, and I desire to live in unity with the Church, never departing therefrom. In witness whereof my sign manual.

It is difficult to believe that such a cynical act of deception could be exceeded, but it was; someone was later to substitute in the official record a much longer confession, purporting to show Joan admitting countless further crimes to which she had never confessed.

Despite the court's promise that if she confessed she would not be punished, Joan was thereupon sentenced to 'perpetual imprisonment with the bread of sorrow and the water of affliction'. That night, lodged once again in the English prison, she was made to assume women's clothing. Her hair, which had grown long in captivity, was shaved off and she was put in irons. What happened next is unclear, but four days later Joan was found to be wearing men's clothes. When questioned about this by a secretly jubilant Cauchon, Joan is said to have admitted changing voluntarily, but there is reason to doubt this. A later trial was told that she had complained of having been treated violently in prison, 'molested, beaten and ill-used; and that an English lord had insulted her'. The court was also told that her woman's clothes had been removed and that men's clothes had been left in a sack in her cell. Whatever the truth of the matter, one must ask, where else would a prisoner who was serving a sentence of life imprisonment under close confinement for, among things, wearing men's clothing get such clothing from?

Even this relapse was not enough for Joan's enemies; a few days later she was visited in her cell by Cauchon, the vice-inquisitor and several assessors, who asked her whether she had heard her voices again. In the court record she is shown to have answered 'yes', and against this word the court reporter noted *Responsio mortifera* ('the fatal reply'). Cauchon now had to ask the assessors what should be done. Of the forty who answered, only two were of the opinion that the court should proceed straight to judgment. Cauchon overruled the majority. On leaving the prison that day he was heard to call out to his paymasters in English, 'Farewell. Be of good cheer. It is done.' Events moved swiftly thereafter.

THE STAKE

Charged with a serious relapse, Joan repudiated her confession, which she had made only 'for fear of the fire'. She would, she said, 'rather do penance by dying than bear any longer the agony of imprisonment'. The following day she was permitted for the first time to receive Holy Communion. At eight o'clock on the morning of 30 May 1431 she was taken to the Old Market at Rouen, where she was informed 'in the name of the Lord' that as a relapsed heretic she was to be cast forth and rejected from the Church as an infected limb and handed over to secular justice, 'praying the same to treat you with kindness and humanity in respect of your life and your limbs'. (This was the common formula in such circumstances, not meant to be taken seriously.) Without further ceremony an English official ordered that she be taken to the stake that had already been prepared nearby. As Joan was about to mount it, she asked for a crucifix. An English soldier roughly put two pieces of wood together and handed it to her; she tucked it inside her dress. Later, as the brands caught fire, a priest held out before her a cross that he had brought from a nearby church. She died crying, 'Jesus. Jesus'. 'And many', the court record states, 'both noble and peasant, murmured greatly against the English'.

Legend has it that at the moment of death a white dove flew up from the square towards the French lines.

'COZENAGE, INIQUITY, INCONSEQUENCES AND MANIFEST ERRORS'

It is not necessary to graft modern ideas of justice onto fifteenth-century court procedures to conclude that Joan's trial was as defective as a trial could be.

The principal judge was appointed by and secretly in the pay of the prisoner's enemies. Joan faced the most serious charges without benefit of representation, even though this was her right at canon law. (Manchon's notes state that she refused the offer of counsel, but it seems likely that this referred to the advice of the clerical authorities rather than to independent counsel.) Evidence was deliberately suppressed and the court record tampered with. The assessors, whose job it was to advise on guilt, were not all present throughout the proceedings and were shown only a doctored version of Joan's testimony, as were the university authorities. Contrary to canon law and against the advice of most of the assessors, Joan was denied her right of appeal to Rome. It is doubtful whether Joan had any opportunity to comment on the charges (the Articles) in their final form. Certainly, they had little, if any, foundation in the evidence. The confession that this illiterate young woman was forced to sign without reading had been obtained under threat of torture and a horrific death. Her later renunciation of that confession was almost certainly obtained by trickery. Finally, she was executed illegally by the English without the order of a court that was required by law.

It took nearly a quarter of a century before the faults in this scandalous process were officially acknowledged. With the passage of time it became politically expedient for a newly appointed Pope to order an inquiry into Joan's trial. It consisted of a bishop and an archbishop, but the investigations were actually carried out by the Inquisitor, Jean Bréhal. Joan's family were the formal prosecutors, and the former judges were represented by their legal successors or, in the case of the now deceased Cauchon, his family.

After hearing many witnesses over several months the court declared on 7 July 1456 that

> the said Processes and Sentences [were] full of cozenage, iniquity, inconsequences, and manifest errors, in fact as well as in law; We say that they have been, are, and shall be – as well as the aforesaid Abjuration, their execution, and all that followed – null, non-existent, without value or effect.

Despite the existence of 'manifest malice against the Roman Church and indeed even of heresy' no one involved in the former proceedings was punished for this appalling miscarriage of justice.

By this judgment Cauchon's inquisition was condemned as the travesty of justice that it undoubtedly was. But the retrial did not validate Joan's visions, her orthodoxy or her sanctity; its purpose was primarily secular, to advance the legitimacy of the French King. It took over four centuries more for Joan to be beatified (in 1909). She was canonised a year later and is now the patron saint of the country she gave her life for, France.

CHAPTER SIX

The Starry Messenger

The Trial of Galileo, 1633

Once it was realised that the earth was not flat but spherical, 'common sense' suggested that the sun, which daily rises in the east and sets in the west, must revolve around the earth; the idea that the earth goes round the sun was manifest nonsense. At least that was the view of the second-century astronomer, Ptolemy. Fifteen hundred years later this view was challenged in a book written by the Polish astronomer and mathematician Copernicus. His Little Commentary *suggested that the sun and not the earth was at – or, strictly, near – the centre of the universe and that the rotation of the earth accounted for the apparent movement of the stars. It took nearly two decades before this theory could be confirmed by observation, and the confirmation was to cost its discoverer dearly.*

Galileo Galilei was born in Padua in 1564, the oldest son of a distinguished mathematician and musician. When his family moved to Florence, Galileo contemplated joining a monastic order, but his father sent him to Pisa to study medicine instead. The subject did not grip the boy, and a chance lecture in geometry drew him to his father's love, mathematics. In 1585 lack of means forced Galileo to leave the university without taking a degree, but he was determined to succeed. Private study eventually resulted in his obtaining, first, a lectureship in mathematics and then the chair of mathematics at Pisa, where he proved Aristotle wrong in suggesting that objects fall at a speed proportional to their weight. (The story of his having demonstrated this at the leaning tower may be as apocryphal as that of Newton's apple.) In 1592 he became professor of mathematics at his home town, Padua, where he worked and prospered for eighteen years.

Galileo's interest in the stars was prompted by the appearance in 1604 in the constellation Serpentarius of what is now known to be a supernova. The following January, having established that the new star was further away than the moon, he gave three lectures arguing that the heavenly bodies could not, as traditionally taught, be eternal and unchanging. What he lacked to confirm this was an instrument for observing the heavens better than the unaided eye. Fortuitously, a Dutch spectacle-maker, Hans Lippershey, had just developed a new design of spyglass. Hearing about this in 1609, Galileo had a similar device made with improved magnification; by the end of the year he had increased its power thirty-fold. But it was what Galileo saw through what had come to be called the telescope that mattered.

THE 'STARRY MESSENGER'

In January 1610 Galileo observed through his 'telescope' from his garden four small 'stars' near Jupiter that he quickly came to realise were satellites of that planet. He published his findings in a book entitled *Sidereus Nuncius* (or 'Starry Messenger'). One of Galileo's former pupils was the Grand Duke of Tuscany, Cosimo II de Medici. Hoping that the Duke would become his patron, Galileo diplomatically named the satellites *Sidera Medicea* after him. The flattery worked; despite an offer of a salary increase and life tenure at Padua, Galileo chose to take up the appointments of chief mathematician of the University of Pisa and philosopher and mathematician to the Grand Duke, and forsook Padua once again for Tuscany.

Never one to hide his light under a bushel, Galileo exhibited his telescope in the gardens of the Quirinal Palace in Rome. Although it received a frosty reception from a few – there were some who even refused to look through the instrument – his sightings were confirmed by the Jesuits of the Roman college, although their interpretation of what they saw was understandably different from Galileo's. The next few years were a period of great achievements for the astronomer – his discovery of sunspots, in particular, confirmed his view of the mutability of the heavens. But problems were about to emerge.

The Church had not been unduly bothered by Copernicus' theories concerning the place of the earth in the solar system. He was, after all, a canon in a monastery who had dedicated his book to the Pope. Contrary to popular belief, many churchmen of the day had enquiring minds and were broadly read. Unorthodox views were tolerated – within bounds. But every organisation has its obscurantists and for some the new science had gone too far; it seemed to them to contradict the Bible, at least when understood literally. They quoted, for example, Joshua 10: 12–13, which reads,

> Then spake Joshua to the Lord in the day when the Lord delivered up the Amorites before the children of Israel, and he said in the sight of Israel, Sun stand thou still upon Gibeon; and thou, Moon, in the valley of Ajalon. And the sun stood still, and the moon stayed, until the people had avenged themselves upon their enemies. Is not this written in the book of Jasher? So the sun stood still in the midst of heaven, and hastened not to go down about a whole day.

Voices gradually began to be raised against the new astronomy, and on All Souls' Day 1613 Niccolò Lorini, a Dominican friar and professor of ecclesiastical history, preached a sermon in which he asserted that the heliocentric (or sun-centred) theory violated scripture. Galileo's response took the form of a letter to his former student and friend Benedetto Castelli, a Benedictine monk – the so-called, 'Letter to Castelli'. Expressing sentiments that some could still read with profit today, he wrote,

> I think it would be the better part of wisdom not to allow anyone to apply passages of Scripture in such a way as to force them to support, as true, conclusions concerning nature the contrary of which may afterward be revealed by the evidence of our senses or by necessary demonstration. Who will set bounds to man's understanding? Who can assure us that everything that can be known in the world is known already?

It did not silence the objectors; the following year Tommaso Caccini, another Dominican friar, preached a sermon from the pulpit of Santa Maria Novella in Florence denouncing Galileo's views as heretical. Despite a letter of apology to Galileo from the preacher-general of the order, the damage had been done.

THE COMPLAINT

Lorini now complained formally about Galileo to the Sacred Congregation of the Universal Inquisition, better known simply as the Inquisition, enclosing a doctored version of the astronomer's 'Letter' that made it seem as if Galileo was deliberately criticising scripture. Despite Lorini's assurance that he was motivated by 'nothing but zeal for the sacred cause', a worried Galileo thought it prudent to write at length to a friendly Vatican official, Monsignor Piero Dini, defending his views. But the winds were shifting. When in March 1615 a Carmelite friar, Paolo Antonio Foscarini, published a letter claiming that the Copernican universe was compatible with scripture, both Galileo and he were warned by an influential friend that such views represented a 'very dangerous attitude'. 'Write freely,' the friend advised, 'but keep outside the sacristy.' The friend was Robert Cardinal Bellarmine, the Church's principal theologian, who was to play such a significant role in Galileo's story. Bellarmine was no obscurantist, but he made it clear that he would want strong proof before he himself ventured beyond the plain words of scripture.

Meanwhile, Father Vincenzo Maculano di Firenzuola, the Church's Commissary-General, had stepped in. He referred the Copernican theories advanced by Galileo to a committee of eleven theologians ('the qualifiers'). In language that will long stand as a model of obscurantism, the qualifiers concluded that the notion that the sun was the centre of the universe was

> foolish and absurd in philosophy, and formally heretical since it explicitly contradicts in many places the sense of Holy Scripture, according to the literal meaning of the words and according to the common interpretation and understanding of the Holy Fathers and the doctors of theology.

While the idea that the earth rotates around the sun 'receives the same censure in philosophy, and that in regard to theological truth it is at least erroneous as to faith'.

The qualifiers' conclusions were confirmed by decree of the Congregation of the Index, omitting only the dangerous word 'heretical'. Eventually, the problem reached the ears of the Pope. The Roman Church can boast of many great minds, but Paul V was not among them. He was once described by the Florentine ambassador as 'so averse to anything intellectual that everyone has to play dense and ignorant to gain his favour'. His actions, however, were to have a profound effect on Galileo.

On 25 February 1616 Cardinal Bellarmine summoned Galileo to his residence in Rome in response to instructions from the Vatican. What was said at that meeting was to be central to Galileo's trial. But this was only the first step. A few weeks later a papal decree was issued denouncing Copernicus' views as heretical and proscribing his great work, *De revolutionibus orbis coelestium* ('On the Revolution of the Celestial Spheres'), until 'corrected'. (Interestingly, the 'corrections' were few and the work was never actually proscribed.) Foscarini's book was banned utterly. From all of this the still favoured Galileo emerged unscathed; indeed, he was even given the honour of an audience with the Pope. In 1618 the appearance of three comets prompted the astronomer to further fruitful research. He was flattered when his long-time friend and admirer Cardinal Maffeo Barberini sent him a poem that he had composed in his honour.

In 1623 the old Pope died. To the delight of Galileo, his friend Barberini was elected in his place, taking the title Urban VIII. Galileo, who in his own words had led a life of studious retirement for seven years, was now permitted to publish a book, *Il saggiatore* ('The Assayer'), on the merits of observational astronomy. It was innocent of any reference to Copernicus and even included a preface from the new Pope, who had honoured the author with a series of long audiences. Papal pensions were granted both to him and to his illegitimate son. But he was not to bask in the Vatican sunlight forever, and for this Galileo himself was, at least in part, responsible.

THE DIALOGUE

For some time Galileo had been preparing his masterwork, *Dialogo dei due massimi del mondo* ('Dialogue Concerning the Two Chief World Systems'). He had been encouraged in this by the Pope's Secretary of the Briefs, Ciampoli, and by the Pope's chief licenser, Niccolò Riccardi. It was even hinted to Galileo that the new Pope regretted the warning of 1616 ('If it had been up to me . . .').[1] When Riccardi read the book in draft, however, he was horrified to find that the views about the universe that it put forward were far from hypothetical. He at once insisted that the preface and conclusions be revised. Eventually, in February 1632 Riccardi, whose understanding of astronomy was not deep, gave his reluctant approval to a revised text, and the book was published. At this time few of the Vatican intelligentsia subscribed to the Ptolemaic view of the universe, preferring instead the compromise of the Danish astronomer, Tycho Brahe, whose observations led him to teach that the planets were in orbit around the sun and the sun around the earth. It has even been said that Galileo's real sin lay in criticising the Tychonic system.

Despite its great merits as a work of science, as an exercise in diplomacy the *Dialogo* was a disaster. No one reading it could believe its author to be anything other than a convinced heliocentrist, dismissive of all other opinions. As if this was not enough, the book went out of its way to offend the author's most influential patron. The *Dialogo* took the form of conversations, spread over four days, between three Venetian gentlemen. They were, respectively, the reasonable Salviati (a thinly disguised Galileo), the obtuse and pompous Simplicio (representing traditional views) and an intelligent layman, Sagredo. (Salviati and Sagredo were the names of two of Galileo's friends, then dead. Simplicio was named after a sixth-century commentator on Aristotle.) It was not a happy choice. The Pope was a learned man who had written, among other things, on the origins of the tides. The astronomer took the incredibly discourteous, not to say stupid, step of putting his patron's views on this subject into the mouth of Simplicio, whose very name suggested simple-mindedness. He even made it clear to whom he was referring by stating that these laughable opinions originated from a 'very exalted and learned personage'. The criticism must have bitten deep.

Galileo's offence was compounded by the fact that the *Dialogo*, which had been written in the vernacular, had become an instant best-seller among lay as well as clerical readers. (As one friendly cleric remarked, 'If he had only written in Latin!'[2]) The Jesuits, Galileo's most bitter critics, were up in arms, and an offended Pope was not disposed to stand in their way. Publication of the book was suspended forthwith. Riccardi was severely reprimanded, and Ciampoli was removed to a position far from Rome. Worse, a Preliminary Commission was appointed to examine Galileo's views. Its report was damning. The principal findings were that

- Galileo had disobeyed the warning of 1616 in deviating from a hypothetical treatment by unequivocally maintaining that the earth moves and that the sun is stationary;
- he had erroneously ascribed the phenomenon of the tides to the stability of the sun and the motion of the earth;
- he had been deceitfully silent about the command laid upon him by the Holy Office in 1616.

The whole 'disgraceful' affair was now put into the hands of the Holy Inquisition.

THE TRIAL

The Pope himself chaired the meeting of the Inquisition that summoned Galileo to appear before it in Rome. Now almost seventy years of age, the astronomer was bitterly regretting his temerity. 'I curse the time devoted to these studies in which I strove and hoped to move away somewhat from the beaten path. I repent having given the world a portion of my writings; I feel inclined to consign what is left to the flames and thus placate at last the inextinguishable hatred of my enemies.' After an unsuccessful attempt to have the case referred from Rome to Florence, Galileo claimed that he was too feeble to attend the hearing and provided a medical report to this effect from three physicians. The Inquisition was not impressed and directed that if the astronomer failed to appear he would be arrested and brought to them in chains. So far, Galileo had been supported by Niccolini, ambassador to Ferdinand, Cosimo's successor as Grand Duke of Tuscany and Galileo's good friend. But now even he realised that it was time to fall into line, and Galileo was reluctantly persuaded to go to Rome. When he got there, he was permitted, as a favour to the Duke, to reside until the trial in the Duke's Villa Medici.

Galileo surrendered to the Congregation of the Holy Office on 12 April 1633 and was immediately transferred to the Inquisition's own quarters, which the astronomer himself acknowledged to be most comfortable. The examination was conducted by Father Firenzuola and three assistants. (Contrary to the impression given in some paintings of the event, these were the only people present at the trial.) The proceedings began by Galileo being asked on oath about the meeting with the now dead Bellarmine sixteen years before. It was put to him that he had been commanded by the Cardinal not 'to hold, teach, or defend [the Copernican view] in any way whatsoever'. The astronomer denied this strenuously; Bellarmine had instructed him, he said, that, while these views could not be held or defended, they might be held 'suppositionally'. This was a common stratagem in those days tolerated by a liberal Church as a means of avoiding accusations of heresy. Galileo then produced what he must have believed to be his trump card.

Shortly after his interview with Bellarmine the Cardinal had provided Galileo with a certificate for use against 'slanderous' foes who were putting out misleading reports of their meeting. It read:

> We, Robert Cardinal Bellarmine, have heard that Mr Galileo Galilei is being slandered or alleged to have abjured in our hands and also to have been given salutary penances for this. Having been sought about the truth of the matter, we say that the above-mentioned Galileo has not abjured in our hands, or in the hands of others here in Rome, or anywhere else that we know, any opinion or doctrine of his; nor has he received any penances, salutary or otherwise. On the contrary, he has only been notified of the declaration made by the Holy Father and published by the Sacred Congregation of the Index, whose content is that the doctrine attributed to Copernicus (that the earth moves around the sun and the sun stands at the centre of the world without moving from east to west) is contrary to Holy Scripture and therefore cannot be defended or held.

On the face of it, the certificate seemed to be conclusive proof that Galileo had not received any warning from the Cardinal. To Galileo's surprise, however, the document seemed to cut no ice with his inquisitors, who went on to ask whether anyone else had been present at the meeting with the Cardinal. A puzzled Galileo replied that some Dominican friars were present but that he had not known them. Asked whether anything else was said to him, Galileo replied that 'it may be that a command was issued but I do not remember it, for it is several years ago . . . I do not think that I have in any way disobeyed the command, that is have not by any means held or defended the said opinion that the earth moves and that the sun is stationary.' Speaking almost like a present-day best-selling author, he added that, 'although I was receiving profitable offers from France, Germany, and Venice, I refused them and spontaneously came to Rome three years ago to place [my book] into the hands of the chief censor'. With a belated attempt at humility, he added that any flaws in the book were 'not introduced through the cunning of an insincere intention, but rather through the vain ambition and satisfaction of appearing clever above and beyond the average among popular writers'.

Turning to the accusation that, when seeking permission to publish his book, he had failed to tell the chief censor about the Bellarmine injunction, Galileo said, somewhat disingenuously, that it was because 'with the said book I had neither held nor defended the opinion of the earth's motion and sun's stability; on the contrary, in the said book I show the opposite of Copernicus's opinion and show that Copernicus's reasons are invalid and inconclusive'. This was not the impression gained by a dispassionate reader. At the direction of the Inquisition, the book had been studied by three counsellors, who had reported that it plainly supported Copernicus. One particular critic complained that the author had even held up those who maintained accepted opinion as 'dumb mooncalves' hardly deserving to be called human beings.

The Italian Professor of the History of Science at the Massachusetts Institute of Technology, Giorgio de Santillana, conjectures that at the end of his interrogation Galileo was getting rattled. 'He no longer knows where he stands, and this is no time to cite the Pope's ill advised encouragements or to implicate the authorities.' Galileo's shaky signature on the depositions of that day speaks volumes as to his state of mind.

An extraordinary meeting now took place in private between the Commissary-General and Galileo at the instigation, it has been suggested, of Barbarini. Firenzuola's report of this meeting records that,

> after many and many arguments and rejoinders had passed between us, by God's grace, I attained my object, for I brought him to a full sense of his error, so that he clearly recognised that he had erred and had gone too far in his book. And to all this he gave expression in words of much feeling, like one who experienced great consolation in the recognition of his error, and he was also willing to confess it judicially. He requested, however, a little time in order to consider the form in which he might most fittingly make the confession, which as far as its substance is concerned, will, I hope, follow in the manner indicated.[3]

At this meeting it seems clear that Galileo had been led to believe, whether explicitly or by implication, that if he made a full confession his penalty would be light. Later, when Firenzuola's 'deal' unravelled, Galileo was to think badly of him, but there are those who believe the Commissary-General acted in good faith but was overruled by the anti-Galileist party in the Vatican. De Santillana, who has looked at this more closely than most, is less confident. Firenzuola, he wrote, 'remains an undecipherable figure, wrapped in the hood of his Order and the mystery of his service'.[4] Galileo was now once again allowed in view of his infirmity to stay at the ducal villa, though under house arrest.

At his second interrogation a fortnight later, Galileo changed his tune; a bit of grovelling seemed to be called for. After 'thinking continuously and directly' about the earlier interrogations for several days, he said, 'it dawned on me to re-read my printed Dialogue'.

> Not having seen it for so long, I found it almost a new book by another author. Now, I freely confess that it appeared to me in several places to be written in such a way that a reader, not aware of

my intention, would have had reason to form the opinion that the arguments for the false side, which I intended to confute, were so stated as to be capable of convincing because of their strength, rather than being easy to answer.

He had done so, he admitted, 'out of the natural gratification everyone feels for his own subtleties and for showing himself to be cleverer than the average man' and he quoted Cicero: 'I may be more avid for glory than right.' He claimed that, if he were to write the book now, he would weaken the erroneous arguments so as not to confuse the ordinary reader. Returning to his quarters, Galileo must have had doubts that his confession had not gone far enough. (Did he perhaps reflect on the fact that it was only some three decades since Giordano Bruno, Galileo's predecessor in the chair of mathematics at Padua, had suffered the *auto-da-fé* in Rome for suggesting that the earth rotates around the sun?) Within minutes he returned to his inquisitors and offered to write an addendum to his book, making clear that he did not hold Copernicus' opinions as true. The repentant astronomer must have thought that this had done the trick, for he was now permitted to return to the Villa Medici.

When Galileo was next brought before the Inquisition on 10 May, he seems to have recovered his courage sufficiently to challenge the official version of the Bellarmine meeting once again. His understanding, he said, was consistent with the decree of the Congregation and he felt 'very reasonably excused' (a good lawyer's phrase) for not having brought the Bellarmine injunction to the attention of the censor. He then switched from defence to a plea in mitigation.

> I am left with asking you to consider the pitiable state of ill health to which I am reduced, due to ten months of constant mental distress, and the discomforts of a long and tiresome journey in the most awful season and at the age of seventy; I feel I have lost the greater part of the years which my previous state of health promised me.

Galileo hoped that if his judges' 'sense of justice perceives anything lacking among so many ailments as adequate punishment for my crimes, they will, I beg them, condone it out of regard for my declining old age . . .'. A somewhat biased summary of the proceedings was then sent to the Pope and to the Congregation, unaccompanied by the trial papers.

A final interrogation followed on 21 June at which Galileo was instructed to speak the truth, 'otherwise one would have recourse to torture'. This phrase appears to have been a formality. Torture was certainly not used on Galileo; indeed, he was never even shown the instruments. Perhaps still hoping for the Commissary's deal, Galileo repeated: 'I do not hold and, after the determination of the authorities, I have not held the condemned opinion.' It was to do him no good.

THE SENTENCE

The final act took place the next day before a large assembly in the convent of Santa Maria sopra Minerva. Galileo, dressed in the white shirt of penitence, knelt before his judges to receive his sentence. It was not what he had expected. The court's judgment poured scorn on his 'pretended' understanding of the wording of the Cardinal's certificate. ('One is supposed to believe that . . .'.) The prisoner was condemned for having failed to notify the censor about the injunction he was under. He had rendered himself 'vehemently suspect of heresy' for having held and believed a false doctrine. The *Dialogo* was prohibited and Galileo was sentenced to 'formal imprisonment in this Holy Office at our pleasure. As a salutary penance we impose on you to recite the seven penitential Psalms once a week for the next three years.'

The astronomer was then shown a form of confession that he was expected to make, 'abjuring, cursing and detesting' his errors and heresies. A shaken Galileo nevertheless had the temerity to ask for two concessions, both of which were granted him: first, not to be required to state that he was not a good Catholic; and, secondly, not to be required to confess to having deceived anyone about his book. We shall never know whether, when rising from his knees, he muttered the famous qualification 'Eppur si muove!' (And yet it moves!). It seems unlikely.

Galileo was not in fact imprisoned as the sentence required, but released into the custody of the Duke and, later, of the Archbishop of Sienna; his friendship apparently still counted for something in the Vatican. He was nevertheless to spend the rest of his days under house arrest. The proceedings had affected him badly but the depression soon lifted. Maria Celeste, one of his illegitimate daughters, now a nun, obtained permission to relieve her father of his duty to recite the penitential psalms, and he began work on a new project, the *Discorsi e dimostazioni matematiche intorno a due nuove scienze* (*Discourses on Two New Sciences*). In the following year he published his ground-breaking treatise on mechanics. In 1636 he suggested how longitude at sea could be determined by using the eclipses of the satellites of Jupiter. The following year he announced his discovery of a new libration (oscillation) of the moon. His personal life, however, became increasingly sad.

In 1634 his beloved Maria had fallen victim to a deep depression brought on in part by her father's plight and, at the age of thirty-three, succumbed to a fatal illness. Three years later, having lost the vision in his left eye, the great astronomer became totally blind. His petition for clemency was refused but he was permitted to retire to his farmhouse in Arcetri. Almost at the end of his days he proposed the use of pendulums in clocks. He died in January 1642 within a few months of the birth of Isaac Newton.

THE 'FALSE INJUNCTION'

No one reading the record of Galileo's trial can fail to be puzzled – as indeed Galileo was at the time – by the direction the inquisitors' questioning took and why their conclusions seemingly ignored the plain terms of Bellarmine's certificate. We now know why: the court had received a key piece of evidence that was never shown to Galileo. It consisted of an unsigned minute, produced, it was claimed, from the Vatican files, which gave an impression of the 1616 interview entirely different from the one the astronomer recalled and the Cardinal's certificate confirmed. This minute recorded that the Lord Cardinal, in the presence of the Commissary-General of the Holy Office, had

> warned Galileo that the above-mentioned opinion was erroneous and that he should abandon it; and thereafter, indeed immediately, before me and witnesses, the Most Illustrious Lord Cardinal himself being also present still, the aforesaid Father Commissary, in the name of His Holiness the Pope and the whole Congregation of the Holy Office, ordered and enjoined the said Galileo, who was himself still present, to abandon completely the above-mentioned opinion that the sun stands still at the centre of the world and the earth moves, and henceforth not to hold, teach, or defend it in any way whatever, either orally or in writing; otherwise the Holy Office would start proceedings against him. The same Galileo acquiesced in this injunction and promised to obey.

If this was a correct record, it confirmed Galileo's guilt in respect of the two most important charges against him. The document is, however, suspect for a number of reasons. First and foremost, it is in terms contrary to the papal instructions to Bellarmine, which are still extant. They required the Cardinal,

> to call Galileo before himself and warn him to abandon these opinions; and *if he should refuse to obey*, the Father Commissary, *in the presence of a notary and witnesses*, is to issue him an injunction to abstain completely from teaching or defending this doctrine and opinion or from discussing it; and further, *if he should not acquiesce*, he is to be imprisoned. (Emphasis added)

It is important to understand exactly what this instruction demanded. First, it required that Galileo be warned to abandon his Copernican views. *Only if he refused to comply with this warning* should an injunction be issued requiring him to abstain from teaching, defending or discussing these views. The unchallenged Inquisition minute of what took place confirms that Galileo 'had acquiesced when warned'. Therefore there could not possibly have been any need, under the terms of his instructions, for Bellarmine to issue the injunction. Since there was no need for the injunction, the necessity to make the threat of imprisonment did not arise. To think otherwise would imply that Bellarmine had taken a cavalier attitude towards his instructions from Rome. Disregarding papal instructions is not a characteristic of cardinals in general and was certainly not characteristic of the saintly Robert Bellarmine.

And there were other anomalies. Galileo's vehement denial that he had been warned not to discuss Copernicus's views 'in any way whatsoever' is entirely consistent with what we know of the Church's attitude towards this issue. The alleged minute was not signed or notarised as the papal instruction demanded; indeed, a notary does not seem to have been present at the meeting. (Is that, perhaps, why the inquisitors were so interested in who was there?) Finally, the minute appears on the Vatican record for the same day as the entry for the previous day, whereas all other minutes have a page to themselves.

After a careful examination of the evidence, de Santillana concludes that the unsigned minute was forged in 1616 by the commissary of the day or one of his assistants. If that is true, the principal charge against Galileo was baseless. And, if that charge was removed, the need to disclose the injunction to the censor fell away also. In other words, Galileo was not guilty of the two main charges against him; his conviction had been secured by forged evidence. But that was not the only defect in these proceedings.

The finding that someone was 'vehemently suspect of heresy', though odd-sounding to modern ears, was an offence under canon law only slightly less serious than outright heresy. However, it was a strange finding in this case, as the present-day Roman Catholic Church frankly acknowledges. Its website cautiously comments on the decision of the Inquisition: 'The choice of words was debatable, as Copernicanism had never been declared heretical by either the ordinary or extraordinary Magisterium of the Church.'[5] Since the Inquisition had no power in its own right to declare doctrines heretical, there can be no basis for its finding of heresy.

THE JUDGEMENT OF HISTORY

The modern impression of Galileo's trial derives, more than anything else, from Bertolt Brecht's powerful play *Galileo*, but it is a misleading one. The seventeenth-century Church was by no means wholly averse to new ideas; many of its most prominent officials were well informed, forward looking and tolerant, at least so long as (what they would no doubt have thought of as) the proprieties were maintained.[6] And Galileo had many friends at the Vatican. But the astronomer's short-sighted pride had no time for the sensibilities of such as these. Galileo, the good Catholic, believed, somewhat naively in the circumstances, that his friends in the Vatican would preserve him from attack, but he failed to take account of the extent to which his own ill-judged writings and actions had alienated his most influential patron. Nevertheless, his trial was blatantly unfair. It had received evidence in secret which was almost certainly forged and it had exceeded its powers in declaring Galileo's actions heretical. Fortunately, the sentence was a merciful one by the standards of the day.

The Church withdrew its objection to the teachings of Copernicus in 1757 and the Dialogo *was removed from the index of proscribed books in 1822. But it was not until 1932 that the sentence on Galileo was officially expunged.*

PART THREE

The Clash of Arms

Introduction

Speaking in the House of Lords, the great judge Lord Atkin said, 'In this country amid the clash of arms, the laws are not silent. They may be changed but they speak the same language in war as in peace.'[1] Well, not quite. Even the most law-observing nation accepts that the niceties of the law must sometimes bend to the necessities of war. During the American Civil War, for example, the President of the Republic, the attorney Abraham Lincoln, thought himself justified in doing away with the writ of habeas corpus, even though it was regarded as being at the heart of his country's liberties, as it is of Britain's. The British did much the same during the Second World War with the notorious regulation 18B (administered, it should be remembered, by that judicial icon Lord Denning). But it is not the ordinary courts of law with which this section is concerned, but rather with a singular type of court set up and administered by the armed forces.

When the military tribunes of Republican Rome went on campaign, they had their own quarters in the great square camps that the army threw up wherever it halted. Before those quarters there was a reviewing stand; in time, this came to be known as the tribunal. Contrary to popular prejudice, there is nothing inherently unjust in someone being tried by a military tribunal, but such courts can fall into error as much as any other. The system of courts martial that has laboured to do justice since at least the sixteenth century failed disgracefully in the case of Admiral Byng, whose government was cynically prepared to misrepresent his military dispatches and even to see him shot rather than expose its own dereliction of duty. If the court had been advised by a better lawyer, Byng's life might have been saved – but then the world would have had to forgo Voltaire's most famous aphorism, quoted below.

British readers may not realise that the six men and a woman charged with involvement in the assassination of Abraham Lincoln were tried, not in an ordinary court of law, but by a military tribunal; it was a controversial decision at the time and the controversy has not gone away. Did the widow Surratt deserve to hang for her supposed part in the conspiracy to eliminate the leadership of the US government? And was Dr Mudd really the innocent medical practitioner he claimed to be? Guilty or innocent, the Lincoln 'assassins' were treated with less than humanity.[2]

The most celebrated military tribunal of all was the International Military Tribunal at Nuremberg, which was set up at the end of the Second World War to hear charges of the gravest nature against the most prominent of the Nazi leaders. Nowadays, such cases would go to the International Criminal Court, but no such institution existed in 1945 and the Allies had to create one *ad hoc*, as well as decide what crimes it could try and by what procedures. It was a challenge: the scope and the nature of the atrocities involved made this truly the trial of the twentieth century. The volume of evidence presented to the tribunal is too great even to be summarised here; instead, the following account concentrates on some of the more momentous issues raised by the trial, as seen through the stories of four of its most controversial defendants. Hermann Goering described the trial as 'victors' justice'. Was he right?

CHAPTER SEVEN

The Scapegoat

The Trial of Admiral Byng, 1757

When a combined fleet of twenty-seven French and Spanish ships put out of Toulon harbour one evening in February 1744, Admiral Thomas Mathews immediately set sail with the intention of stopping them landing troops to fight Britain's allies, the Austrians. But mismanagement and an adverse wind meant that his vessels were so strung out that he could not get them into proper station for an attack.

By the next morning the wind had increased still further the gap between the van and the rear of the British fleet. Nevertheless, when his leading ship was abreast of the enemy's centre, Mathews opened fire on the rear of the enemy fleet. The French van then turned back, and Mathews was forced to draw off. Owing to a misunderstanding over flags, the British rear under command of Admiral Lestock failed to come into action throughout the engagement.

According to the somewhat hidebound rules of engagement of those days, Mathews was in the wrong in not waiting to engage the enemy until his van was abreast the enemy's. As a result, he found himself put on trial, as well as Lestock and a number of other officers. Following a series of courts martial Lestock was acquitted and Mathews convicted; along with several captains, the Admiral was dismissed the service.

And so it seemed that the officer who had bravely engaged the enemy was punished, while the officer who had hung back was let off. One of the members of the court martial that tried Mathews was Rear Admiral John Byng. He learned the lesson only too well; ten years on it was to return to haunt him.

Over a decade later France and Britain were at each other's throats. Again. Hardly had the War of the Austrian Succession come to an end than the two countries were glaring at each other around the world. In India, the French were threatening the English merchants. In America, they were stopping the English from crossing the Alleghenies. In Europe, France had joined Russia and Spain in a coalition that threatened Britain's ally, Prussia. But there was a more proximate threat to British interests.

The island of Minorca in the Mediterranean enjoyed one of the world's finest natural harbours. Guarded by the strong defences of Fort St Philip, Port Mahon was a natural target for the French. Nevertheless, despite repeated attacks on British shipping in the western Mediterranean and other warnings, the British government, under Thomas Pelham-Holles, 1st Duke of Newcastle, had failed to take any action to protect the island. Only when the City of London protested at the dangers to its commercial interests did it act, reluctantly and inadequately, and it led to England's involvement in what came to be known as the Seven Years War. This is the story of how it began.

The British forces in Minorca were under the command of General William Blakeney, a competent and courageous officer but now in his eighty-second year and so crippled with gout that he had to spend much of his day in bed. His force of four regiments of foot and a few marines was seriously under strength. The lieutenant governor of the island and the colonels of all four regiments were absent for various reasons. Of the subalterns, nineteen had not yet joined their units and nine more were away on recruiting duties. The British squadron in the Mediterranean was in just as parlous a state, comprising as it did only three ships of the line and a few smaller craft. Reinforcements were urgently needed, but who should take command of them?

The obvious choice was John Byng, the fourth son of George Byng, Viscount Torrington, a former First Lord of the Admiralty. Plump, confident and rather fussy, Byng at the age of forty-two was not universally admired. Horace Walpole, who had only met him once, 'thought his carriage haughty and disgusting'.[1] More worryingly, as a flag officer he had in the words of the naval historian Dudley Pope, 'one professional shortcoming . . . he had never commanded a ship, squadron or fleet in action'.[2]

Byng had entered naval service in 1718 at the age of fourteen. Aided no doubt by his father's influence, his rise had been swift; lieutenant in 1723, captain in 1727, Rear Admiral in command of the Mediterranean fleet in 1745, Vice-Admiral in 1747 and Admiral in 1755. On 9 March 1756 he was ordered by the Admiralty 'to take the ships lately ordered to fit for the Mediterranean under his command'. A few days later he was promoted Admiral of the Blue.[3] The respected Rear Admiral Temple West, who had served with and enjoyed the confidence of Byng, was to be his second in command.

Byng's orders were to take his squadron of ships to Gibraltar. If the French fleet had left for America, which the Admiralty plainly believed to be their intention, Byng was to follow and seize them. If the French had not left the Mediterranean but had attacked Minorca, he was to go to the relief of that island. Otherwise, he should prevent the French from leaving Toulon. He was to exercise 'the utmost vigilance' in protecting Minorca and Gibraltar from hostile action. The government was now belatedly alive to the possible consequences of its neglect.

Arriving at Portsmouth to take up his command, Byng discovered that his force consisted of ten, largely ill-founded, ships of the line. One of his vessels, the *Intrepid*, was actually unfit for a foreign voyage. Worse, he was over 700 sailors short, and his orders specifically prevented him from appropriating seamen from other ships. (They were thought to be needed to deal with a threat of invasion that never materialised.) Protests from Byng led to his being granted a mere 300 more sailors. However, he was ordered to disembark his vital marine contingent in order to take on board a regiment of fusiliers. When he left Portsmouth on 2 April 1756 Byng's squadron was still short of 336 men and unsupported by any marines, then as now a vital part of a fighting ship's defences. A last-minute dispatch from London reported that the French force known to be fitting out in Toulon was believed – erroneously as it turned out – to be heading for America.

THE FRENCH INVADE

The day after Byng and his inadequate force left England twelve French ships of the line under Admiral de la Galissonière, with transports containing 16,000 troops under the duc de Richelieu, sailed out of Toulon. When they dropped anchor off the port of Ciudadella, at the north-western end of Minorca, General Blakeney, who had received warning of the intended attack only two days before, immediately concentrated all his forces in Fort St Philip. Three days later the British government dispatched a squadron of five ships under Rear Admiral Broderick to reinforce Byng. It was too late; the squadron sailed from England the day that Byng was to fight his fateful engagement with the French fleet.

Reaching Gibraltar on 2 May, Byng found to his dismay that the dockyard from which he had hoped to reprovision and revictual his ships was badly decayed and without the necessary supplies. Learning that Minorca had already been invaded, Byng reported to the Admiralty that, even if it could be done, reinforcement of the Minorca garrison would only lead to the loss of more men. It was not what his superiors wanted to hear; the Admiral, they assumed, was a defeatist. It was the first in a series of misjudgements that was to seal Byng's fate.

To make matters worse, the orders given to the governor of Gibraltar, General Fowke, were in plain contradiction to those given to the Admiral. Byng had reason to believe the fusiliers to be part of his own force; Fowke and his military advisers thought otherwise. A council of war called by the General concluded that to send the fusiliers to Minorca would be insufficient to relieve that island and would weaken Gibraltar's defence, particularly if the French fleet were to inflict damage on Byng's squadron.[4] Byng weakly acceded to the governor's view and his small force, bolstered by a few additional ships and little more than 200 soldiers, left Gibraltar on 8 May for the relief of Minorca. As Pope comments, 'A greater man would have taken a broader view; but the Hon. John Byng was, unfortunately, only the son of a great man.'

THE ENGAGEMENT

When Byng arrived at Minorca, Fort St Philip was being heavily bombarded by a number of French batteries but was still flying the British flag. The French fleet then hove into sight and any hope Byng had of getting in touch with the shore had to be abandoned. It was now about six o'clock in the evening. During the night the two fleets separated, but they came into contact again the next morning, and the line of battle was formed on both sides.

The battle began in the manner customary at that time, with the two fleets in line ahead but converging on each other at an angle of some 35 degrees. The Permanent Fighting Instructions required each ship in turn to cross in front of an enemy's bow and rake it with cannon fire, but this proved impossible with the British fleet being further strung out than the French. When Byng gave the signal, the van of his fleet engaged the enemy, but because they were so nearly head-on to the French their fire was largely ineffective, whereas they themselves suffered great damage. *Intrepid* had its foretopmast shot away, causing confusion among the rear, which had to back their topsails to avoid running into each other and thus never actually engaged the enemy. Despite this débâcle Byng failed to rescind the order of line ahead. His misjudgement undoubtedly had it origins in part in his recollection of Admiral Mathew's court martial, as witnessed by his remark on the quarterdeck:

> You see, Captain Gardiner, that the signal for the line is out, and that I am ahead of the ships *Louisa* and *Trident* [which should have been ahead of him]. You would not have me, as admiral of the fleet, run down as if I were going to engage a single ship. It was Mr Mathews's misfortune to be prejudiced by not carrying down his force together, which I shall endeavour to avoid.[5]

The French got away relatively unscathed and the battle proved indecisive.

BYNG'S COUNCIL OF WAR

The losses in killed and wounded in this encounter were nearly equal. However, the French lost no senior officers, whereas in Byng's squadron Captain Andrews of the *Defiance* was killed outright and Captain Noel of the *Princess Louisa* mortally wounded. The British ships had also suffered much more damage than the French. Byng now called a council of war consisting of his military and naval staff. The questions debated and the conclusions arrived at were recorded as follows:

1. Whether an attack on the French fleet gave any prospect of relieving Mahon? Unanimously resolved that it would not.
2. Whether, if there were no French fleet cruising at Minorca, the British fleet could raise the siege? Unanimously the opinion was that the fleet could not.
3. Whether Gibraltar would not be in danger by any accident that might befall this fleet? Unanimously agreed that it would be in danger.
4. Whether an attack with our fleet in its present state of it upon that of the French will not endanger the safety of Gibraltar, and expose the trade in the Mediterranean to great hazards? Unanimously agreed that it would.
5. Whether it is not most for His Majesty's service that the fleet should immediately proceed for Gibraltar? We are unanimously of opinion that the fleet should immediately proceed for Gibraltar.[6]

Fortified by these opinions, Byng sailed for Gibraltar, where he discovered Broderick's ships awaiting him. Thus reinforced, he felt able to challenge the French fleet again and began to make his preparations accordingly. They were to be in vain.

On 25 May Byng had sent to the Board of Admiralty a detailed dispatch claiming victory in the naval engagement, reporting the conclusions of his council of war and offering to seek out the enemy as soon as he had been resupplied. It was not received before his superiors had already acted upon altogether different information. They had received a copy of an intercepted report from the marquis de la Galissonnière that painted a misleading picture of a British squadron much stronger than the French force it had fought. Byng, it seemed to the Board, had made a hash of his task, and it immediately resolved to replace him. Sir Edward Hawke and Captain Saunders, advanced for the purpose to Rear Admiral, were sent to Gibraltar on board the *Antelope* with orders for Byng's immediate arrest and return to England along with Admiral West. News of this action was leaked to the press.

As soon as he arrived at Spithead, Byng was placed under arrest. At this juncture personal tragedy was to be piled upon professional. Byng's brother Ned, who had come to inform him of their mother's death, took sick and died of a fever. The bereaved Admiral was then taken to Greenwich Hospital, where he was imprisoned under conditions of strict confinement. (Henry Fox, the Secretary of State, had sought to have him thrown into the Tower of London.) The government, fearful of public reaction to the loss of the island and, even more, of the implications for itself, then committed the first in a series of infamies that were to conclude with what can only be described as an act of judicial murder.

THE MUTILATED DISPATCH

Byng's dispatch had reached London too late to affect the decision to recall him.[7] The government, fearful of public reaction, nevertheless published it in the *London Gazette* of 26 June, but in a severely mutilated form. It is necessary to print here only the following extracts, which the government deliberately withheld, in order to understand how Byng's words had been traduced and misrepresented.

> His Majesty's colours were still flying at the castle of St Philip; and I could perceive several bomb-batteries playing on it from different parts. French colours I saw flying on the west part of St Philip. I dispatched the *Phoenix, Chesterfield,* and *Dolphin* ahead, to reconnoitre the harbour's mouth; and Captain Hervey to endeavour to land a letter for General Blakeney, to let him know the fleet was here to his assistance; though every one was of the opinion we could be of no use to him; as, by all accounts, no place was secured for covering a landing, could we have spared the people.
>
> . . . it was found impracticable either to succour or relieve the former with the force we had. So, though we may justly claim the victory, yet we are much inferior to the weight of their ships, though the numbers are equal; and they have the advantage of sending to Minorca their wounded, and getting reinforcements of seamen from their transports, and soldiers from their camp; all which undoubtedly has been done in this time that we have been lying to refit, and often in sight of Minorca; and their ships have more than once appeared in a line from our mast-heads.
>
> I send their Lordships the resolutions of the council of war, in which there was not the least contention or doubt arose. I hope, indeed, we shall find stores to refit us at Gibraltar; and, if I have any reinforcement, will not lose a moment of time to seek the enemy again, and once more give them battle, though they have a great advantage in being clean ships that go three feet to our one, and therefore have their choice how they will engage us, or if they will at all; and will never let us close them, as their sole view is the disabling our ships, in which they have but too well succeeded, though we obliged them to bear up . . .
>
> I cannot help urging their Lordships for a reinforcement, if none are yet sailed on their knowledge of the enemy's strength in these

Socrates. Plato quotes a tipsy Alcibiades comparing Socrates to a satyr with swaggering gait and roving eye. Others speak of his snub nose, thick neck, outspread nostrils and protruding eyes. Perhaps that explains why the British Museum (where this statuette can be found) describes it as 'an idealized later version of the philosopher's appearance'. (British Museum)

Joan of Arc. This sketch, said to have been drawn by Clément de Fauquembergue after Joan's relief of the siege of Orléans, is not consistent with her known appearance at that time. However, it is the only surviving contemporary portrait. (ET Archives, London)

Thomas More's household. Holbein's wonderful conversation piece of More in the middle of his extended family, though destroyed, is preserved in the form of copies and original sketches. This engraving by Édouard Lièvre differs from the painting in both composition and skill, but retains its liveliness of detail. (Mary Evans Picture Library)

Galileo. This engraving of a 1636 painting by the Medici portraitist Justus Sustermans manages an upwards glance, which could be interpreted either as an astronomer's scrutiny of the heavens or as the frightened appeal of an accused to a higher power. (Popperfoto)

King Charles I. This engraving of the King leaving Westminster Hall a condemned man is of course a romantic reconstruction. The axe is almost certainly an invention, but the menacing attitudes of the crowd seem authentic. (Getty Images)

The Tolpuddle Protest. The largest demonstration in support of the Martyrs set off from Copenhagen Fields on 21 April 1834, a month after the trial to deliver an address to the Prime Minister. Copenhagen Fields later became the site of the Caledonian market. (Mary Evans Picture Library)

The SHOOTING of ADMIRAL BYNG. on board the MONARQUE. *London Mac.*

Admiral Byng's execution. This engraving by an unknown artist is a fair representation of the scene on the deck of the Monarque, *with the condemned man almost up against the mouths of the muskets. The kneeling Byng gave the signal to fire by dropping his kerchief. (Mary Evans Picture Library)*

The Lincoln conspirators. The hanging of four of the Lincoln assassins, three men and a woman, in the Old Arsenal Penitentiary, Washington, was recorded by Alexander Gardner. Major-General Hantranft, the officer in charge, clapped his hands three times, and the poles that supported the trap doors were knocked away. After twenty-five minutes the bodies were taken down and pronounced dead. (Library of Congress)

Sacco and Vanzetti. The short, dapper Sacco (right) and the taller, lugubrious Vanzetti (left) following their arrest for the South Braintree robbery. They managed to elude death by assiduous legal manoeuvres for another seven years. (Getty Images)

Roger Casement in the dock. Sir Roger Casement KCMG, with Private Daniel Bailey on his right. Following Casement's conviction no evidence was offered against Bailey and he was duly acquitted. (Mary Evans Picture Library)

William Joyce in 1938. Was it his face only that was scarred? (Getty Images)

The Nuremberg accused. Back row (from left): Raeder (just visible); Schirach (speaking); Sauckel; Jodl; von Papen; Seyss-Inquart; Speer; Neurath; Fritzsche. Front row (from left): Goering; Hess; Ribbentrop; Keitel; Kaltenbrunner; Rosenberg; Frank; Frick; Streicher; Funk and Schacht. (A Picture Post photo from Getty Images)

Julius and Ethel Rosenberg. A handcuffed kiss in the back of a prison van just after their arraignment. Their passion was not confined to communism. (Getty Images)

seas, and which, by very good intelligence, will in a few days be strengthened by four more large ships from Toulon, almost ready to sail, if not sailed, to join these.[8]

In the absence of these and other passages the reader would have gained an altogether less favourable view of Byng's efforts and intentions than his original dispatch warranted. As the *Newgate Calendar* was later to record, 'when published, every expression tending in any way to cast blame on the ministers was carefully expunged'. Public reaction was predictable. The *Calendar* went on:

> Their object was accomplished to the full; the public mind took fire, and the rage and clamour against the admiral was unbounded. This feeling was artfully fomented by hired emissaries, who were sent into all classes of society and places of amusement to denounce the offender, and mobs were actually hired to hang and burn him in effigy.

Byng's Hertfordshire seat, Wrotham Park, barely escaped ruin. Even at this remove it is difficult to contemplate with equanimity the cynicism of politicians who could so misrepresent a military dispatch in an attempt to save their own skins.

CAPITULATION

On 29 June, after a gallant defence that lasted seventy days and cost the enemy dearly, the garrison of Fort St Philip was forced to surrender. The British force, which was accorded all the honours of war, embarked for Gibraltar in French ships. News of the loss of the island reached England on 14 July. King George II was enraged, Newcastle was thrown into a panic, city and country were horrified. On 9 August a grand jury in Buckinghamshire resolved that its MPs should promote an inquiry into why 'the important island of Minorca, for the want of timely succour, hath been totally lost'. Similar demands were made by other counties and by the City of London. The government was now only too conscious that, if what was left of its reputation was to be preserved, something dramatic had to be done.

Fowke was court-martialled on 10 August. He was found guilty of disobeying his orders and suspended from duties for one year. Observing that 'If he is unfit for service for one year, he is certainly so forever', the King dismissed him altogether from the service.[9] Now it was Byng's turn. On 3 December the House of Commons was informed that Byng (who, in addition to his naval duties, was also one of its Members) was in custody pending court martial. The Admiral was charged under Article 12 of the

Articles of War; he knew well the consequences if he should be convicted. In its original form, Article 12 read:

> Every person in the Fleet, who, through cowardice, negligence, or disaffection, shall, in time of action, withdraw, or keep back, or not come into fight, or engagement, or shall not do his utmost to take or destroy every ship which it shall be his duty to engage; and to assist all and every of his Majesty's ships, or those of his allies, which it shall be his duty to assist and relieve; every such person, so offending, and being convicted thereof by the sentence of a court martial, shall suffer death *or such other punishment as the circumstances of the offence shall deserve, and the court-martial shall judge fit.*

However, the concluding words, here in italics, had been repealed by a later Act. If an officer was convicted under this Article, therefore, his fate was death unless the royal prerogative of mercy were exercised in his favour.

COURT MARTIAL

On 23 December Byng was taken back to Portsmouth, where his trial began five days later on board the *St George*, a vessel he had once commanded. The court martial comprised Vice-Admiral Thomas Smith (president), three rear-admirals and nine captains. All had been appointed by Admiral Lord Anson, the First Lord of the Admiralty. The Judge Advocate was a Mr Charles Fearne, on whose report of the proceedings this account is principally based. The court was to sit until 27 January the following year, Sundays only excepted.

Byng was charged that, contrary to the twelfth Article of War, he,

> *on 20th of May last* did withdraw and did not do what was in his power to destroy the French Fleet, nor assist His Majesty's ships engaged with them, and that he did not do his utmost to succour St Philips Fort, in the island of Minorca . . . but acted contrary to and in breach of his instructions. (Emphasis added)

In an extraordinary ruling at the outset of the proceedings the court determined by a vote of 11:2 that, notwithstanding that the charge was confined to the date of the battle, 'by the general words in it and by the enclosure of Admiral Byng's letter of 4 May' the order for trial 'seems to indicate the inquiry to be made from the time of the Squadron's sailing from St Helen'. This manifestly unjustifiable decision (which Byng appears not to have been given the opportunity to challenge) was, as we shall see, only the first in a series of legal blunders.

Vice-Admiral West was the first witness to be called to give evidence. His account of the action was broadly supportive of Byng's. He confirmed that on the arrival of the British squadron off Minorca the enemy were 'so masters of Mahon harbour as to prevent the English fleet from making use of it with security to themselves'. If the troops had been landed, they would not have been 'fit' (presumably in the sense of 'adequate') to engage the enemy. Nor would they have been sufficient to defend Fort St Philip. Finally, West confirmed the parlous state of the squadron's ships.

General Lord Blakeney, as he had now become by reason of his gallant defence of the island, was then called to give evidence. At first, he said that Byng's 100 troops would have been of considerable service in defending the castle. Recalled later at Byng's request, he added that it was 'impossible to say' whether, had the Gibraltar detachment been landed, his force could have 'saved the island'. He said that its landing would have allowed him to hold out until relieved but went on: 'Without force enough to drive the enemy out of the island there was no saving it.'

An important witness was the Hon. Captain Augustus Hervey. Hervey, a former protégé of Byng and now his most faithful supporter, gave evidence backing the Admiral's tactics and confirming his exemplary conduct throughout the battle. He was not to be pressed into injudicious opinions. Asked whether the battle could have been won with different tactics, he replied that it was 'a matter of opinion founded upon the event and chance of battle, where even two equal fleets meet'.

Captain Arthur Gardiner, who had been on the quarterdeck with Byng during the action, confirmed the Admiral's personal courage and lent support to his decision not to pursue the French. It was also Gardiner, however, who reported Byng's remark to him during the action concerning the court martial of Admiral Mathews. This could only have left an impression in the court's mind of a commander made timorous by this experience. (Perversely, the court in the earlier case seems to have given no heed to the effect of their decision on the morale of future commanders.)

A great many other witnesses were called, from flag rank down to midshipmen, gunners and carpenters, but without adding much to what had gone before.

At the request of Byng, who was suffering from an eye condition, the Judge Advocate read out the Admiral's written defence. It was a frank and powerful document.

Byng claimed that he was labouring under 'a popular and almost national prejudice'. The prejudice was 'convenient, nay I may say, necessary for some persons to shelter themselves [from the charge of losing Minorca].' As to the battle, the French fleet was superior to his own in almost every respect. Rather than retreating from an inferior force, he claimed, a superior force had retreated from him. He had been sent out with 'so inadequate a force' because his orders from the Admiralty never 'supposed probable' that the fleet in the Mediterranean would see action with the French. 'Fighting was the least intentional part of my instructions.' He had not 'loitered' at Portsmouth or Gibraltar. Arriving off Minorca, it was clear that the island, apart from Fort St Philip, was lost. His report to the Admiralty had been 'at first hushed up in silence, afterwards represented (without producing it) as the desponding letter of a man who would not fight'. After the battle he could have attacked the French once more but only with the near certainty of defeat at sea and at risk of the security of Gibraltar. He could not in any event have landed his small reinforcements. In this view he had been supported by a council of war.

Byng called only two witnesses, Gardiner and his own secretary, to confirm his statements. The court adjourned to consider its verdict.

HONOUR, HUMANITY AND JUSTICE

At this point there occurred a remarkable intervention in the form of a letter to the court from Byng's former adversary, the duc de Richelieu. The letter came under cover of a note from the French philosopher and writer François Marie Arouet or, as he was better known, Voltaire. It read,

> Sir, although I am almost unknown to you, I think it is my duty to send you a copy of the letter I have just received from the Maréchal de Richelieu: honour, humanity, and justice demand that it should reach your hands. This noble and unsolicited testimony of one of the most honest and generous of my fellow-countrymen makes me conclude that your judges will render you the same justice. I am, with respect, *Voltaire.*

In his famous novel *Candide*, written two years after the trial, Voltaire's eponymous hero comments – in an obvious reference to Byng – 'Dans ce pays ci il est bon de tuer de temps en temps un amiral pour encourager les autres' (In this country it is thought well to kill an Admiral from time to time to encourage the others).

The enclosure from Richelieu stated,

> I am much concerned, Sir, about the case of Admiral Byng. I can assure you that all I have seen and heard of him is entirely honourable to him. Since he had done all that could reasonably be expected of him, he was not to be blamed for having suffered defeat. When two generals engage in battle, though both are equally men of honour, one must be beaten: it is not in the least to M. Byng's discredit that he was. His conduct was throughout that of a clever

sailor, and worthy of all admiration. The strength of the two fleets was about the same: the English had thirteen vessels: we had twelve, but ours were much better equipped and smarter. Fortune – which is the goddess of all battles – particularly of sea-battles – was more favourable to us than to our enemies, in causing our fire to have a much greater effect on their vessels than their fire on ours. I am convinced – and it is the general opinion – that, had the English persisted in the fight, their whole fleet would have been destroyed. Nothing could be more unjust than the present campaign against Admiral Byng. All men of honour, all officers in the services, should take a special interest in it.[10]

This unprecedented intervention by the former enemy commander confirmed one of the main planks of Byng's defence. Unfortunately, it was intercepted and referred to the authorities in London. By the time they had reviewed its contents it was too late to influence the court martial. Whether it would have had any effect if it had been received in time we can only speculate.

'A PROPER OBJECT OF MERCY'

On 27 January 1757 the court martial announced their unanimous findings in the form of thirty-seven resolutions that concluded as follows:

32. That after the ships which had received damage in the action were as much refitted as circumstances would permit, the Admiral ought to have returned with his squadron off St Philip's, and endeavoured to open communication with that castle, and to have used every means in his power for its relief, before returning to Gibraltar.
33. That Byng did not do his utmost to relieve St Philip's Castle.
34. That he did not do his utmost to take, seize and destroy the ships of the French King which it was his duty to have engaged, and to assist such of His Majesty's ships as were engaged in fight with the French ships, which it was his duty to have engaged.
35. [. . .]
36. That the Admiral appears to fall under the 12th Article of War; to wit, 'or shall not do his utmost to take, or destroy, every ship which it shall be his duty to engage, and to assist and relieve all and every of His Majesty's ships which it shall be his duty to assist and relieve . . .
37. As that Article positively prescribes death, without any alternative left to the discretion of the court, under any variety of circumstances Admiral Byng should be shot to death, at such

119

time and on board such ship as the Lords Commissioners of the Admiralty should direct . . . But as it appears by the evidence of Lord Robert Bertie, Lieutenant-Colonel Smith, Captain Gardiner and other officers of the ship, who were near the person of the Admiral, that they did not perceive any backwardness in him during the action, or any marks of fear or confusion and from other circumstances, the court do not believe that his misconduct arose either from cowardice or disaffection; and do therefore unanimously think it their duty most earnestly to recommend him as a proper object of mercy.

The court then sentenced the Admiral to death in accordance with the Act of Parliament. Byng, who had received advance notice of the verdict, bore it well; he made a low bow and left the court. Some of its members were seen to be in tears. Immediately after, in the hope of undoing the obvious injustice of their sentence, the members of the court wrote unanimously to the Board of Admiralty in the following terms:

We cannot help laying the distresses of our minds before your lordships on this occasion, in finding ourselves under the necessity of condemning a man to death from the great severity of the 12th Article of War, part of which he falls under, and which admits of no mitigation, *even if the crime should be committed by an error in judgment*; and therefore, for our own consciences' sake, as well as in justice to the prisoner, we pray your lordships in the most earnest manner to recommend him to His Majesty's clemency. (Emphasis added)[11]

Realising, perhaps for the first time, the full consequences of their actions, the members of the Board of Admiralty presented a memorial to the King, but, instead of addressing the central issue of injustice, raised only what appeared to them to be a legal defect in the proceedings. They requested that the opinions of the judges should be taken, 'doubts having arisen with regard to the legality of the sentence, particularly whether the crime of negligence, which is not expressed in any part of the proceedings, can, in this case be supplied by implication'. (Although the royal reference to the judges enquired in terms as to the legality of the *sentence*, it is apparent from the rest of its wording that what they were being asked about was in fact the legality of the *verdict*.) The King accordingly requested judicial opinion, and a panel of twelve judges under the distinguished Lord Mansfield upheld the order of the court martial. Why they did so we shall never know since the panel gave no reasons for their decision.

Several members of the court martial now made frantic efforts to secure a reprieve. At the last minute a Bill was presented to Parliament that would have allowed them to speak publicly about the court's recommendation of mercy. It was passed by the Commons but thrown out by the Lords under an extraordinary procedure that involved an intimidating examination of the officers' views at the bar of the House. Continuing public clamour for a scapegoat meant that pleas by Captain Hervey, Byng's sister, Sarah, the Secretary of State and William Pitt were also ignored. The Board of Admiralty was finally told that 'the King was pleased to signify his pleasure' that the sentence should be carried out. Moved no doubt by popular sentiment and his own prejudices, the monarch had declined to exercise the mercy towards the prisoner that all of those competent to judge had recommended.

On 16 February the Board of Admiralty confirmed the sentence of death. One of its members, Vice-Admiral Forbes, refused to sign the death warrant on the ground that the court martial 'does in express words, acquit Admiral Byng of cowardice and disaffection, and does not name the word, "negligence"'. Admiral West resigned his appointment in protest, 'rather than serve on terms which subject another officer to the treatment shown Admiral Byng . . .'. None of this had any effect; the sentence was to be carried out.

THE FIRING SQUAD

The day of 14 March 1757 was stormy, with high seas running. (Byng's former flagship, the *Ramillies*, actually broke her moorings half an hour before the execution.) The execution was to take place on the *Monarque*, a ship that Byng had once commanded. At first, it had been ordered to take place on the fo'c'sle of the ship, which would have put Byng on a level with the ordinary seamen. After representations it was removed to the quarterdeck. The *Newgate Calendar* described the scene:

> The unfortunate Admiral being thus abandoned to the stroke of justice, prepared himself for death with resignation and tranquillity. On the day fixed for his execution, the boats belonging to the squadron at Spithead being manned and armed, containing their captains and officers, with a detachment of marines, attended this solemnity in the harbour, which was also crowded with an infinite number of other boats and vessels filled with spectators. About noon, the Admiral having taken leave of a clergyman, and two friends who accompanied him, walked out of the great cabin to the quarter-deck, where two files of marines were ready to execute the sentence. He advanced with a firm deliberate step, a composed and resolute countenance, and resolved to suffer with his face uncovered, until his friends, representing that his looks would possibly intimidate the soldiers, and prevent their taking aim properly, he submitted to their request, threw his hat on the deck, kneeled on a cushion, tied one

white handkerchief over his eyes, and dropped the other as a signal for his executioners, who fired a volley so decisive, that five balls passed through his body, and he dropped down dead in an instant. The time in which this tragedy was acted, from his walking out of the cabin to his being deposited in the coffin, did not exceed three minutes.

Thus fell, to the astonishment of all Europe, Admiral John Byng; who, whatever his errors and indiscretions might have been, was at least rashly condemned, meanly given up, and cruelly sacrificed to vile political intrigues.

Byng wrote to the Admiralty Marshal shortly before his death:

My enemies themselves must think me innocent . . . If my crime is an error in judgement, or differing in opinion from my judges; and if yet the error in judgement should be on their side, God forgive them, as I do; and may the distress of their minds, and uneasiness of their consciences, which injustice to me they have represented, be relieved and subside, as my resentment has done.

As Fortescue pithily wrote in his magisterial *History of the British Army*, 'the unfortunate Admiral was shot because Newcastle deserved to hang'.

How on earth did a failure to win a naval battle – not even the loss of a battle – lead to the execution by firing squad of a British commander? The short answer is that it was a combination of a number of things, notably, a tribunal that lacked independence; serious errors of law and procedure in the conduct of the trial; an oppressive law that imposed the death sentence regardless of the degree of guilt; but, most of all, a national mood of prejudice against the defendant brought about by a mendacious blame-shifting exercise on the part of a government that was ultimately responsible for the débâcle that was the loss of Minorca.

THE LACK OF INDEPENDENCE

After Byng's trial an anonymous writer in the *Evening Post* pertinently asked, 'Are not the naval ministers Admiral Byng's prosecutors? May they not be deeply interested in finding him guilty to screen themselves? Were not his judges, as well as all the witnesses, immediately dependent on the Admiralty for now, for all their future prospects? Might not an undue influence be apprehended?' There was force in this comment; the members of Byng's court martial seem to have been deliberately chosen from among those with an interest in his conviction. As well as the president of the court, the three rear admirals were known to be favourites of Anson. Augustus Hervey was later to comment, 'It was observed throughout [the trial] that not one question had been asked by the court that could give an opening to favour the prisoner, and yet not one reply was given that could tend to accuse him of any one crime.' The night before the trial a member of the Board of Admiralty and critic of Byng, Lord Boscawen, was heard to say at dinner, 'Well, say what you will, *we* shall have a majority, and he will be condemned.'[12] He was to be proved correct.

Just as serious were the errors made by the court, notably their misunderstanding of the nature of the charge.

WAS BYNG GUILTY OF 'NEGLIGENCE'?

If Byng was to be found guilty, the Articles of War required it to be shown that he had acted through 'cowardice, negligence or disaffection'. The Admiral had been expressly acquitted of the first and last of these – cowardice and disaffection – and the only one remaining was negligence. As was noted at the time, the court's written reasons for their decision did not mention the word 'negligence'. However, this alone was not sufficient to invalidate the judgment. As the King's reference to the judges correctly implied, lack of the word 'negligence' in the resolutions would not matter if the court martial's findings could be read as clearly *implying* negligence. But did they?

Neither the officers present at Byng's council of war nor his gallant adversary, Richelieu, saw fit to criticise the Admiral's conduct of the engagement at Port Mahon. The members of the court martial were perfectly entitled to take a different view if they felt that the evidence warranted it, but even if they had, could such a conclusion have amounted to an offence under Article 12? To answer this question it is necessary to understand what the word 'negligence' meant in Article 12.

An officer who fails to do his duty is, in ordinary language, neglecting his duty. But Article 12 required *both* a failure on the part of the officer to do his duty *and* a finding of negligence. The reason for this is the obvious fact that a failure to do one's duty need not be culpable: to take merely two examples, were an officer to fail to do his duty by reason of sickness or wounds, no one would think any the less of him. But what was the position if he simply made the wrong decisions?

The Lord Chief Justice recently affirmed: 'It is a salutary principle that conviction of serious crime should depend on proof not simply that the defendant caused (by act or omission) an injurious result to another but that his state of mind when so acting was culpable.'[13] It cannot be too strongly emphasised that from time to time everyone, including the most able, is liable to fall into error or commit acts of misjudgement. A law that punished the common currency of human behaviour, particularly where the only punishment was death, would be as pointless as it would be inhumane, since it would be seeking to enforce the unenforceable. If anyone is responsible for an incompetent's lack of ability, it should surely be the person who appointed him to his post.

The most likely meaning of 'negligence' in Article 12, therefore, was *culpable* failure to do one's duty. A culpable failure might be anything from gross negligence at one extreme, to blameworthy inattention at the other, but would certainly not include professional misjudgement or simple lack of skill. If His Majesty's judges thought otherwise, they were wrong.

'IN TIME OF ACTION'

But, even if Byng had been guilty of culpable negligence, he should still not have been convicted in the circumstances charged. What the court martial failed to take account of was that Article 12 of the Articles of War was confined to neglect of duty only '*in time of action*'; there is no mention there of renewing a naval engagement after it had been broken off, or of an officer's duty to go to the aid of His Majesty's forces on land, or even of failing to obey orders. As an Australian judge has pointed out, the court martial's resolutions simply did not refer to a 'time of action', which is the only situation with which Article 12 was concerned.[14] (Resolution 34, it is true, speaks of actions at sea, but it could not possibly refer to anything other than Byng's failure to renew the naval action, which, as pointed out above, was beyond the scope of the Article.) Determined to convict the defendant of something, the court appears to have worded this resolution so as to fudge the boundary between the sea action and the defendant's conduct thereafter. The court had access to legal advice, and it is difficult to believe that it acted in this respect otherwise than with a deliberate intention to mislead.

The conclusions are inescapable: Byng was not given a fair trial before an independent tribunal, and the court martial's decisions – of law and procedure – were insupportable and unconscionable. Nor can there be any excuse for the King's failure to grant the mercy that the court martial had unanimously recommended.

Byng was not an outstanding naval commander, but he was an unquestionably brave man who did his imperfect best in a difficult situation not of his choosing. It is clear that, from the start, those in authority saw in his failure to prevail at Port Mahon an opportunity to conceal their own disgraceful failure properly to ensure the defence of their country's interests. Byng's death was the price that had to be paid for their incompetence.

Byng's tomb is in the family crypt in the Church of All Saints in the quiet Bedfordshire village of Southill. There is a local tradition that the inscription on the monument was written by Dr Johnson himself[15] and it is easy to see why. The words read:

TO THE PERPETUAL DISGRACE OF PUBLIC JUSTICE, THE HON. JOHN BYNG, ESQ., ADMIRAL OF THE BLUE, FELL A MARTYR TO POLITICAL PERSECUTION, MARCH 14TH, IN THE YEAR MDCCLVII [1757]; WHEN BRAVERY AND LOYALTY WERE INSUFFICIENT SECURITIES FOR THE LIFE AND HONOUR OF A NAVAL OFFICER.

CHAPTER EIGHT

The Assassins

The Trial of the Lincoln Conspirators, 1865

Waking up after a restless night, America's President Abraham Lincoln told his wife, Mary Todd, of a disturbing dream.

> About ten days ago I retired very late. I had been up waiting for important dispatches from the front. I could not have been long in bed when I fell into a slumber, for I was weary. I soon began to dream. There seemed to be a death-like stillness about me. Then I heard subdued sobs as if a number of people were weeping. I thought I left my bed and wandered downstairs. There the silence was broken by the same pitiful sobbing, but the mourners were invisible. I went from room to room; no living person was in sight, but the same mournful sounds of distress met me as I passed along. It was light in all the rooms; every object was familiar to me; but where were all the people who were grieving as if their hearts would break? I was puzzled and alarmed. What could be the meaning of all this?
>
> Determined to find the cause of a state of things so mysterious and so shocking, I kept on until I arrived at the East Room, which I entered. There I met with a sickening surprise. Before me was a catafalque, on which rested a corpse wrapped in funeral vestments. Around it were stationed soldiers who were acting as guards; and there was a throng of people, some gazing mournfully at the corpse, whose face was covered, others weeping pitifully. Who is dead in the White House? I demanded of one of the soldiers. 'The President,' was the answer; 'he was killed by an assassin!' Then came a loud burst of grief from the crowd, which awoke me from my dream. I slept no more that night; and although it was only a dream, I have been strangely annoyed by it ever since.[1]

It was the second week of April 1865. Within days, Lincoln was dead, killed by an assassin's bullet. His body, guarded by soldiers, was laid out in the East Room of the White House. National mourning was on an unprecedented scale. A funeral train carried the murdered President's body from Washington DC to its final resting place in Springfield, Illinois. All along the 1,700-mile route the people turned out in their thousands and tens of thousands, some out of curiosity, but most in order to pay their respects to a man they had come to regard as the saviour of their nation and – though it was not strictly true – the Great Emancipator of the slaves. Lincoln's assassin was soon to be dead and most of his fellow conspirators rounded up, but the questions of who was behind the conspiracy and whether all those arrested were guilty as charged are to this day the subjects of bitter dispute, even litigation in one case. What lay behind the first assassination of an American President?

A HOUSE DIVIDED

Throughout the first half of the nineteenth century tension had been building up between the slave-owning economy of the Southern states and the rapidly industrialising North. In 1856 the country attorney Abraham Lincoln joined the Republican Party that had been formed two years earlier to resist the spread of slavery. Lincoln disliked slavery but he feared the break-up of the Union more. In a series of debates around the country he proclaimed: 'A house divided against itself cannot stand. I believe this government cannot endure, permanently half slave and half free. I do not expect the Union to be dissolved. I do not expect the house to fall. But I do expect it will cease to be divided.'[2]

Within two years Lincoln had been elected President with a mandate to prevent at all costs the dissolution of the Union. But it was already too late. The Southern states decided that they could not remain in a Union set upon abolishing the institution of slavery. South Carolina had seceded in 1860 and a Confederacy of seven states was formed the following year, Virginia, North Carolina and Arkansas joining shortly afterwards. When in April 1861 the Union garrison of Fort Sumter on an island in Charleston Harbour, South Carolina, refused to surrender to the Confederacy, the shore batteries opened fire in what were to be the opening shots of a terrible civil war.

Modern technology (rifled muskets and cannon, breech-loading rifles and the Gatling gun) made the ensuing conflict one of the bloodiest in history. America was to lose far more of her sons in its civil war than in the Second World War and Vietnam put together. Families were divided in their loyalties. Officers who had trained and fought together now found themselves on opposite sides. The South's foremost general, Robert E. Lee, had actually been offered command of the Union armies before resigning his commission to fight for his home state of Virginia.

Desperate times called for desperate measures. A raid ordered by Lincoln on the Southern capital, Richmond, had as its aim the assassination of the Southern president and his cabinet. A future governor of Kentucky deliberately sold clothing to Union troops knowing it to be infected with smallpox and yellow fever. Both sides behaved disgracefully towards their prisoners of war. The closing months of the conflict particularly were shrouded in acrimony. In the defeated South some suspected Lincoln of having personally ordered the destruction of their towns during General Sherman's march to the sea. In such a climate it seems unsurprising that the Confederate secret service should have contemplated the assassination of Lincoln. At the heart of the conspiracy was the improbable figure of America's most prominent Shakespearian actor, John Wilkes Booth.

'AN IMPERFECT ACTOR ON THE STAGE'

John Wilkes Booth was born in Maryland on 10 May 1838. He grew up the son of an indulgent mother and a heavy-drinking father, the noted English actor Junius Brutus Booth. His eldest brother Edwin had played Othello to Henry Irving's Iago.

As a young man, Booth had been told by a gypsy that he would live a fast life and die young. Fired with a desire for fame, he went on the stage at the age of seventeen. As he became better known, he moved to Richmond, where he came to admire the Southern way of life. During the 1850s Booth was attracted to the Know-Nothing Party, which aimed to preserve the country for native-born whites.[3] In 1859 he enlisted in the Richmond Grays, apparently in order to witness the hanging of the violent, unhinged abolitionist John Brown. With the civil war looming, Booth moved north for reasons that have never been satisfactorily explained. (It is variously said that he had promised his mother not to get involved with the army and that he was fearful of being disfigured. It is also possible that he was already involved with the Confederate secret service.) He began smuggling quinine to the Confederate forces and in the spring of 1862 was arrested for making anti-government remarks. The actor became increasingly obsessed with Abraham Lincoln and complained of the President's 'appearance, his pedigree, his coarse low jokes and anecdotes, his vulgar similes and his frivolity'.[4] In November 1863, when Lincoln and his wife went to see him in a play at Ford's Theater, Washington DC, Booth was seen to approach the President's box and mutter threats.

In October 1864 Booth went to Montreal, where he held meetings with representatives of the Confederate secret service; it seems likely that it was at these meetings that the idea of action against President Lincoln was first mooted. By January of the following year the 26-year-old Booth had put together a team to do whatever was decided, although at this stage assassination was not yet on the agenda.

Booth had assembled a team that included some long-standing acquaintances. Lewis Thornton Powell, also known as Paine or Payne, was a long-time friend of Booth, having first met the actor at the theatre in Richmond. A Confederate soldier, he had been injured and taken prisoner at Gettysburg. After escaping from the Union Army Hospital in Baltimore, he had enlisted in Mosby's Virginia cavalry in the autumn of 1863. A year later he became involved with the Confederate secret service; shortly afterwards, he took the Oath of Allegiance to the Union. Tall, handsome, with a thatch of dark hair and no small degree of dash even in confinement, Powell was the most striking among the plotters in both character and looks.

The unemployed Samuel Arnold had been a classmate of Booth. He had joined the Confederate army, but was discharged for health reasons. Another childhood friend, Michael O'Laughlen had grown up in the same street as Booth. A small, rather delicate man with a heavy black moustache, he had been discharged from the Confederate army in 1862 and returned to Baltimore to work as a clerk in a feed store.

At the outbreak of war John Surratt was a college student. On the death of his father he was briefly appointed as a local postmaster. His principal activity during the war, however, was as a courier for the Confederate secret service. Surratt's mother Mary and her husband owned a tavern and post office in Surrattsville, a small Maryland settlement named after her husband's family. The husband died in 1862 and in October 1864, along with her daughter Anna, the widow Mary moved to his three-storey property in Washington, where she let out rooms. She rented the Surrattsville tavern to a heavy-drinking ex-policeman named John Minchin Lloyd.

The German-born George Atzerodt was the semi-literate operator of a carriage repair business. During the war he used his boat to help Confederate agents cross the Potomac. One of those he helped was John Surratt, who invited him to Washington, where he stayed at Mary Surratt's boarding house. He was asked to leave when Mary discovered that he had been drinking alcohol in his room.

'Ned' Spangler, a long-time friend of Booth, was a carpenter at Ford's Theater.

At twenty-two years of age the chemist's clerk David E. Herold was the youngest of the conspirators. His photograph suggests a weak-willed man.

THE KIDNAP PLOTS

Towards the end of the war the South had become desperately short of soldiers. Booth's first plan in October 1864 was not to kill Lincoln, but to kidnap him on the way to his summer retreat at a former banker's residence outside Washington, known as the Soldier's Home, and offer him in exchange for Confederate prisoners of war. For whatever reason, this plan came to naught. A few months later he met John Surratt at a Washington hotel, together with a Dr Samuel A. Mudd and Louis Wiechmann, a War Office employee who shared a room with Surratt in

Mrs Surratt's lodging house, and let them into the plot. (Wiechmann – known to the reporters as Weichmann – was later to claim that he had been excluded from the vital part of the conversation.)

Booth's hopes were raised again when in March the following year he learnt that the President proposed to attend a play at Ford's Theater in Washington. The original plan was to turn off the gas lights in the theatre, to seize the President in his box and to lower him, trussed up, to the stage from where he would be taken to an awaiting carriage. Ned Spangler was to build accommodation for the buggy that would convey the captured President to the South. Atzerodt was to ferry Lincoln over the river. Herold was to use his intimate knowledge of the back roads in Maryland to drive the President away and the formidable Powell was to be the team's strong man. Not everyone supported this daft proposal, and it was agreed instead to seize Lincoln in his carriage on the way to a soldiers' hospital near Washington and to take him to Richmond, using Herold's boat to ferry the President across the river. This scheme was frustrated in its turn when the President changed his plans at the last minute and remained in the capital. John Surratt lost heart after this abortive venture and went back to carrying dispatches for the South. (In later years he was to boast that the kidnapping had actually been attempted and that he had taken part in it, but this seems unlikely.) When the plot was abandoned, O'Laughlen and Arnold returned to their homes; it was to save them from the gallows.

On 9 April 1865 Robert E. Lee surrendered to the Union general Ulysses S. Grant at Appomattox Courthouse. Despite the fact that his forces amounted to only one-sixth of the Confederate army, the war was effectively over and an exchange of prisoners was now pointless. But Booth's feelings still ran high. Two days later he was present outside the White House, where, along with Herold and Powell, he heard Lincoln make his inauguration address. When the President suggested that voting rights should be granted to 'the more intelligent blacks and to those who had served the Northern cause', Booth was outraged. His diary entry that day read: 'Something decisive and great must be done.' He was soon to get his chance.

'THE PLAY'S THE THING'

On 13 April Booth learned that the President and General Grant were planning to attend the evening performance of a British play, *Our American Cousin*, in Ford's Theater the following day. It was a splendid opportunity; Booth knew the theatre well and could expect easy access. This time the actor's objective was more ambitious and far more deadly; it was nothing less than the removal of the leadership of the Union government by means of three synchronised assassinations. As he explained the plan to his now reduced gang, Booth would kill Lincoln and Grant at the theatre while Atzerodt killed the Vice-President, Andrew Johnson, at his hotel. At the same time Powell, accompanied by Herold, was to kill Secretary of State William Henry Seward at his residence.[5] That evening was a night of celebration and fireworks to mark the end of the war. Booth, however, did not share in the rejoicing; instead, he went to Ford's Theater and bored a peephole in the door of the state box.

The following day the President's party arrived at the theatre at around 8.30 p.m., about half an hour after the play had started. It was Good Friday, 14 April. On learning that the difficult Mrs Lincoln was going to be present, General Grant had cried off, possibly saving his life. (His wife had refused to sit with 'that crazy woman'.) He was replaced at the last minute by a 28-year-old army officer, Major Henry R. Rathbone, and Rathbone's fiancée, Clara Harris, whose fates were to become tragically linked with Lincoln's. The presidential party went to the second-tier state box (actually two boxes joined together), the outside of which was decorated with flags and a portrait of George Washington. After a standing ovation and a rendering of 'Hail to the Chief', the President sat down in a rocking chair, wearing his characteristic long black coat and top hat. His bodyguard for the night was John Parker of the Metropolitan Police Force.

About an hour later Booth arrived at the theatre armed with a single-shot derringer and a hunting knife. After fortifying himself with a drink at a saloon next door, he entered by the front of the theatre. At about 10.15 p.m., after showing his card to a footman, he entered the corridor leading to the state box, wedging the outer door shut behind him with a wooden rod he had left there the night before. He found the internal door unguarded, John Parker having left his post, possibly for a better view of the play. (This far from diligent officer, who had already been the subject of disciplinary action, seems to have obtained his appointment by the favour of Mrs Lincoln.) Booth entered the box, took aim and fired a single shot into the President's head through his left ear. The bullet lodged behind Lincoln's right eye; he never regained consciousness.

As the President slumped forward out of his seat grasping one of the flags draped in front of him, Major Rathbone struggled with Booth, who stabbed him in the breast and shoulder. Mrs Lincoln screamed. Booth then jumped from the box some 11 feet onto the stage. Although this was a feat that the actor had performed professionally many times before, on this occasion one of his spurs caught in the flags decorating the box and he landed clumsily, breaking a bone in his left leg just above the ankle. Panic reigned as Booth waved his bloody knife and shouted something to the audience before stumbling off the stage and out of the back door of the theatre. Some heard him declaim the Virginia state motto, *Sic semper tyrannis* ('Thus always to tyrants'); others, 'The South is revenged'.

The President did not die at once. A medical examination found him to be too seriously wounded to be taken to hospital, and four soldiers were summoned to carry him across the road to a room in a boarding house, where his great length was placed diagonally on an all-too-small bed. Here, he lay on his back, the upper part of his head covered with a cloth and the lower jaw dropping down. Soon, Lincoln's powerful Secretary of War, Edwin M. Stanton, appeared, along with other members of the Cabinet. Mrs Lincoln sat at her husband's bedside, but had to be removed from the room after becoming distressed. At her request, her son, Robert Todd Lincoln, was brought to the bedside. At 7.22 a.m. the next morning, despite the efforts of sixteen doctors, the President's laboured breathing stopped. 'Now,' said Stanton, 'he belongs to the angels.' (In later reports the last two words were edited to 'the ages').

The nervous Atzerodt had been drinking all day. On learning of the death of Lincoln he finally lost his nerve, threw his revolver in the gutter and hastened to get drunk. Next day he fled the state without having made any attempt to kill the Vice-President. Powell, however, did proceed with his allotted task, the murder of the Secretary of State. Though ultimately unsuccessful, the attempt was remarkable for its determination and ferocity.

Seward was at home in bed recovering from a carriage accident. At about the time that Booth shot the President, the would-be assassin arrived at his door claiming that he was delivering medicine from the Secretary's doctor. Refused entry, Powell pushed his way in and ran upstairs while Herold waited outside. The Secretary's older son, Frederick (who was Assistant Secretary of State), tried to keep Powell from his father's bedroom and was pistol whipped for his pains. Major W.B. Seward Jr, the Secretary's younger son who was inside the room, rushed to his father's aid. Despite all the son's efforts and those of a convalescent soldier who was also present, Powell managed to slash the Secretary's throat twice, leaving him badly scarred for life; only a leather-covered metal surgical collar saved Seward from death. Shouting, 'I'm mad. I'm mad,' Powell then fought his way out of the house past Seward's third son, Augustus, and a State Department messenger, injuring both severely. Mounting his horse, he was heard to echo the cry 'Sic semper tyrannis'. About a mile from the Navy Yard Bridge he took shelter in a tree.

Herold met up with Booth and around midnight the two of them stopped at the Surratt tavern to collect field glasses and carbines that had been left there for them earlier. Booth drank some whiskey to dull the pain in his leg. At about 4 a.m. they arrived in the small settlement of Bryantown at the house of the physician Dr Mudd.

According to Mudd's later account, Booth had disguised himself in a shawl that hid the lower part of his face. Herold, who did all the talking, gave false names and claimed that his companion had been involved in a riding accident. Mudd set and splinted Booth's broken leg and insisted that his visitors stay the night. Next morning he got his handyman to make rude crutches for Booth and lent him his razor to shave off a moustache. After an unsuccessful attempt to hire a carriage, the two fugitives left by a short cut through a swamp that Dr Mudd pointed out to them. He claimed that they pressed $25 on him for his services.

Later that day Dr Mudd told his wife Sarah Frances that he had suspicions concerning his two visitors. She persuaded him not to abandon her that night but to send word the following day to the soldiers who were searching the district. After church the next morning Mudd confided his 'suspicions' to a friend, but when a Lieutenant Lovett arrived to question him the doctor failed to mention them. He also misled them concerning the direction the two men had gone. When the Lieutenant returned three days later, Sarah Mudd produced a left riding boot that had been cut off the visitor's leg three days before. The turned-down top of the boot bore the name 'J Wilkes'. Dr Mudd claimed that he had not noticed the writing. He also denied recognising photographs of the two fugitives. Soon, orders came for his arrest. Meanwhile, Secretary Stanton, who had effectively taken over the government of the country, had been organising the largest manhunt in America's history. It was greatly helped by the fact that Booth's last act before the assassination had been to send a letter to the press in terms virtually admitting his part in the plot. It was signed, 'Men who love their country better than gold or life. JW Booth – Payne – Atzerodt – Herold.'

Unfortunately for him, Lewis Powell turned up at the door of Mrs Surratt's boarding house at the very moment the soldiers arrived. He was carrying a pickaxe and claimed to be a labourer hired by Mrs Surratt to dig a gutter. At 11.30 at night this seemed an unlikely story, especially as Mrs Surratt solemnly denied hiring or even knowing him. The two of them were arrested, along with Wiechmann and Lloyd. After being kept in solitary confinement and threatened with being charged with the murder of the President, Wiechmann and Lloyd agreed to give evidence against Mrs Surratt. The extent of their involvement in the conspiracy, if any, will probably never be known.

Most of the other conspirators were swiftly rounded up. An incriminating letter from 'Sam' found in Booth's hotel room led the authorities to Samuel Arnold, who was known to be one of Booth's close friends. On searching his rented room the police found a loaded pistol and several bowie knives. He was arrested at the Maryland home of his cousin. Ned Spangler, who had helped prepare the President's box and had held Booth's horse outside the theatre on the night of the assassination, was also arrested after it came to light that he had been a long-time employee at the Booth family farm in Maryland. O'Laughlen surrendered himself to the federal authorities.

Only Booth, Herold and Surratt remained at large. On 20 April Secretary Stanton offered a $100,000 reward for their capture. Persons 'harbouring or secreting' them would be 'subject to trial by a military commission and the punishment of DEATH'. In all, several hundred people were arrested, including the proprietors of Ford's Theater. Most had to be released for lack of evidence.

The search for the principal conspirator was pursued with great vigour through swamp and forest, but he and his companion managed to elude capture for some time with the help of Confederate sympathisers. Strangely, none of these was ever prosecuted.

GARRETT'S BARN

Early in the morning of 26 April a troop of cavalry commanded by First Lieutenant Edward Doherty caught up with Booth hiding in a barn used as a tobacco warehouse at Garrett's Farm near Port Royal, Virginia. At first, the officer did not realise that Herold was inside as well. Doherty takes up the story:

> We threatened to burn the barn if he did not surrender; at one time gave him ten minutes to make up his mind. Finally, Booth said, 'Oh; Captain, there is a man here who wants to surrender awful bad.' I answered, and I think Mr Baker did at the same time, 'Hand out your arms.' Herold replied, 'I have none.' Baker said, 'We know exactly what you have got.' Booth replied, 'I own all the arms, and intend to use them on you gentlemen.' After some little parley I said, 'Let him out.'

His report went on:

> Almost simultaneous with my taking Herold out of the barn the hay in the rear of the barn was ignited by Mr Conger, and the barn fired. Sergt. Boston Corbett, Company L, Sixteenth New York Cavalry, shot the assassin Booth, wounding him in the neck. I entered the barn as soon as the shot was fired, dragging Herold with me, and found that Booth had fallen on his back. Messrs Conger and Baker, with some of my men, entered the barn and took hold of Booth. I proceeded with Herold to find a rope to secure him, there being no irons for that purpose. The assassin Booth lived about two hours. In the meantime, a doctor was procured, who remained with Booth till he died.

Booth's spinal cord had been severed by the shot, and, when he asked his captors to raise his hands before his face, he was heard to mutter, 'Useless! Useless!' In his dying moments he whispered, 'Tell my mother I did it for my country.'

The remaining conspirators were at first imprisoned on the ironclads *Montauk* and *Saugus* and later in the Arsenal Penitentiary in Washington.

Secretary Stanton ordered 'for better security against conversation' that they should be shackled and their heads covered by canvas hoods. The hoods, which were not removed even for washing or eating, reached down nearly to their waists, with openings only for breathing and eating. Inside the hoods, the prisoners' ears and eyes were covered with cotton wool, pressing hard on their eyeballs; it must have been excruciatingly uncomfortable. When Powell attempted to kill himself by banging his head against the cell wall, his canvas hood was replaced with a padded one. It is difficult to think of any genuine security reason for this barbaric treatment.

THE MILITARY TRIBUNAL

Secretary Stanton decided that a military rather than a civil tribunal should try the accused. It was a controversial decision even within government, but the Attorney General, James Speed, upheld its legality. The Commission comprised three major-generals, four brigadier generals and two colonels. Major-General David Hunter (Judge Advocate and Recorder) presided, assisted by two special judge advocates.[6] The chief prosecutor was the Judge Advocate General of the US army, Joseph Holt. Photographs of these gentlemen show them in military uniform, differentiated only by the length of their beards.

On 9 May at around midnight the prison governor made a surprise visit to the prisoners' cells; their hoods were removed and the charges read to them. They were each accused of 'maliciously, unlawfully and traitorously and in aid of the existing armed rebellion', conspiring together to kill and murder Lincoln, Johnson, Seward and Grant; murdering Lincoln; assaulting with intent to kill and murder Seward; and lying in wait to kill and murder Johnson and Grant. Significantly, the accused were said to have been 'incited and encouraged by [the Southern President] Jefferson Davis'. (In fact, though he spent two years in prison, Davis was never to be charged with any crime.) Since it was Seward's constitutional duty as Secretary of State to call an election on the death of Lincoln, his murder would have prevented the election of a new President of the Union, and this fact was reflected in the indictment. The charges were read to the prisoners, and then their hoods were replaced and they were plunged once more into darkness. They were to face trial the following day.

The trial took place in a large improvised courtroom on the third floor of the Washington Arsenal Penitentiary. It lasted from 10 May until 30 June.[7] The defendants, who all pleaded 'not guilty', were permitted lawyers and to call witnesses, but in accordance with contemporary practice were not allowed to testify in their own defence. Conviction was to be by simple majority, but the death sentence would require a two-thirds majority.

The accused sat together in court, each separated by a soldier; only the modestly veiled Mary Surratt was kept apart from the rest. Even in court all except Mary remained shackled at ankles and wrists. Powell and Atzerodt bore the additional burden of an iron ball that had to be carried into and out of court by the military escort. At first, the authorities wanted to hold the trial in secret, but public pressure forced them to admit the press and chosen individuals. The dashing Powell was said to have been the subject of much female interest.

At the outset, Mudd's counsel, General Thomas Ewing Jr, made a significant challenge to the court's jurisdiction. In peacetime, he said, a non-military citizen was entitled to be judged in a civilian court. Since the state of Maryland was not part of the Confederacy and since the local civilian courts remained open, a military tribunal had no power to try the case. His submission was rejected and the prosecution began to call their evidence.

Powell was identified by Seward's butler as his master's assailant, a fact that he could hardly contest. The accused fell back on the only plea remaining to him, insanity, relying on his cry of 'I am mad'. Medical evidence suggested that, on the contrary, he was only feigning madness. Herold's pitiful defence was that as a 'constitutional coward' he was incapable of participating in murder. The case against Atzerodt was equally damning. He had stayed in a hotel room above that occupied by Andrew Johnson. He had been heard to enquire about the Vice-President's habits and schedule and had boasted that he would soon become rich and famous.

Sam Arnold's letter to Booth was produced to the court. It announced his backing out of the conspiracy, ostensibly for financial reasons and because suspicion was beginning to settle on him. The defence argued that from the date of that letter Arnold bore no further responsibility for the plot. Unfortunately for him, the rest of the letter made it clear that his withdrawal from the plot was not due to any lack of enthusiasm on his part, 'Time more propitious will arrive yet. Do not act rashly or in haste . . . and 'ere long I shall be better prepared to again be with you.' There was written evidence clearly linking O'Laughlen with the earlier kidnap plan, but of his complicity in the assassination there was none. The case against the horse holder Ned Spangler consisted mainly of evidence that he had slapped a stagehand after the assassination and warned, 'Don't tell which way he went.' The defence called contradictory evidence, but it was not believed.

The case against Mrs Surratt consisted principally of evidence of her close associations with the other conspirators. Early in 1865 Booth and his friends had been frequent visitors to Mary's boarding house. Powell had stayed there using the alias 'Reverend Wood'. A visiting card with Booth's picture on it was found tucked behind another picture in the house. Wiechmann claimed that on 11 April he and Mrs Surratt had gone to Surrattsville, meeting John Lloyd on the way. Three days later, on the day of the assassination, the two of them had again visited the town. But there was more. Lloyd testified that two carbines and ammunition had been left with him by John Surratt, Herold and Atzerodt. On the day of the assassination, he claimed, Mrs Surratt 'told me to have those shooting-irons ready that night, there would be some parties who would call for them. She gave me something wrapped in a piece of paper, which I took upstairs, and found to be a field-glass. She told me to get two bottles of whisky ready, and that these things were to be called for that night.' Mrs Surratt's explanation was that she had gone to Washington to collect a debt. However, when a defence witness, who had earlier given an entirely different version of the 'shooting irons' story, later withdrew his statement in the witness box, Mrs Surratt's defence was thrown into disarray.

The doctor had met Booth for the first time in Bryantown in November 1864, when he had spoken to him and Surratt in a dark passage. Mudd told the investigators: 'I have never seen Booth since [the November meeting] to my knowledge until last Saturday morning.' Wiechmann gave the lie to this when he testified that they had met again the following month in Washington. Several witnesses established conclusively that his association with Booth had been far closer than he had admitted.

A former slave of Dr Mudd gave evidence that John Surratt was at the doctor's house almost every weekend during the war and that when soldiers came from the South she and others had been told to stand watch. (This was later challenged by defence witnesses.) More than one ex-slave of the doctor's spoke of Confederate soldiers having been allowed to rest in the woods near his house and of their having received succour from him. Even more incriminating was how the doctor had responded to questioning. Lieutenant Lovett told the court, 'When we first asked Dr Mudd whether two strangers had been there, he seemed very much excited, and got pale as a sheet of paper and blue about his lips, like a man frightened at something he had done.' Colonel Wells, who had also interviewed Mudd, gave evidence of his 'very extraordinary' attitude: 'I found that, unless I asked direct questions, important facts were omitted.' Despite having met Booth more than once, Dr Mudd denied recognising his photograph. Both officers confirmed that Mudd had later admitted to having recognised the assassin. Evidence was also heard of the doctor's personal antipathy towards the President.

The court adjourned for four weeks to consider its verdicts, during which time the prisoners remained, hooded and shackled, in their cells.

THE LAST ACT

Before being announced, the verdicts and sentences of the court martial had to be submitted to the new President, Andrew Johnson, for approval;

he confirmed them all. Powell, Herold, Atzerodt and Mary Surratt were found guilty of conspiracy and murder and sentenced to hang. Samuel Arnold, Michael O'Laughlen and Dr Mudd were found guilty of conspiracy (but not murder) and sentenced to hard labour for life. 'Ned' Spangler was sentenced to six years' imprisonment. Dr Mudd had escaped the death penalty by one vote.

The accused were informed of their sentences in prison. To their horror, those condemned to death learned that they were to die the following day. Powell met his fate stoically, but Mary Surratt wept uncontrollably.

Five of the nine members of the Military Commission recommended that 'in consideration of [her] sex and age' Mary Surratt's sentence should be commuted to life imprisonment. President Johnson would have none of it. Signing the death warrant, he commented that she had 'kept the nest that hatched the egg'. Later, he was to maintain that he had never been shown the plea for mercy. Mary Surratt's lawyers, now desperate, sought and obtained from Judge Wylie of the Supreme Court of the District of Columbia a writ of habeas corpus – that is to say, an order to produce their client to the court. When informed of this, the President, prompted by his bellicose Secretary of War, signed an order declaring the writ of habeas corpus 'suspended in cases such as this'. (Lincoln had acted in a similar unconstitutional manner during the war.) Attempts by Mary's distraught daughter to approach the President were blocked.

On 7 June in the large courtyard of the Old Arsenal Building in Washington the condemned, three men and a woman, ascended the scaffold in sight of their awaiting coffins and open graves. The weather was hot and steamy and in a macabre gesture of courtesy an umbrella was held over the condemned woman. The findings of the Military Commission were read out, the prisoners were bound at the arms, ankles and knees, and hoods were placed over their heads. The trap was sprung shortly before 1.30 p.m. Mary Surratt's last pathetic words were, 'Please, don't let me fall!' Powell went to his death as befitted a soldier, maintaining to the last the innocence of Mary; his end was not to be a merciful one. The noose failed to snap his neck and, like Herold, he suffered a slow death by strangulation.

Afterwards, the executioner made a brisk trade cutting the nooses into short pieces for sale as souvenirs.

John Surratt's whereabouts on the night of the assassination are still unknown. He himself later claimed to have been in New York and to have fled to Canada upon hearing of Lincoln's death. What is clear is that on 15 September he sailed to England and thence to Rome, where he joined the Papal Zouaves. On being traced and arrested, he escaped his captors by diving into a 100-foot-deep ravine. He was finally caught in Alexandria and brought back to the United States to face trial in a civilian court.

After a month's hearing the trial ended in a hung jury. The federal government eventually dropped all charges and Surratt was released from custody in the summer of 1868, thereafter turning a pretty penny by going round the country lecturing on the assassination. He died of pneumonia in 1916, the last of the conspirators. Throughout his life, John Surratt maintained that his role had been confined solely to the unsuccessful kidnap plot. Guilty or innocent, he seems to have made precious little effort to help his mother in her hour of need.

FORT JEFFERSON

Samuel Mudd and Michael O'Laughlen were taken to Fort Jefferson to serve their sentences. The military prison was America's 'Devil's Island' in the Gulf of Mexico where prisoners were held in appalling conditions. Surrounded by a 70-foot-wide moat containing sharks, it was, in the words of Mudd's lawyer, 'beyond the reach of the law'. The loyal Mrs Mudd petitioned continually for her husband's release, but to no effect. On 25 September Dr Mudd attempted to escape by concealing himself in a visiting ship. He was quickly discovered and returned to custody in conditions harsher than before. It seemed that he would never get out, but fate was about to take a hand.

In the summer of 1867 yellow fever swept the island, claiming the lives of O'Laughlen and the prison doctor among many others. Dr Mudd, now working in the carpenter's shop, agreed to stand in for the doctor and, by all accounts, performed heroically. He himself came down with the disease but recovered. The entire garrison of the island signed a glowing petition in support of the doctor and sent it to the President; it seemed to have no effect and in September 1868 Mudd failed in an attempt to obtain a writ of habeas corpus. Eventually the good doctor's efforts reaped their reward. On 8 February 1869, in what was to be almost his last official act before leaving office, President Johnson signed an unconditional pardon releasing Dr Mudd from prison where he had served somewhat less than four years. Mudd resumed his medical practice in his home town and fathered five more children. In 1876 he was elected to the Maryland legislature. In 1883 at the age of forty-nine he died of a fever and was buried in St Mary's Cemetery next to the Bryantown church where he had first met Booth.

Arnold too was pardoned by President Johnson in 1869. He lived until 1906. Ned Spangler was pardoned at the same time. He worked in Baltimore until 1873 when he sought help from Dr Mudd, who gave him 5 acres of land on which he lived until his death in 1875; it was the place where Mudd had hidden the rebel soldiers.

Dr Mudd's descendants, notably his grandson Richard Mudd – also a doctor – worked tirelessly to clear their forebear's name. Not only was his grandfather innocent of the conspiracy, Richard claimed, but he was tried by a tribunal that had no jurisdiction over him.

The American Secretary of War has power to correct any military record 'when the Secretary considers it necessary to correct an error or remove an injustice', and the Army Board for Correction of Military Records was set up to advise on such applications. In 1992 the Board recommended that Samuel Mudd's conviction should be set aside on the ground that the Hunter Commission's jurisdiction did not extend to non-combatant civilians like him. The Assistant Secretary of the Army thought otherwise: the assassination had been committed, he determined, by an unlawful belligerent as an act of war.

A District Court declined to overturn the Secretary's decision. Upon the death of the 101-year-old Richard Mudd, his son Robert, Samuel's great-grandson, took the case to a Federal Appeal Court. In November 2002 that court dismissed his application on the ground that Dr Mudd was not a 'member or former member of the armed forces . . . [and that] neither the grandson nor the great-grandson is an heir or legal representative of the type of "claimant" contemplated by the statute'.[8] It is unlikely therefore that we will ever get a definitive view of the legality of his trial. But that should not prevent its being examined.

WAS THE TRIAL LAWFUL?

In 1866, less than a year after the trial of the conspirators, the US Supreme Court ruled that a military court had no jurisdiction in civil cases if the civil courts were open at the time – exactly the objection raised at the trial by Dr Mudd's counsel.[9] When the Hunter Commission was appointed, the civil courts in the District of Columbia had been open. It would be presumptuous of an English lawyer to pontificate upon such a difficult point of federal law, but there is a strong, though not unanimous, body of legal opinion in America that the Supreme Court's decision is conclusive of the illegality of the Commission.

The appointment of the Hunter Commission brought with it another problem that was perhaps not obvious at the time, that of unjust bias. All the members of the tribunal had recently been engaged in a senior capacity in a war against the Confederacy that was accused of being behind the very conspiracy they were appointed to try. The president of the court and another of its members had been close to the victim of the crime, had even accompanied the body of their assassinated friend to its final resting place. This act had led to General Hunter being branded a war criminal by the South and threatened with death. One does not have to suspect the tribunal members of actual partiality to conclude that the composition of the court fell short of the standards of independence to which every judicial body should aspire.

Moreover, another member of the Commission was a noted phrenologist who saw fit to study the shape of the defendants' heads throughout the trial. He was to write of Dr Mudd that he 'had the appearance of a born liar and deceiver'. Nowadays, such 'evidence' would be instantly discounted by a court of law, but – who knows? – he may have been right.

WAS THE TRIAL FAIR?

Just as important is the issue of whether the proceedings were conducted fairly. This is a question that must be answered, not in the light of today's more testing standards, but by the laws and usages of the time, which were broadly those of the English courts from which the American legal system derived many of its basic principles.

The first defects concerned the drafting of the charges against the accused. As defence counsel pointed out at the time, the charges seemed to combine accusations of both conspiracy and murder. It is always important in law for the charges against an accused to be drafted with the greatest clarity. If murder was being alleged as well as conspiracy, it should have been the subject of separate charges. Further, the charges used – and repeated – the word 'traitorously'. Once again, if treason was being alleged, it should have been charged as such, not least because there were strict rules concerning the proof necessary to establish treason.

An equally serious problem was the failure of the court to give the defendants sufficient time to prepare their defence. Article 6 of the American Bill of Rights repeats the common-law requirement that an accused person must be 'informed of the nature and cause of the accusation'. It is implicit in this right that the accused should be given the information in good time to prepare his defence. The complexity, and possible misdrafting, of the charges against the accused made it more than usually important that they should have had adequate time for the preparation of their defence, yet the prisoners were wakened from their sleep to be informed of the accusations only hours before the opening of their trial and with no time properly to instruct legal representatives, who at that time had not even been appointed.

Mary Surratt was effectively denied the right to choose her own representative. When an opposition senator from Maryland sought to act on her behalf, General Hunter announced that a colleague had objected to his doing so on the ground that the senator had no respect for the oath of loyalty. Though this objection was later withdrawn, the senator's position had been weakened and he eventually left the court.

Another serious error was the failure to make clear to the tribunal the distinction between the projected, but not attempted, kidnap plots and the successful assassination. Evidence of the former was admitted seemingly to prove the latter. This failure on the prosecution's part can only have been deliberate, since Booth's diary, setting out his plans in detail, was already in government hands. Why that diary was not tendered in evidence no one can know; it certainly should have been. It may be significant that, when the existence of the diary came to light long after the trial, some eighteen of its pages were found to be missing, apparently torn out.

Equally improper was the way in which the prosecution intervened in the sentence passed on Mary Surratt. The chief prosecutor, Holt, retired and deliberated with the tribunal. After the trial her attorney reported 'on good authority' that the Commission had decided not to impose the death penalty on this defendant, but that Holt had successfully argued for this decision to be reconsidered. Even then, the initial decision in favour of death was only taken by a bare majority. By the tribunal's rules this should have ruled out that sentence. However, the same source reported that Holt then persuaded the Commission to impose the death penalty, but to add a rider recommending mercy. If this is what happened, it was the most egregious interference with the course of justice, which, as we have seen, resulted in this poor woman's death. After the trial Holt declared that, contrary to what Johnson had claimed, the President had been shown the plea for mercy. But, given his determination to see Mary hang, Holt's statement smacks of self-serving.

There can be no doubt that the military court was improperly constituted and that its proceedings were unjust in many important respects, even by the standards of the day. But were the accused in fact guilty of the crimes of which they were convicted? The only real doubt concerns Mary Surratt and Dr Mudd, both of whom have their ardent supporters still.

BUT WERE THEY GUILTY?

Geography cannot be ignored in considering the complicity of Samuel Mudd and Mary Surratt. Maryland was a border state, its loyalty split between North and South.[10] In 1861 President Lincoln had authorised the arrest without formal charge of suspected dissidents in the state. (Dr Mudd had given sanctuary to one of them.) And during the war the stationing of federal troops in the state had given rise to great resentment. In view of its geographical position between North and South and the discontent of many of its population, it is not surprising that the Confederate spy network ran from Washington to the Potomac River and thence to the South by way of Surrattsville, where Mary's tavern was situated, and Bryantown, where Dr Mudd had his home.

It seems likely that both were used as Confederate safe houses. It may also be significant that the injured Booth departed substantially from his planned escape route in order to get to Mudd's house, bypassing on the way the houses of three other medical practitioners.

As well as the evidence given against her, there are two facts that tend to confirm Mrs Surratt's guilt. Following the trial, Louis Wiechmann made a written statement to the effect that, after the investigators had left her tavern on the first occasion, Mary Surratt had exclaimed to her daughter, 'Anna, come what will, I am resigned. I think J. Wilkes Booth was only an instrument in the hands of the Almighty to punish this proud and licentious people.' And in 1977 the written statement that George Atzerodt had given to the authorities during his interrogation came to light for the first time – the so-called 'lost confession'. It contained the entry, 'Booth told me that Mrs Surratt went to Surrattsville to get out the guns (two carbines) which had been taken to that place by Herold, This was Friday.'[11]

It seems certain that Mary Surratt was party to the plot to kidnap the President and it seems likely that she was aware of, if not actually taking part in, the assassination plot, though the evidence here, had it been properly weighed, is unlikely to have been enough to satisfy the high standard of proof required for such a serious crime. Her sentence and the failure to consider the recommendation for mercy resulted in a horrible injustice.

And the doctor?

Samuel Alexander Mudd was born in Maryland in 1833 and graduated as a doctor in 1856. After two years' postgraduate work he returned home to Bryantown to practise as a physician. He married in 1857 and had four children. It would be wrong to think of Mudd solely as a doctor, however. Like many other physicians at the time, he was also a slave-owning tobacco farmer. Following Lincoln's Emancipation Proclamation in 1863, tobacco farming became far less profitable, and Dr Mudd was forced to cut back his acreage; it was bitterly resented. In a letter to the press of 1862, which did not come to light until years later, Mudd accused the North of pride, short-sightedness and hypocrisy and of having caused the destruction of 'one of the most glorious nations upon the face of the earth'.

There is no question that Mudd had met Booth, not once as he had claimed, but at least twice. His story of not having recognised a man whom he had known and to whom he gave medical treatment over a period of some twelve hours was simply incredible. His failure to answer official questions straightforwardly and the fact that he lied about the identity of his patient to at least two military interrogators amount to substantial confirmation of his guilt. A Captain Dutton later made a sworn affidavit that on the way to prison Mudd had confessed to having recognised the injured Booth. He had lied, he said, 'to protect himself and his family'. (The doctor was later to deny this.) Some thirty-six years after the event Samuel Cox Jr, who had been twelve at the time, recounted that Dr Mudd had told him that he had recognised Booth when he treated him but that, improbably, he had believed the assassin's story of a riding accident.[12] Yet more damning evidence was to emerge.

When interviewed about the case in 1883, Thomas Ewing, Mudd's attorney, said:

> The court very nearly hanged Dr Mudd. His prevarications were painful. He had given his whole case away by not trusting even his counsel or neighbors or kinfolk. It was a terrible thing to extricate him from the toils he had woven about himself. He had denied knowing Booth when he knew him well. He was undoubtedly accessory to the abduction plot, though he may have supposed it would never come to anything. He denied knowing Booth when he came to his house, when that was preposterous. He had been even intimate with Booth.[13]

And the 'lost confession' of George Atzerodt contained the sentence, 'I am certain Dr Mudd knew all about it as Booth sent . . . liquor and provisions for the trip with the President to Richmond about two weeks before the murder to Dr Mudd's.'[14]

While there may be doubt as to Dr Mudd's part in the conspiracy to kill the President, there can be little question that he was privy to the abduction plot and, in the old term, an accessory after the fact to the assassination.

THE CONTINUING ENIGMA

Conspiracy theories still abound concerning the assassination of America's most revered President. Most are groundless, like the 'Papal Conspiracy' that rests on nothing more than the fact that some of the conspirators were Catholics and that John Surratt found employment with the Papal Zouaves while on the run from the American authorities. That Booth's plan was aided and funded by the Confederate secret service is now pretty well established. But did he have assistance from other sources? People have asked, for example:

- Why did Stanton lie to Lincoln in saying that the officer he first requested to accompany him to the theatre was not available? (His defenders would reply that Stanton wanted to prevent the President from going.)
- Why was the wholly incompetent officer Parker assigned to guard Lincoln? Why did he absent himself at the crucial moment and why

is there no record of disciplinary action being taken against him? (It is said that his duty was to guard the President only on the way to and from the theatre.)

- Why was Booth's diary not produced at the trial and who removed the missing pages? (It was of course possible that Booth himself removed the pages.) And, most puzzling of all,
- Why did Booth imagine that he could, unaided and armed only with a single shot pistol, assassinate a President whom it was reasonable to assume would be well protected?

Questions like these have given rise to speculation that Booth was assisted in his endeavours by highly placed officials of the federal government, possibly Stanton or even Johnson, who had both opposed Lincoln's liberal attitude towards the defeated enemy. Until further facts come to light, however, suggestions like these must remain no more than speculation.

Even the supporting players in this tragedy had interesting stories to tell.

- Boston Corbett, the army sergeant who shot Booth, was an odd character. A religious eccentric, he had castrated himself to avoid sexual temptations. On leaving the army he lived in a cave on a hill. Later, after discharging a weapon at people he believed to have mocked a prayer, he was declared insane and committed to an asylum from which he shortly escaped. He was last heard of leaving for Mexico.
- Within a year of the trial one of the two men who had denied Mary Surratt's daughter access to the President to plead her mother's case was to tie a bag of shot around his neck and drown himself in the Hudson River. The other killed himself by a shot to the temple.
- William A. Petersen, the German tailor in whose house the President died, committed suicide in 1871.
- Clara Harris and Henry Rathbone, who had been Lincoln's guests in the box at Ford's Theater, married in 1867, seemingly to live happily ever after. But Henry, tormented by paranoid delusions, blamed himself for the President's death and in 1883, when he was US Consul General in Germany, stabbed Clara to death. For the rest of his life he was confined to an asylum for the criminally insane.
- Mary Todd Lincoln, like her husband, was a lifelong depressive. In 1875 she was declared insane on the application of her son and committed briefly to a sanatorium. She spent the last months of her life in a darkened room dressed in widow's weeds.
- Ford's Theater literally collapsed in 1893, killing twenty-two people and injuring sixty-eight others. It has since been rebuilt.

But the assassination was to have wider consequences.

THE MISSED OPPORTUNITY

Andrew Johnson's first task after taking over as President was to reconcile his divided country. In origin a poor white Southerner, Johnson's feelings towards blacks were at best mixed. He was certainly more concerned with the maintenance of the Constitution than the abolition of slavery. When in 1866 laws were passed to protect the rights of ex-slaves, Johnson vetoed them as unconstitutional. His own plans for reconstruction were frustrated by his Secretary of War, Edwin Stanton, and others within his Cabinet.

Even when Johnson eventually freed the slaves, it was a botched job. The decision as to how to cope with emancipation was left in the hands of white Southerners, and the result was a series of repressive 'Black Codes' that made mockery of the rights of the former slaves. A century and a half later, many African Americans still feel themselves second-class citizens in a white society and many in the South remain resentful of the North. It is ironic that the last dying kick of the Confederacy should have resulted in such a repressive post-bellum regime as would hold back the advancement of the South for decades.

It could all have been very different. During his second inaugural speech only six weeks before his death President Lincoln had urged:

> With malice toward none, with charity for all; with firmness in the right, as God gives us to see the right, let us strive on to finish the work we are in: to bind up the nation's wounds, to care for him who shall have borne the battle, and for his widow and his orphan, to do all which may achieve and cherish a just and lasting peace among ourselves, and with all nations.[15]

And what he proclaimed publicly he affirmed privately. At a Cabinet meeting on the morning of his assassination, Lincoln said of his former enemies:

> I hope there will be no persecution, no bloody work after the war is over. No one need expect me to take part in hanging or killing those men, even the worst of them. Frighten them out of the country, open the gates, let down the bars, scare them off, enough lives have been sacrificed. We must extinguish our resentment if we expect harmony and union.[16]

It was not to be.

CHAPTER NINE

The Nazis

The Nuremberg Trials, 1945

At 8 p.m. on 31 August 1939, a group of SS commandos, crudely disguised as Poles, launched a simulated attack on the German radio station at Gleiwitz on the border with Poland. The deception was not a particularly sophisticated one, but that did not matter, for it was not intended to be kept up for long.

At 3.30 a.m. the following morning in response to this 'unprovoked aggression' the German battleship Schleswig-Holstein, *on a 'good-will' visit to the Polish port of Gdansk,[1] opened fire on the fort at Westerplatte. Just over an hour later a force of some 3,200 German tanks, motorised infantry and 10,000 artillery pieces invaded Poland. It was an unequal contest; all Poland could call on were a few light tanks and its incredibly brave cavalry. Two days later, Britain and France declared war on Germany. The Second World War had begun.*

The First World War between Germany and its neighbours had ended in 1918 with what many Germans saw as a treacherous betrayal, followed by vindictive peace terms. Out of the ensuing maelstrom of economic disaster and social and political unrest there emerged a charismatic leader whose paranoid view of the world was mired in all the ancient bigotries of Europe. Even his megalomaniac ambitions might have been contained, however, had it not been for the head-in-the-sands attitude of the British.

Adolf Hitler came to power as Chancellor of Germany quite lawfully on 30 January 1933. At first, many Germans and not a few Englishmen saw him as a reinvigorating influence. The unemployed were given jobs, the economy, assisted by an inspired choice of economics minister, began to recover and the armed forces were won over by an ex-soldier determined to restore their former standing. In March 1936 a still inadequately equipped German army reoccupied the Rhineland. Neither the one-time Allies nor the instrument they had set up to keep the peace, the League of Nations, raised a finger to stop it. Three years later, almost to the day, Germany took over Austria in what was known as the *Anschluss* (or annexation); apart from a few diplomatic bleats, the world shrugged its shoulders, writing it off as merely another piece of German unification. The same could not be said of the rape of Czechoslovakia, which actually took place with the written consent of Britain's appeasing Prime Minister.

In a radio broadcast of September 1938 Neville Chamberlain, the one-time mayor of Birmingham, gave voice to popular opinion in this country when he said, 'How horrible, fantastic, incredible, it is that we should be digging trenches and trying on gas-masks here because of a quarrel in a far-away country between people of whom we know nothing!'

Encouraged by his first seemingly effortless successes, Hitler turned his sights towards his eastern neighbour, Poland, a country whose historical fate it has been to occupy a position between two of Europe's most powerful nations. In August 1939 the leaders of Soviet Russia and Nazi Germany, who hitherto had been at daggers drawn, signed a non-aggression treaty, which was known, after the names of their foreign ministers, as the Molotov–Ribbentrop Pact. When in 1939 German troops crossed the Polish border, Britain and France found themselves compelled by treaty obligations to declare war on the aggressor. It was too late; within a fortnight the Poles had surrendered to overwhelming force and the reluctant Allies were left fearfully to await Hitler's pleasure.

Nine months later, with his eastern front secure, Hitler's panzers brought the Blitzkrieg (or lightning war) they had so successfully waged in Poland to France and the Low Countries. Despite stiff resistance, the French were swiftly brought to their knees, and the small British Expeditionary Force was ignominiously kicked out of the continent. In London the elderly, and by many mistrusted, Churchill was asked to form a government.

'FIRST THEY CAME FOR THE JEWS'

The horror had begun slowly. Who in the 1930s could get seriously worked up about the burning of a few books in a 'faraway' country or the proscription of 'decadent' modern art? Even when the first concentration camp was built at Dachau in 1933, its declared purpose was the relatively innocuous one of containing political dissidents. But in the same year non-Aryans, which primarily meant Jews, were barred from government service, and a start was begun on the forcible sterilisation of gypsies and other 'inferior' races. Also targeted was a range of other minorities, such as homosexuals and Jehovah's Witnesses. Laws were passed (the Nuremberg laws) designed 'to assure the purity of German blood and German honour and to clarify the position of Jews in the Reich'. Three years later a carefully orchestrated wave of attacks, later to be known as *Kristallnacht* after the many broken windows, was carried out on synagogues and Jewish shops and businesses throughout Germany.

With the growing demands of military service, labour was scarce in the Third Reich, and men were brought in by the tens of thousands from the conquered territories – which by now comprised most of Western Europe – to perform all manner of work, often for Germany's most reputable companies. While some were recruited voluntarily, most were taken forcibly. They laboured under appalling conditions and with inadequate diet. Bad work could result in brutal punishment, even death. Some who were forced to build huge concrete defences and underground factories found their final resting places in the very concrete they had poured. But there was worse.

When Hitler finally invaded Russia in June 1941, his shock troops were closely followed by special squads, or *Einsatzgruppen*, whose sole purpose was the systematic murder of Jews, gypsies and communist commissars (or political officers). Mass killings took place, often with the cooperation of the army. But shooting proved to be an inefficient method of mass murder and stressful for those carrying it out. On 20 January 1942 at a conference, in a mansion on the side of a lake near Berlin (the Wannsee Conference), plans were laid for 'the final solution to the Jewish question', as the Nazis were pleased to call their attempt to murder an entire race. The concentration camps at Auschwitz–Birkenau, Treblinka, Sobibor, Belzec and Majdanek–Lublin were soon given over to a programme of mass 'extermination' by poison gas.

THE TURN OF THE TIDE

But even before Wannsee the entry of America into the war in 1941 had demonstrated, not only the worldwide nature of the conflict, but also, for anyone with an eye to see, the impossibility of the Axis powers (as Germany and Italy were called) ever triumphing in the long run. Hitler's promised Thousand Year Reich was not to be.

The tide began to turn in 1942 with a reinvigorated Britain's victory over Hitler's General Rommel at El Alamein. It was followed a year later by Russia's crushing defeat of the German army at Stalingrad. And on 6 June 1944 the greatest armada in history crossed the English Channel to descend on Hitler's 'West Wall' in Normandy. In less than a year American and Russian troops had met in the heart of Germany. Hitler committed suicide five days later. On 7 May 1945 Colonel General Alfred Jodl signed an unconditional surrender of the remaining German forces. After this, the capitulation of the 'government' of Hitler's successor, Grand Admiral Dönitz, was a mere formality. The time for reckoning had come.

Just before the Normandy invasion the Allied Joint Chiefs of Staff had instructed their Supreme Commander in Europe, the American General Eisenhower, to 'search out, arrest and hold, pending receipt . . . of further instructions as to their disposition, Adolf Hitler, his chief Nazi associates, other war criminals and all persons who have participated in planning or carrying out Nazi enterprises involving or resulting in atrocities or war crimes'.

The Deputy Führer, Rudolph Hess, was already in custody. He had been detained in England since his arrival there by air in 1941 in a futile attempt to convince the British to make peace. Eventually, most of the other Nazi leaders and generals were rounded up or surrendered, though some of them escaped justice altogether. The propaganda chief, Joseph Goebbels, had followed his leader to the grave, after first killing his wife and children. The arch-villain, Heinrich Himmler, head of the repressive SS (*Schutzstaffel* or protective squad) and Gestapo (*Geheime Staatspolizei* or secret state police), bit on a cyanide pill shortly after capture. Martin Bormann, Hitler's powerful secretary, was assumed to have fled abroad, but is now known to have been killed trying to escape from a beleaguered Berlin. The absence from the dock of Adolf Hitler meant that it has been left to historians to seek to understand how one man, however talented and charismatic, could almost single-handedly have taken a civilised country down the road to hell, dragging most of the world with him.

The arrested men were confined at one or other of two detention centres codenamed contemptuously 'Ashcan' and 'Dustbin', without anyone at this stage having much idea what should happen to them.

WHAT TO DO WITH THEM?

In a memorandum written just before the end of hostilities, Winston Churchill had suggested, 'The best way to bring about the fall of the present High Command in Germany is to draw up a list of war criminals who will be executed if they fall into the hands of the Allies. The list need not be more than fifty to a hundred long (apart from the punishment of local offenders). This would open a gulf between the persons named in it and the rest of the population.'[2] Some senior American figures were inclined to be even more radical. Stalin, however, insisted on a show trial of the type he was so fond of in Russia, and the Americans, who for long had been the dominant Allied power, sided with the Russians, albeit from nobler motives. (They wanted representatives of all aspects of the Nazi regime to appear in the dock.) At a conference in Yalta in February 1945 the Big Three, as Roosevelt, Churchill and Stalin were known, finally agreed on the arrangements to bring the Axis leaders to trial before a specially created tribunal.

To placate the Russians, who wanted the trial to take place in their zone of the defeated Germany, it was agreed that, while Berlin would be the permanent seat of the court, the first trial would take place in Nuremberg, which was in the American sector of Germany. (The Cold War was to put an end to the idea of any subsequent trials of this nature.) Despite extensive bomb damage, the city still possessed a largely undamaged court and prison in the same complex. It also had the dubious distinction of having been the site of the huge Nazi party rallies of the 1930s. A few months later a formal agreement was signed in London, setting up an International Military Tribunal (IMT) with four members, one from each of the signatories, 'for the trial and punishment of the major war criminals of the European Axis countries'.

NEW CRIMES, NEW CRIMINOLOGY

After much debate it was decided that the trial should proceed by the Anglo-American adversarial system rather than the inquisitorial system favoured by the French and Soviets, that the defendants should have the right to be legally represented, the right to have the proceedings conducted in their own language and the right to give evidence and cross-examine witnesses – another Anglo-Saxon practice. The defendants were to be served in advance of the trial with a detailed summary of the evidence and with many of the documents. These provisions were embodied in a Charter annexed to the Agreement. But with what offences should the prisoners be charged? As well as violations of the laws or customs of war, which had for centuries been recognised as crimes in international law, the framers of the Charter included two novel offences:

- *Crimes against peace.* These were defined, broadly, as planning or waging a war of aggression or a war in violation of treaties. The concept of aggressive war was controversial.
- *Crimes against humanity.* These included deportation for slave labour, religious and other persecution and the ill-treatment of prisoners, as well as the commission of more 'ordinary' crimes such as murder.

In addition, the Charter permitted defendants to be charged with conspiracy to commit any of the listed crimes. This caused difficulties with the French and Soviets, because a separate crime of conspiracy was unknown in their countries.

THE DEFENCES

A source of potential embarrassment to the Allies was the possibility that the defendants might wish to claim that their conduct had been no worse than that of the victors, the *tu quoque* or 'you did it too' defence. Germany's invasion of Norway in 1940, for example, had barely anticipated Britain's own intentions for that country. And the last thing Russia wanted was any reference to be made to the Molotov–Ribbentrop Pact. (Scandalously, Stalin insisted on having some of the defendants charged with the massacre of some 4,000 Polish officers at Katyn in the

Soviet Union, knowing full well that it was his own countrymen who were the sole authors of that atrocity.) In fact, the *tu quoque* 'defence' is not admissible in any court, since the guilt of others cannot be relevant to whether the defendant committed the crime of which he is charged. This was recognised in the Charter, which provided that 'the Tribunal shall . . . confine the trial strictly to an expeditious hearing of the cases raised by the charges . . .'.

It was anticipated that some of the defendants would seek to shift responsibility from themselves onto their late, and conveniently absent, Führer. As Hans Franck had said in 1935, 'I have no conscience. Adolf Hitler is my conscience.' The Charter cut the ground from this defence by providing that 'the fact that the Defendant acted pursuant to orders of his government or of a superior shall not free him from responsibility, but may be considered in mitigation of punishment if the Tribunal determines that justice so requires'. Any other rule would have rendered the trial nugatory.[3]

It remained only to decide who should stand trial.

THE DEFENDANTS

After much agonising a list of twenty-four defendants was produced by the Allies, of whom only twenty-two would, in the event, be tried, one of them, Martin Bormann, in his absence.

Robert Ley, former chief of the German Labour Front, was to commit suicide before the trial began, professing Nazism to the end. (His last touching letters to his wife make one wonder at men's ability to compartmentalise their minds.) It had been intended to indict Alfred Krupp, the armaments manufacturer and employer of mass slave labour; incredibly, the wrong Krupp was named in the indictment. (There was not much of a case against the 'right' Krupp, and in any event the accused was, as it turned out, too ill to stand trial.) Nor is it easy to understand the inclusion among the defendants of the economics minister, Hjalmar Schacht. He was known to dislike the Versailles treaty, to have argued for a regenerated German army and to have supported the *Anschluss*, but none of these was a crime and it is not surprising that he was acquitted.

A singular feature of the Nuremberg trial was the indictment as defendants of organisations as well as individuals. The idea was that proven membership of a convicted organisation should count against an individual in the trials that were to follow Nuremberg. After much debate, a list of Nazi organisations was drawn up. It had not been well thought out. The list included the Reich Cabinet, despite the fact that this body had last met in 1937. The SA (*Sturmabteilung* or Storm Troopers, otherwise known as the Brownshirts) appears to have been included only on the basis of their role as street fighters in the early 1930s. The inclusion of the General Staff and High Command of the German army was the result of a misunderstanding. The much-feared German General Staff of 1918 (which, despite its name, had actually exercised command of the army) had been banned by the Versailles treaty. The new high command (*Oberkommando der Wehrmacht*, or OKW) was completely under the thumb of Hitler.

Of the corporate accused, only the SS, the Gestapo and the Leadership Corps of the Nazi Party were in the end convicted. Contrary to expectations, however, no individual was subsequently found guilty solely on the basis of his membership of any of these organisations. The exercise, in other words, had been pretty much a waste of time.

The Trial Begins

In October 1945 the Tribunal elected as its president the British nominee, the ascetic but greatly respected appeal court judge Lord Justice Geoffrey Lawrence. The indictments were issued shortly after. When the trial began on 20 November all the defendants pleaded 'not guilty'.

Each of the Allies had its own chief prosecutor. *The Times*'s obituary of the British chief prosecutor Sir Hartley Shawcross was later to claim that he 'was adjudged to have performed the most effectively. The Russian prosecutor was continually on the end of the phone being briefed by his political masters in Moscow. The American was really a civil lawyer, relatively new to criminal proceedings and thoroughly out of his depth. And the French chief prosecutor was changed after two months, so the French contribution was inevitably reduced.'[4] The task of outlining the case against the accused, however, was to fall to the American, Mr Justice Jackson. He met the challenge well.

> The wrongs which we seek to condemn and punish have been so calculated, so malignant, and so devastating, that civilization cannot tolerate their being ignored, because it cannot survive their being repeated. That four great nations, flushed with victory and stung with injury, stay the hand of vengeance and voluntarily submit their captive enemies to the judgment of the law is one of the most significant tributes that Power has ever paid to Reason.
>
> This Tribunal, while it is novel and experimental, is not the product of abstract speculations nor is it created to vindicate legalistic theories. This inquest represents the practical effort of four of the most mighty of nations, with the support of 17 more, to utilize international law to meet the greatest menace of our times, aggressive war. The common sense of mankind demands that law shall not stop with the punishment of petty crimes by little people.

It must also reach men who possess themselves of great power and make deliberate and concerted use of it to set in motion evils which leave no home in the world untouched. It is a cause of that magnitude that the United Nations will lay before Your Honours.

In the prisoners' dock sit twenty-odd broken men. Reproached by the humiliation of those they have led almost as bitterly as by the desolation of those they have attacked, their personal capacity for evil is forever past. It is hard now to perceive in these men as captives the power by which as Nazi leaders they once dominated much of the world and terrified most of it. Merely as individuals their fate is of little consequence to the world.

What makes this inquest significant is that these prisoners represent sinister influences that will lurk in the world long after their bodies have returned to dust. We will show them to be living symbols of racial hatreds, of terrorism and violence, and of the arrogance and cruelty of power. They are symbols of fierce nationalisms and of militarism, of intrigue and war-making which have embroiled Europe generation after generation, crushing its manhood, destroying its homes, and impoverishing its life. They have so identified themselves with the philosophies they conceived and with the forces they directed that any tenderness to them is a victory and an encouragement to all the evils which are attached to their names. Civilization can afford no compromise with the social forces which would gain renewed strength if we deal ambiguously or indecisively with the men in whom those forces now precariously survive.[5]

This is not the place for a detailed account of this monumental and momentous trial that in the course of some 218 hearing days received evidence from 360 witnesses. Two issues dominated the proceedings, the Nazi plan for the conquest of Europe and the concentration-camp atrocities.

THE WARS OF AGGRESSION

The Charter failed to define the concept of a war of aggression, which gave rise to much controversy. The Tribunal was to make the dubious claim that aggressive war was already a crime under international law but this was hotly disputed.[6] The prosecutors got round this problem neatly by charging the accused with the separate and uncontroversial offence of planning or waging wars of aggression *that were also* wars in breach of treaties.

Historians disagree about the extent to which Hitler's territorial aggrandisements were planned. The historian A.J.P. Taylor, for example, made a convincing case for Hitler as an inspired opportunist, and his early military adventures certainly appear to bear that out. However that may be, the Führer made no secret of his long-term ambitions. In his rambling manifesto, *Mein Kampf* ('My Struggle'), he made it plain that 'the restoration of the frontiers of 1914 could be achieved only by blood'. We must assume that the peaceniks of 1930s Britain had never read this work.

Paul Schmidt, official interpreter of the German Foreign Office, confirmed his former leader's ambitions when he wrote:

> The general objectives of the Nazi leadership were apparent from the start, namely the domination of the European Continent to be achieved, first by the incorporation of all German speaking groups in the Reich, and secondly, by territorial expansion under the slogan 'Lebensraum' [room to live]. The execution of these basic objectives, however, seemed to be characterised by improvisation. Each succeeding step was apparently carried out as each new situation arose, but all consistent with the ultimate objectives mentioned above.[7]

As Hitler told his military commanders well before the war, 'The question for Germany is where the greatest possible conquest can be made at the lowest cost.'[8]

'I DIDN'T KNOW'

The court heard and saw evidence of the systematic mass murder, torture and medical experimentation carried out in the concentration camps of a barbarity that no one had dreamed possible in twentieth-century Europe. It was plain from the evidence that these were not the acts of isolated individuals but an integral part of a policy deliberately embarked upon by the Nazis under directions from the top, but willingly executed at almost every level.

Some of the accused pleaded ignorance of what had been going on. The facts were against them, as R.E. Conot has noted.

> When more than 45,000 members of the *Waffen SS* had served in concentration camps, when *Einsatzgruppen* reports had been extensively distributed among the leadership, when thousands of men had witnessed the exterminations in the East, when Himmler had made an unequivocal declaration to the party leaders, when Goebbels had been forced to issue broadsides in response to rumours, and when reports from foreign sources had been readily available to any top Nazi who wished to educate himself, whatever ignorance had existed had been voluntary.[9]

Below are a few snapshots of these 'ignorant' men.

THE ART COLLECTOR

Unquestionably, the dominant character among the defendants was the head of the Luftwaffe, Reichsmarschall Hermann Goering. An outstanding fighter pilot during the First World War, Goering had taken over Von Richtofen's squadron after the death of the 'Red Baron'. Engaging and forceful, he became one of the Führer's earliest supporters, retaining his confidence despite his disastrous – and possibly fatal – mishandling of the air war against England in 1940. A wound in the groin during what is known as the Beer Hall Putsch of 1923 had led to long-term drug addiction, and Goering spent much of the latter days of the war at his palatial hunting lodge, Karinhall, in perfumed silk pajamas and with painted toenails, organising the plunder of artworks throughout conquered Europe.

Goering's extrovert, even genial persona was at odds with his actions. He founded the Gestapo, was heavily implicated in the slave-labour programme and played a significant part in the 'final solution of the Jewish problem'. He was even directly responsible for using concentration-camp prisoners in high-altitude experiments. Ironically, a forced withdrawal from drugs after capture led to an emergence at the trial of the old Goering, who sought with some success to impose his will on his fellow prisoners. When the trial began, he made an attempt to make a speech instead of entering a plea, but was slapped down by the president of the court. When he gave evidence later it was with unabashed nerve, but Goering's guilt was not to be evaded by his skill in standing up to cross-examination; it had been established conclusively by a mass of objective documentary and oral evidence.

THE ARCHITECT

Albert Speer was and remains an enigma. As a young man of twenty-eight he had caught the eye of Adolf Hitler, who made him his official architect. As Speer later wrote, 'For the commission to do a great building I would have sold my soul like Faust. Now I had found my Mephistopheles.'[10] Although he joined the Nazi Party, Speer's loyalty was always to the Führer rather than to Nazism. From the start there was between the two men a feeling of mutual admiration that seems never to have fully left either of them.

As well as designing public buildings, a particular interest of the Führer, Speer was responsible for the dramatically successful Nazi party rally in Nuremberg in 1934. Following his achievements as a department head in the German Labour Front, Speer was appointed Reichs minister of armaments and war production on the death of his predecessor in a plane crash. He proved to be an organisational genius in that post, raising Germany's military output dramatically. (It has been said that his efforts prolonged the war by two years.) When at the end of the war Hitler finally lost touch with reality, Speer deliberately sabotaged his Führer's 'scorched-earth' policy and even claimed to have planned his assassination.[11] The plot failed for technical reasons, and in a quixotic gesture the now suspect Speer took the brave step of visiting his one-time hero in his bunker in Berlin, even though it had nearly been overrun by the invading Russians.

Those who interrogated Speer after the war were left with the impression of an intelligent, if somewhat cold, man whose regret for his part in the Hitler regime was sincere but whose willingness to accept his full guilt was always elusive. Major Airey Neave of British Intelligence described him thus: 'He was the exception . . . the only man in Hitler's entourage who sacrificed neither his will nor his reason . . . a man of great talent who did his most to enable the Nazi dream to become a reality.'[12]

Although charged on all four counts, the weightiest evidence against Speer concerned the use of slave labour. In the witness box he spoke proudly of his industrial achievements, but his replies to questions were revealing. He had been glad of the workers that others had produced for him, but how they had been acquired was not his concern; and others were to blame for any maltreatment they may have received. The only concentration camp he had visited during the war (Mauthausen) had given him 'a model impression of cleanliness'. Confronted with examples of the brutal treatment of slave labour, he responded coldly, 'You would not expect me to be intimately acquainted with what happened.'

From the start of the trial Speer accepted collective responsibility as a member of the Nazi government but said that he left it to the court to declare what individual responsibility he should bear. Among the members of the tribunal the Russian and American judges pressed at first for the death penalty, but the American, possibly influenced by the man's undoubted charm and intelligence, changed his vote to one of imprisonment. While Speer was clearly not an initiator of atrocity, doubt remains to this day about his proclaimed ignorance of the horrors of the regime he had served so faithfully. The writer Gitta Sereny, who probably came to know Speer better than anyone, quotes from an affidavit that he made long after the war in 1977: 'to this day I still consider my main guilt to be my tacit acceptance of the persecution and the murder of millions of Jews.' She commented, 'If Speer had said as much in Nuremburg, he would have been hanged.'[13]

THE GENERALS

There is a myth particularly attractive to some Germans that, while atrocities may have been committed by the Nazi party leadership and its military arm, the SS, ordinary German soldiers, whose skill and bravery were unquestioned, were above that sort of thing. Certainly, there are many examples of individual soldiers refusing to go along with the Nazis' racial extermination policy, and not a single one seems to have suffered anything worse than being relieved of his post. On the other hand, there is ample evidence of regular military units routinely aiding the extermination squads, even of committing their own atrocities. The picture was similar at the top of the command chain.

Field Marshal Wilhelm Keitel, Hitler's Chief of Staff, was an artillery officer who had participated fully in the planning of the war at the highest level. His lack of command qualities as a soldier was made up for in Hitler's eyes by his willingness to go along with whatever his master required. (Privately, he was called *Lakeitel*, or 'the nodding ass', by the staff officers.) Keitel was the archetype of a Prussian Junker with an in-built sense of loyalty to his superiors. In 1934 he had welcomed the murder of the SA leader Ernst Röhm (who was thought to be planning a coup against Hitler), but remained silent about the murders at the same time of two retired generals. In the witness box he claimed that the crime of waging aggressive war could not apply to a soldier; the facts argued against him. In 1941 he was responsible for the infamous 'Commissar' order that condemned to death the communist political officers, and for the *Nacht und Nebel* ('Night and Fog') decrees that resulted in the summary execution of prisoners of war. He ordered that attacks on soldiers in the East should be met by putting to death fifty to a hundred communists for every German soldier killed. In 1942 he issued a directive that enemy paratroopers were to be turned over to the SD. After the landing in Normandy, Keitel reaffirmed this order, extending it to Allied missions fighting with partisans. In court he admitted that he did not believe the order to be legal but claimed that he could not stop it; it had been done in obedience to Hitler's orders. In answer to Lord Justice Lawrence, however, he could recall only one instance when he had protested to Hitler in writing.

Even as late as July 1944 Keitel acted vigorously to protect Hitler after an unsuccessful attempt to assassinate him by discontented officers. For this Prussian officer, loyalty to his leader was all.

The background of Alfred Jodl, Chief of the Operations Section of the *Wehrmacht*, could not have been more different from Keitel's. He was a Bavarian grammar-school boy of farming stock, and the more capable soldier of the two. He had been enthusiastically involved in the *Anschluss* and in the unprovoked invasions of Czechoslovakia, Greece and Yugoslavia. In 1941 he signed an order refusing to accept an offer of surrender of Leningrad or Moscow, which he insisted should be completely destroyed. He also participated in the infamous order under which commandos were to be put to death without trial. Though initially an admirer of the Führer, Jodl became increasingly disillusioned as the war progressed and fell out with him violently over the fiasco of the Russian campaign, but his repeated requests to be sent to the front were ignored. Jodl shared with Keitel an unswerving loyalty to his leader. At the end of his cross-examination in court he said, 'It is not the task of a soldier to be the judge of his Commander-in-Chief. May history or the Almighty do that.' He would leave the court, he said, with his head held as high as when he entered it.

Jodl's attorney, Dr Exner, made a telling point:

It is true that without his generals Hitler could not have waged the wars. But only a layman can construct a responsibility on that basis. If the generals do not do their job, there is no war. But one must add: if the infantryman does not march, if his rifle does not fire, if he has nothing to clothe himself with and nothing to eat, there is no war. Is therefore the soldier, the gunsmith, the shoemaker, the farmer guilty of complicity in the war? The argument is based on a confusion between guilt and causation. All these persons, and many others too, effectively co-operated in the waging of the war. But can one therefore attribute any guilt to them?

However, as the President of the Court remarked to another advocate, the German people were not on trial; the defendants were.

The generals knew from the start of the trial that they were doomed. Their only hope was that their end would be the soldier's death by firing squad, not a criminal's death by hanging. In this, they were to be disappointed.

THE VERDICTS

The trial ended on 31 August 1946 and the verdicts were announced on 30 September and 1 October, the Jewish Day of Atonement. Three of the defendants (Schacht, von Papen and Fritsche) were acquitted but later sentenced to various terms in a labour camp by a German court. Four of the defendants, including Speer, were given terms of imprisonment ranging from ten to twenty years. Three were sentenced to life imprisonment (Hess, Funk and Raeder) and the remaining twelve, including Goering, the two generals and the absent Bormann, to death by hanging.[14] On 13 October the Allied Control Council, which had power to reduce or commute sentences, rejected all the appeals. With one exception, those sentenced to die were hanged in Nuremberg three days later. Those sentenced to imprisonment were to serve their time in the grim Spandau prison in Berlin. Goering characteristically cheated justice. On the day before the executions he swallowed cyanide.[15] He left a written note:

> To the Allied Control Council:
> I would have had no objection to being shot. However, I will not facilitate execution of Germany's Reichsmarschall by hanging! For the sake of Germany, I cannot permit this. Moreover, I feel no moral obligation to submit to my enemies' punishment. For this reason, I have chosen to die like the great Hannibal.

The fortunes of those not sentenced to death varied widely. Von Neurath, the former Reich Protector for Bohemia and Moravia, was sentenced to fifteen years' imprisonment but was released from Spandau in 1954 because of failing health. He died in 1956. Raeder, the former Commander-in-Chief of the Navy, was released from his life sentence in 1955 because of failing health. He died in 1960. Walther Funk, the former Minister of Economics, was released in 1957 and died in 1960. Baldur Von Schirach, the former Hitler Youth leader, served his entire term of twenty years in Spandau and died in 1974. Albert Speer was sentenced to twenty years' imprisonment. He too served the full term and died in 1981. Finally, Rudolf Hess served over forty years of his life sentence at Spandau, where he committed suicide in 1987 at the age of ninety-three. It had been obvious even at his trial that he was mentally incompetent, and he did not get any better afterwards; only Soviet intransigence prevented the Western powers from releasing him from prison long before his end.

VICTORS' JUSTICE?

Procedurally speaking, there can be no criticism of the conduct of the Nuremberg trial; the terms of the Charter stand up well, even today. The problems lay elsewhere.

Goering had told the court, 'This is a political trial by the victors and it will be a good thing when Germany realizes that . . .'. A more reasoned case was made by the German lawyer Professor Jahrreiss, who had been chosen to summarise the arguments for the defence. He submitted, first, that it was impossible for the defendants to get a fair trial in the immediate aftermath of war and against the prejudicial background to which the revelation of atrocities had given rise. He also claimed that it was unjust for the accused to be tried by representatives of the victorious powers. Lastly, he challenged the retrospective nature of some of the offences. They had, he suggested, been specially devised to convict the offenders before the court, thus offending against the principle that the law should be of general application and not tailor-made to the individuals before the court. Each of these objections deserves to be considered.

It is impossible to deny that at Nuremberg the representatives of the victorious nations were trying the leadership of the country they had so recently defeated. From a dry legal point of view, the Allies could claim that they were simply exercising the sovereign power of the German state when there was no other authority to do so. Such an answer, however correct it may be, does not remove the bitter taste that always accompanies the spectacle of the victor trying the vanquished. The inclusion of a Soviet judge was particularly regrettable when Russia itself had been guilty of the most egregious act of aggression towards Poland, not to mention countless appalling war crimes. The choice of Iola T. Nikitchenko in particular was doubly unfortunate in view of his part in Stalin's disgraceful show trials of the 1930s.

But what alternatives were there? The appointment of a German judge, even an anti-Nazi, was at the time unthinkable. In the end the issue was academic: Article 3 of the Charter ruled out any challenge to the jurisdiction of the Tribunal.

RETROSPECTIVE JUSTICE

Perhaps the strongest criticism of the Nuremberg Tribunal was that the accused were charged with two offences – namely, crimes against peace and crimes against humanity – that did not exist at the time of the acts in question.

There are two main objections to applying the criminal law retrospectively, one ethical, the other utilitarian. The first is that it is simply not fair to punish someone for doing something that at the time of commission was not a crime. The second is that doing so serves no purpose. One of the objects of the law is to deter people from wrongful behaviour; yet nothing is achieved by punishing someone for doing something that at the time he was not forbidden to do. The Tribunal dealt with this by claiming that the legal maxim that there could be 'no crime without a law' was designed to protect the innocent who did not know that their deeds were wrong.

> To assert that it is unjust to punish those who in defiance of treaties and assurances have attacked neighbouring states without warning is obviously untrue, for in such circumstances the attacker must know that he is doing wrong, and so far from it being unjust to punish him, it would be unjust if his wrong were allowed to go unpunished.

But that is like saying that, since people know that telling lies is wrong, untruthfulness may be punished as if it were a crime.

It is certainly true that the continuing struggle to keep up with developments in human wickedness requires from time to time the creation of new criminal offences, but the arguments against applying such new offences retroactively seem overwhelming. Most civilised nations share an aversion to this practice. There is, for example, a long-standing presumption in England against giving a retrospective meaning to an Act of Parliament. And the American Constitution actually prohibits it altogether. But it was accepted wholeheartedly at Nuremberg; as Churchill was to comment to the British General Ismay after the trial, 'You and I must take care not to lose the next war.'[16]

In the end, discussion about the justice of the Charter is academic. The war had been the most destructive in history. The Allies were determined to expose the horrors of the Nazi regime in whatever way they saw fit, and who was to stop them? The idea of retrospective guilt was controversial, but in practice did not give rise to serious disquiet. No one can doubt that those convicted could have been found guilty of other, more conventional crimes, had they been charged with them, and the language of the novel offences did at least do justice to the enormity of the crimes involved. It is a tribute to the drafters of the Charter and to the members and advocates of the International Military Tribunal that so little criticism can justifiably be levelled at their labours.

The Disaffected

Introduction

It is not necessary to resort to political theory to realise that there is a sort of unspoken bargain in society whereby, in exchange for the security that our country attempts to provide for us, we as citizens owe allegiance to our country. But how much allegiance is the state entitled to expect under this arrangement and how is the citizen's allegiance to be reconciled with his right to dissent? There are lessons to be drawn from each of the four trials discussed in this part of the book.

The first and the earliest trial in this part concerns perhaps the most seminal figure in Western civilisation, the Greek philosopher Socrates. It is easy to forget that Socrates, while living in the world's first democracy,[1] actually scorned the form of government he lived under and was the teacher of some of its most prominent enemies. To a modern lawyer the case that Socrates' accusers made out against him at his trial looks weak, so why then did he fail to contest it properly and why, when he was convicted, did he seem almost to invite his own death? Because of the time that has elapsed since the trial and the fact that we have to rely almost exclusively on one source – and that provided by an admiring pupil of the accused – unravelling exactly what happened and why is more than usually difficult. It nevertheless seems worth attempting because of the significance of the man and of the momentous question posed by his trial: how far should people be allowed to go in expressing views that most of his fellow citizens consider to be dangerously subversive?

Sir Thomas More also found himself to be in conflict with the state, in the form of England's most powerful sovereign, Henry VIII. Unlike Socrates, More kept his own counsel, but that was not enough to save him. On an issue that touched him deeply, Henry demanded from his first minister nothing less than a public submission to his will. Against so powerful and determined a man even More's forensic skills proved

163

insufficient and in the end he went bravely to the scaffold. His wife, Alice, could not understand why he had risked his life, his fortune and his family's happiness for something that seemed to her to be of abstract intellectual significance only. What interests us today, however, is not whether More's suffering and death were in vain but the issue of the freedom of the individual to refuse to conform.

Three hundred years later it was not a mighty cleric but a group of farm labourers who had to suffer for their nonconformity. The arrest, trial and transportation of the six farm labourers known as the Tolpuddle Martyrs were regarded even at the time with widespread distaste, and the case is still a beacon for the trade-union movement. Was the trial in that courtroom in Dorchester fair and independent or was it a put-up job on the part of a government determined to stamp out the recently legalised unions?

A far worse fate was to befall two Italian immigrants to early twentieth-century America. Fernando Sacco and Bartolomeo Vanzetti were convicted of the brutal murder of two men in the course of an armed hold-up. After seven years of increasingly desperate appeals they went to the electric chair amid a chorus of public sympathy. Sacco and Vanzetti were viewed by liberal opinion at the time, as they have been ever since, as the innocent victims of power and privilege. Closer examination reveals a surprisingly more complex story.

CHAPTER TEN

The Gadfly

The Trial of Socrates, 399 BC

Until the death of Falstaff, which it strangely prefigures,[1] the death of the Athenian philosopher Socrates is probably the most moving in Western literature. When the gaoler brought him a cup of the poison hemlock,[2] the condemned man asked what to do. Socrates' pupil Plato described to his friend Echecrates what happened next.[3]

> The [gaoler] answered: 'You have only to walk about until your legs are heavy, and then to lie down, and the poison will act.' At the same time he handed the cup to Socrates, who in the easiest and gentlest manner, without the least fear or change of colour or feature, looking at the man with all his eyes, Echecrates, as his manner was, took the cup and said: 'What do you say about making a libation out of this cup to any god? May I, or not?' The man answered: 'We only prepare, Socrates, just so much as we deem enough.' 'I understand,' he said: 'yet I may and must pray to the gods to prosper my journey from this to that other world – may this, then, which is my prayer, be granted to me.' Then holding the cup to his lips, quite readily and cheerfully he drank off the poison. And hitherto most of us had been able to control our sorrow; but now when we saw him drinking, and saw too that he had finished the draught, we could no longer forbear, and in spite of myself my own tears were flowing fast; so that I covered my face and wept over myself, for certainly I was not weeping over him, but at the thought of my own calamity in having lost such a companion.
>
> Nor was I the first, for Crito, when he found himself unable to restrain his tears, had got up and moved away, and I followed; and at that moment Apollodorus, who had been weeping all the time, broke out a loud cry which made cowards of us all. Socrates alone retained his calmness: 'What is this strange outcry?', he said. 'I sent away the women mainly in order that they might not offend in this way, for I have heard that a man should die in peace. Be quiet, then, and have patience.' When we heard that, we were ashamed, and restrained our tears; and he walked about until, as he said, his legs began to fail, and then he lay on his back, according to the directions, and the man who gave him the poison now and then looked at his feet and legs; and after a while he pressed his foot hard and asked him if he

could feel; and he said, no; and then his leg, and so upwards and upwards, and showed us that he was cold and stiff. And he felt them himself, and said: 'When the poison reaches the heart, that will be the end.'

He was beginning to grow cold about the groin, when he uncovered his face, for he had covered himself up, and said (they were his last words) he said: 'Crito, I owe a cock to Asclepius; will you remember to pay the debt?'[4] 'The debt shall be paid,' said Crito; 'is there anything else?' There was no answer to this question; but in a minute or two a movement was heard, and the attendants uncovered him; his eyes were set, and Crito closed his eyes and mouth.

Such was the end, Echecrates, of our friend, concerning whom I may truly say, that of all the men of his time whom I have known he was the wisest, and justest, and best.[5]

For nearly two and a half thousand years people have wondered how a properly constituted court of the world's first democracy could condemn to death the world's most renowned philosopher. To answer this question we must stray far from the realms of philosophy into the realpolitik of ancient Greece.

Socrates was born in 469 BC in the city-state of Athens, then at the height of its power and influence under its great leader Pericles. He was the son of a stone mason and a midwife. As a citizen, Socrates took his turn on the city council but did not take part in its debates; he did, however, serve in the army and in his thirty-eighth year fought as a hoplite (a heavy infantryman), earning the prize for valour. But it was in his capacity as a teacher in the workshops and the marketplace that Socrates made his name. His distinctive style of instruction – still in use at Britain's older universities – consisted of questioning his pupils in order to force them to see the weakness in their reasoning and assumptions. (It can be a bruising experience, challenging as it does the listener's preconceived beliefs and prejudices.) But it was not only his teaching methods that were distinctive. He has been described as 'a squat, ugly, barefoot man who did not bathe often and was easy to spot shuffling through the agora or passing the time in his favourite hangout, the shop of Simon the Cobbler. Looking nothing like a god or hero, he had bulging eyes, a flat, pug nose, prominent lips, and a pot belly.'[6]

Socrates had long been regarded by his fellow Athenians as a rather dotty eccentric. Like Bertrand Russell at the beginning of the twentieth century, he rejected established religion and encouraged his pupils to question their parents' values. Such deviant thinking may be tolerated in peacetime, but Athens had for some thirty years been mired in a savage internecine struggle with a number of other city-states led by Sparta. Dissidents are seldom popular in a society under threat, and this was reflected in Aristophanes' play *The Birds*, in which a group of pro-Spartan youths were described as being 'socratified'. Eventually defeated in battle and laid low by plague, Athens fell to its enemies in 404 BC. Democracy was abolished and replaced by a dictatorship of the 'Thirty Tyrants' under which hundreds were killed and thousands exiled. Socrates, who was close to the leaders of the new regime, was invited to join them but fell out of favour when he refused to do their bidding over the unjust arrest of a citizen whose goods they intended to confiscate. But, when democracy was restored, this act of defiance was not enough to save the philosopher. Three men with personal as well as public motives decided to do something about the nonconformist teacher.

THE ACCUSERS

Of Socrates' three accusers, little is known about Lycon, except that he was an orator, a profession for which Socrates was known to have a low regard. A young poet, Meletus, stung by Socrates' criticism of poetry and religion, also signed the indictment and is sometimes regarded as the chief accuser. But the driving force behind the prosecution was almost certainly the third man, Anytus, a wealthy tanner, politician and, during the war with Sparta, general.

Socrates had openly scorned the Athenian form of democracy under which he lived, and he taught that only wise men, philosophers like himself, were fit to govern. It was not surprising that someone like Anytus, who had suffered greatly from the war, should object to Socrates' constant attacks on the system he had fought so hard to defend. But his language suggests a personal element to his bitterness. After Socrates had referred slightingly to the tanner's 'servile' occupation, Anytus had warned, 'Socrates, I think that you are too ready to speak evil of men, and if you take my advice, I would recommend you to be careful.' Perhaps there was truth in the rumours of some sort of relationship between Socrates and the sons of Anytus and Lycon. (Though normal in Sparta, homosexuality was frowned upon in Athens.)

Before charges could be brought against anyone, Athenian law required that there should be preliminary proceedings (known as the *Anakrisis*) before a magistrate (called the King Archon). Plato, Socrates' most famous pupil, actually describes Socrates meeting a friend on the way to the proceedings, but they fall into discussion and we never hear what happened at the hearing. The usual procedure was for the charge and denial to be attested to under oath, after which the magistrate questioned both parties, who were then entitled to question each other. If, as must have happened in this case, the magistrate saw fit, charges were then drawn up against the defendant.

The actual wording of the indictment against Socrates is long lost but one authority records it as follows:

> This indictment and affidavit is sworn out by Meletus: Socrates the son of Sophroniscus of Alopece is guilty of refusing to acknowledge the gods recognized by the State and of introducing new and different gods. He is also guilty of corrupting the youth. The penalty demanded is death.[7]

There were, in other words, what we would call three counts in the indictment. They were: '*asbeia*' or impiety, which probably meant failing to acknowledge the city's gods; introducing new gods; and corrupting the youth. But was this a good bill? After the restoration of democracy the laws of Athens had been completely revised and an amnesty passed for all prior offences. We must therefore presume that Socrates' offences occurred, or at least continued, after the amnesty. And there is another problem. The American writer I.F. Stone has pointed out that the indictment fails – contrary to all known examples – to specify the text of the law said to be transgressed. This may not be the objection it seems. The Athenian offence of 'impiety' was nebulously broad in scope, and the terms of their oath (see below) left the jurors with great scope for discretion.

THE TRIAL

The trial took place before the people's (or heliastic) court in the public square (agora) of Athens before a jury of some five hundred citizens (known as dicasts) who were chosen by lot. The dicasts were sworn to listen impartially to the case and to vote in accordance with the laws or, if there were no law, in accordance with their sense of what was most just.

In Socrates' day there was little distinction between a court of law and any other organ of government; the same council oversaw both. The proceedings were likely to have been rowdy, with dicasts, parties and spectators talking animatedly among themselves throughout. Unlike today's more clinical approach, the parties to a trial were expected as a matter of course to try to blacken each other's characters and to use emotional as well as intellectual arguments.

After the charges had been read out, the prosecutors were allotted three hours in which to make their case. Socrates then had a similar time to respond. What we don't know is what exactly it was that Socrates was alleged to have done – what we would call nowadays the particulars of the charges. It may be that these important details were expected to emerge in the course of the trial. Since we have no record of the prosecution case, we can only infer it from Socrates' recorded defence, and a very curious defence to a capital charge it was. He actually began by dealing with charges that had not been laid against him. After referring to his accusers, he said,

But far more dangerous are the others, who began when you were children, and took possession of your mind with their falsehoods, telling of one Socrates, a wise man, who speculated about the heaven above, and searched into the earth beneath, and made the worse appear the better cause. The disseminators of this tale are the accusers whom I dread; for their hearers are apt to fancy that such enquirers do not believe in the existence of the gods.

Socrates denied that he was a natural philosopher. Nor was he a paid teacher, although, he said, it would have been an honour to have been one. Why, then, was he being criticised? In answer to his own question Socrates recalled the occasion when the oracle at Delphi had told a friend of his that there was no one wiser than he. He professed to have been puzzled by this, since there were, of course, many who knew more than he did. After much thought he had come to realise that the god Jove

> by his answer . . . intends to show that the wisdom of men is worth little or nothing; he is not speaking of Socrates, he is only using my name by way of illustration, as if he said, 'He, O men, is the wisest, who, like Socrates, knows that his wisdom is in truth worth nothing.' And so I go about the world, obedient to the god, and search and make enquiry into the wisdom of any one, whether citizen or stranger, who appears to be wise; and if he is not wise, then in vindication of the oracle I show him that he is not wise; and my occupation quite absorbs me, and I have no time to give hither to any public matter or interest or to any concern of my own, but I am in utter poverty by reason of my devotion to the god.

In fact, he went on,

> there are plenty of persons, as they quickly discover, who think that they know something, but really know little or nothing; and then those who are examined by them, instead of being angry with themselves, are angry with me: 'This confounded Socrates', they say; 'this villainous misleader of youth!' – and then if somebody asks them, 'Why, what evil does he practise or teach?' they do not know, and cannot tell; but in order that they may not appear to be at a loss, they repeat the ready-made charges which are used against all philosophers about teaching things up in the clouds and under the earth, and having no gods, and making the worse appear the better cause; for they do not like to confess that their pretence of knowledge has been detected – which is the truth; and as they are numerous and ambitious and energetic, and are drawn up in battle array and have persuasive tongues, they have filled your ears with their loud and inveterate calumnies.

Finally he turned to deal, fairly cursorily it must be said, with the individual charges.

Referring to the accusation of impiety, that he was an atheist who claimed that the sun was stone and the moon earth, Socrates observed that such views had long been found in learned books and in the theatre. He pointed to the paradox inherent in the suggestion that he could at the same time be both a complete atheist and an advocate of alternative gods. (Though semantically correct, this argument hardly answered the charge.) Socrates claimed that he did believe that there were gods, but 'in a sense higher than that in which his accusers believed in them'. (We may wonder how attractive such a seemingly patronising argument would have been to the jury.)

Socrates took the 'new gods' in the second charge to be a reference to his practice of listening to what he called his *daimonion* (little divinity), something like his conscience (a conceit later to be shared by Rudyard Kipling). He claimed with some justification that this practice of his was no different from that of those who took their omens from the cries of birds or the voices heard by the oracle at Delphi.

Nor can we be sure what the charge of 'corruption' meant. It does not seem to have referred to sexual corruption, and probably implied no more than that Socrates had led his pupils astray. (Stone suggests the words, 'subverting' or 'alienating'.[8]) Socrates dealt with this charge by making a comparison with the training of horses. Horses are trained, he said, not by anyone, but by those best qualified to do so; the same principle should apply to the training of the young. The implication of this, of course, was that he himself was such a qualified teacher. More cogently, he pointed out that several of his former pupils were present in court and that none of them had complained that he had corrupted them.

'YOU WILL NOT EASILY FIND ANOTHER LIKE ME'

Socrates used the rest of his allotted time, not to defend the charges, but passionately to justify his way of life.

> Some one will say: 'And are you not ashamed, Socrates, of a course of life which is likely to bring you to an untimely end?' To him I may fairly answer: 'There you are mistaken: a man who is good for anything ought not to calculate the chance of living or dying; he ought only to consider whether in doing anything he is doing right or wrong – acting the part of a good man or of a bad . . .' For the fear of death is indeed the pretence of wisdom, and not real wisdom, being a pretence of knowing the unknown; and no one knows whether death, which men in their fear apprehend to be the greatest evil, may not be the greatest good . . .

I do nothing but go about persuading you all, old and young alike, not to take thought for your persons or your properties, but first and chiefly to care about the greatest improvement of the soul. I tell you that virtue is not given by money, but that from virtue comes money and every other good of man, public as well as private.

This is my teaching, and if this is the doctrine which corrupts the youth, I am a mischievous person.[9]

Socrates went on to compare himself to a gadfly, 'a gadfly, given to the state by God; and the state is a great and noble steed who is tardy in his motions owing to his very size, and requires to be stirred into life. You will not easily find another like me . . .'. He had twice risked his life for the sake of justice, but his inner voice had prevented him from becoming a politician. He had taught no one anything, and, significantly, he refused responsibility for the acts of those whom others called his disciples.

Socrates, in other words, chose to defend the formal charges against him with sophistry of the type he had so often condemned, reserving his passionate indignation for what he saw as the hidden prejudice against someone like himself who challenged orthodox beliefs. Although he had a wife, Xanthippe – some say a shrew – and three sons, Socrates refused to parade them before the court in the hope of clemency. The judge's task, he said, is not to make a present of justice, but to give judgment according to law and not according to his own good pleasure.

CONDEMNATION

The jurors voted by placing bronze disks into one of two urns, for conviction or acquittal. The vote went against Socrates by 280 to 221. Had a mere 30 votes gone to the other side, he would have been acquitted. Only the question of sentence remained.

The prosecution had asked for the death penalty. Under Athenian law, the defendant had the opportunity of proposing an alternative sentence, and the court expected Socrates to propose exile; he refused to do the expected. In language that has depressing echoes even today, he said that he was really too honest a man to be a politician and live. Nor could he cease his teaching. 'The unexamined life', he famously remarked, 'is not worth living'.[10] Instead of death, he suggested that the city should provide him with free meals and accommodation for life, such as it was the custom to give to the Olympic champions. Alternatively, he offered to pay a fine of 1 silver mina – a sum that he increased to 30 minae after his friends had offered to help out. He well knew the consequences of these contemptuous proposals.

The jury voted in favour of death, and by a majority even larger than for his conviction, namely 360 to 140. (The disparity between the sum of these figures and those in the voting for the verdict may have been due to abstentions or to people leaving or joining the jury; we simply don't know.) One can only presume that the jury, having formed the view that Socrates was a danger to their city who was not prepared to acknowledge his guilt, must have concluded that nothing but death would stop him.

Socrates met his fate philosophically:

> . . . either death is a state of nothingness and utter unconsciousness, or, as men say, there is a change and migration of the soul from this world to another . . . Wherefore, O judges, be of good cheer about death, and know this of a truth – that no evil can happen to a good man, either in life or after death. He and his are not neglected by the gods; nor has my own approaching end happened by mere chance. But I see clearly that to die and be released was better for me; and therefore the oracle [i.e. his internal oracle or *daimonion*] gave no sign. For which reason also, I am not angry with my accusers, or my condemners; they have done me no harm, although neither of them meant to do me any good; and for this I may gently blame them.[11]

Even *in extremis* he could not resist a touch of humour. When, after the trial was over, one of his pupils said that he found it hard to bear that Socrates was being put to death unjustly, the philosopher replied, 'My beloved Apollodorus, would you prefer to see me put to death justly?'

DID HE SEEK DEATH?

Socrates' conduct at his trial suggests nothing less than a man who almost wanted to die. Offered what appears to have been a proper forensic defence prepared for him by his friend Lysias, Socrates had declined it as a fine speech but unsuitable for him. Asked why, the ascetic philosopher replied, 'Would not fine raiment and fine shoes be just as unsuitable for me?' The defence he actually put up largely ignored the charges in the indictment in favour of an attack on what he saw as the prejudice against a nonconformist like himself.[12] The sentence that he proposed as an alternative to the death penalty seems almost to have been designed to alienate the jury. And in prison he declined his friends' offer of help to escape on the ground that it would be wrong to break the city's laws.

The Greek historian Xenophon speculated that Socrates simply preferred a painless death to the throes of illness or the vexations of old age, but this seems unlikely. Perhaps this curious act of self-immolation can best be explained by Socrates' remarks shortly before his end:

So if you look at it in this way, I suppose it is not unreasonable to say that we must not put an end to ourselves until god sends some compulsion like the one which we are facing now . . .

For I deem that the true disciple of philosophy is likely to be misunderstood by other men; they do not perceive that he is ever pursuing death and dying; and if this is true, why, having had the desire of death all his life long, should he repine at the arrival of that which he has been always pursuing and desiring?[13]

'THE ENVY AND DETRACTION OF THE WORLD'

Socrates himself believed the real cause of the verdict to have been 'not Meletus, nor yet Anytus, but the envy and detraction of the world, which has been the death of many good men, and will probably be the death of many more; there is no danger of my being the last of them'.[14]

But envy alone is unlikely to have been the only reason for Socrates' unpopularity; for that we need to look elsewhere. The Socrates we know from Plato's writings (the *Dialogues*) was a curious mixture of intellectual ability, courage and the capacity to wound that even the greatest can sometimes display. Socrates made great play of his modesty, but a close reading of the *Dialogues* reveals what Stone has referred to as 'the cruelty that lurked behind the Platonic account in its exquisite and aristocratic jesting'.[15] How many of the jurors had been at the sharp end of Socrates' tongue? Contrary to the impression he sought to give, the great man appears to have been very conscious of his abilities, and he was not prepared to hide the fact. But there was worse.

Socrates held the view that government is too serious a matter to be left to the masses, that only the fit should rule. In lesser men such views can be used as justification for the tyrant's will, and many of Socrates' pupils had shown such tendencies. Plato, his most gifted pupil, was later to write *The Republic*, that blueprint for the repressive society. The charismatic but treacherous Alcibiades had been an active supporter of his city's enemies during the Peloponnesian Wars, and the scholarly Critias was perhaps the most bloodthirsty of the Thirty Tyrants. Socrates, in other words, was tarred with the reputation of his pupils. Furthermore, while the philosopher had remained comfortably in the city throughout his friends' bloody reign, his prosecutor Anytus had been driven into exile and his property confiscated. Such thoughts cannot have been far from the minds of the Athenian jury. More than half a century after Socrates' death the historian Aeschines wrote, 'Gentlemen of Athens, you executed Socrates the sophist because he was clearly responsible for the education of Critias, one of the Thirty anti-democratic leaders . . .'.[16]

Socrates, perhaps the world's foremost philosopher in both the strict and the popular senses of the word, met his death as bravely as he had lived, but there is no reason to think that his contemporaries would have regarded his trial and execution as anything but just. His conviction was the inevitable consequence of his character and opinions, and the sentence passed by the court was one that the philosopher himself seems almost to have invited. Some have seen Socrates' fate as the brutal suppression of free speech. It can as readily be regarded as the defensive reaction of a people fearful of teachings that seemed to them to strike at the stability of their freshly restored democracy by a close associate and instructor of those who would destroy it.

CHAPTER ELEVEN

The Good Servant

The Trial of Sir Thomas More, 1535

The prisoner had been brought into the prosecutor's garden and interrogated about his heretical beliefs and the whereabouts of his friends. He caved in only when threatened with the stake, but his conscience did not permit him to maintain this hypocrisy for long, and for his relapse he was burned alive at Smithfield by order of that same prosecutor. In his agony he cried out, 'I die for having said that it is lawful for every man and woman to have God's book . . . that the true key to heaven is not that of the Bishop of Rome but the preaching of the Gospel.'

The prisoner was James Bainham,[1] barrister of the Middle Temple; the prosecutor another barrister, the saintly Thomas More. Yet it is More who is the hero of this story. This paradox lies at the heart of the age of religious reform.

Just as our perception of the pre-Tudor monarchs has been distorted by Shakespeare's stage spectaculars, so our understanding of Thomas More will long be coloured by Robert Bolt's play *A Man for All Seasons*, beautifully realised in film by Fred Zinnemann. If you add to this the difficulty of comprehending More's sixteenth-century turn of mind, it is little wonder that some commentators despair of ever being able to discover the truth behind the legend. Such pessimism leads nowhere; however imperfect the historical record, we must seek to understand this brave and complex man and why he chose to suffer and die at the hands of the king he had served so long and so loyally.

Thomas More was born on or about 7 February 1477 in the City of London, the son of a barrister who was later to become a judge. After serving as a page in the household of Cardinal Morton, Archbishop of Canterbury, the young Thomas was sent to Oxford, where he chose to study Greek and mathematics. These were then considered potentially dangerous subjects, and when his father learnt of this he removed Thomas from the university and enrolled him, first at New Inn and, later, at Lincoln's Inn, of which his father and grandfather had both been members. Thomas became a reader (lecturer) in law and was subsequently called to the Bar. For a while this deeply religious young man toyed with the idea of entering the priesthood and even took to wearing a hair shirt, a practice he was to continue throughout his life.

In 1504 More was elected to Parliament and in 1510 he became Under-Sheriff of the City of London. His career at the Bar took off at about the same time. As his son-in-law William Roper records, 'there was at that time in none of the Prince's courts of the laws of the realm any matter of importance in controversy wherein he was not of the one party of counsel'.[2] Having witnessed More pleading a case (unsuccessfully) against the Crown, the young King Henry VIII, rather than being annoyed, was so impressed that he took More into his service. From then on his advancement was swift. After serving as ambassador to various countries More was appointed Under Treasurer at the Exchequer in 1521 (duly receiving the knighthood that went with the job) and Speaker of the House of Commons two years later. Henry, who was himself no intellectual lightweight, enjoyed More's conversation. He was even seen to walk in his garden with his arm around his minister. But Thomas knew that this conviviality was only skin deep. As he told Roper, 'if my head would win him a castle in France . . . it should not fail to go'. He was not to know how shortly this prophecy would be fulfilled.

THE KING'S GREAT MATTER

Henry's eyes had frequently wandered throughout his long years of marriage to his first wife, Catherine of Aragon, a woman six years his senior. He had already fathered a child out of wedlock by one woman (Elizabeth Blount) and had had an affair with at least one other, Mary Boleyn. When this ended in 1525 he turned his attentions to Mary's younger sister, one of the Queen's ladies-in-waiting, the plain but provocative Anne. The teasing Anne firmly rejected any approach from the King short of marriage. Henry was by no means averse to the idea since Catherine had in his eyes 'failed' in her wifely duty to produce a male heir and was no longer of childbearing age, but the Queen would not hear of divorce and some excuse had to be found that would permit it.

Catherine had previously been married to Henry's brother Arthur, and Henry now claimed to be concerned, on biblical authority, that his marriage was a sin. He cited Leviticus 20: 21: 'And if a man shall take his brother's wife, it is an unclean thing: he hath uncovered his brother's nakedness; they shall be childless.' (He apparently ignored Deuteronomy 25: 5: 'If brethren dwell together, and one of them die, and have no child, the wife of the dead shall not marry without unto a stranger: her husband's brother shall go in unto her, and take her to him to wife, and perform the duty of an husband's brother unto her.') He also claimed to believe that Catherine had lied when she had declared that her earlier marriage to Arthur had not been consummated. It would perhaps be an oversimplification to suspect Henry of hypocrisy in these matters; he appears to have been a man of such enormous self-regard as to be able to convince himself of almost any opinion that was to his advantage. He duly made approaches to Rome, whose authority would be needed for any divorce.

Unfortunately for Henry, Rome at this time was controlled by Catherine's nephew, Charles V, the Holy Roman Emperor. It would be unseemly to refuse Henry a divorce outright, so when the Pope sent a cardinal to England to hear the application for nullity, the papal legate was instructed to proceed slowly. Catherine dug her heels in, and, after a long period of prevarication, the cardinal referred the suit back to Rome. Henry's Lord Chancellor, Thomas Wolsey, had sat along with the papal legate. Henry blamed him for this débâcle. In 1529 Wolsey was replaced as Lord Chancellor by Thomas More, the first layman ever to hold this position.

The English clergy also objected to the idea of Catherine's divorce, but Henry would brook no dissent, and in 1532 they were instructed to accept the King as 'supreme head of the Church and clergy of England'. (The clergy agreed to conform but timorously added the words, 'so far as the law of Christ allows'.) Even this was too much for Thomas More, who believed strongly in the paramountcy of the Church. He well understood the hopelessness of opposing Henry's will in this matter, and on the day after the submission of the clergy More surrendered the Great Seal (the mark of his office of Chancellor) and retired to his house at Chelsea, pleading ill health as his excuse.[3]

The year 1533 was one of portents, of strange sights in the sky and of violence on the streets. In January Henry secretly married the now pregnant Anne, who had succumbed to the King's advances as soon as she had been convinced of the seriousness of his resolve to marry her. An Act in Restraint of Appeals now declared that England owed no allegiance to 'foreign princes or potentates', a measure obviously aimed at the authority of the Pope. And at the King's request the newly appointed Archbishop of Canterbury, the compliant Thomas Cranmer, granted Henry his divorce and declared his remarriage 'good and lawful'. Anne was declared Queen and crowned within days. The Pope responded by excommunicating Henry. All the elements were now in place that were to change forever the face of religion in England. Only one person stood in the way of the King's complete success.

Although now out of office and in straitened circumstances, Thomas More was still a royal councillor and a name to be conjured with. It was thought a great insult, therefore, that, despite the intervention of two bishops, he had declined to appear at the coronation of the new queen. Not being able to punish him directly for this affront, the King's friends determined that he should be attacked from another direction. More was summoned to appear before the Privy Council to answer charges of bribery while acting as a judge. Everyone who knew him would have realised how improbable such accusations were, but the mere fact of their having been made indicates the strength of his enemies' resolve to secure his downfall.

At his trial for bribery More surprised everyone by admitting having received the gift of a gilt cup as a New Year's present from the wife of a litigant. 'Lo! Did I not tell you, my Lords,' cried Anne Boleyn's father triumphantly, 'that you would find this matter true?' More then proceeded to confound them all by explaining that, having drunk a toast to the woman out of the cup, he had given it back to her to give to her husband as a New Year's gift. The next accusation concerned another gilt cup that, again, More admitted having received. This time he was able to show that in exchange for it he had given the donor a cup of far greater value. The final charge was that he had favoured a litigant who had rewarded him with a pair of gloves packed with gold pieces. More admitted receiving the gloves, but explained that he had given the gold back, saying: 'Mistress, since it were against good manners to forsake a gentlewoman's New Year's gift, I am content to take your gloves, but as for your money, I utterly refuse.' But his success was to be only a brief respite in the battle to bring him down.

A young servant girl called Elizabeth Barton, popularly known as the Holy Maid of Kent on account of her ecstatic visions, had incurred the King's displeasure by warning against his divorce. He promptly had her made the subject of a Bill of Attainder, an ancient procedure for condemning people without trial. On learning that Thomas More had been in touch with Elizabeth, the King immediately ordered that his name be attached to the Bill also. More had indeed visited Elizabeth, but was able to show that he had not encouraged her in any way. His name was reluctantly removed from the Bill. The Maid, however, was hanged.

By March 1534 the King had had enough. More was summoned before a committee of the Court of Star Chamber comprising Cromwell, Cranmer and Audley (who had replaced More as Lord Chancellor) and asked to declare his opinion on 'the King's great matter'. More answered that he had given his views to the King personally and would not repeat them. Threatened with painful consequences if he did not conform to the King's wishes, More replied, 'My Lords, these terrors be the arguments for children and not for me.'[4] The Duke of Norfolk tried to browbeat him into supporting the royal view by reminding him that 'the wrath of the King means death'. More's response was, 'Is that all? Then in good faith is there no more difference between your Grace and me but that I shall die today and you tomorrow.'

Later the same month an Act of Succession was passed by Parliament pronouncing the King's marriage to Catherine 'void and annulled' and effectively revoking the Pope's jurisdiction in England. It required anyone called upon to do so to 'make a corporal oath' to maintain 'the whole effects and contents of the Act' and a commission was set up to administer the oath. It was the step that More had feared.

'A HOUSE NIGH HEAVEN'

Almost as soon as the Act was passed More was summoned to Lambeth Palace to swear to the Act of Succession. While being rowed up the Thames from his house at Chelsea he was silent for some time but at last said to his son-in-law, 'Son Roper, I thank Our Lord the field is won.' Roper was at a loss to understand this remark, but it seems that More had conquered his fears and was prepared to accept the worst.

When he appeared before the tribunal More was given permission to study the wording of the Act. To his horror, he found that the oath that he was required to swear contained a rider acknowledging the King as head of the Church in England, something that had not been authorised by the Act of Parliament. To deny the King's claim to the headship of the Church would be to invite a charge of treason. More's reaction was that of a lawyer; he would refuse to take the oath but would not explain why. In this way he would be in breach of the Act, but he hoped that he could thereby avoid the graver crime of treason. As he later explained,

> My purpose was not to put any fault either in the Act or any man that made it, or in the oath or any man that swears it, nor to condemn the conscience of any other man. But as for myself in good faith my conscience so moved me in the matter, that though I would not deny to swear to the succession yet unto the oath that here was offered to me I could not swear without the jeoparding of my soul to perpetual damnation.[5]

The tribunal, however, saw through such lawyers' tricks. More was committed to the custody of the Abbot of Westminster and his lands and goods were forfeited to the Crown. Five days later, he was transferred to the Tower of London. On the way he managed to joke with his gaoler: 'Assure yourself, Master Lieutenant, I do not mislike my cheer; but whensoever I do, then thrust me out of your doors.' Kept in progressively dire conditions in London's ancient prison, he was reduced to writing to his family with charcoal. Others who refused to admit the King's headship of the Church fared worse. After being horribly tortured, they were hung, drawn and quartered within the sight and sound of Thomas More.

In the Tower More was permitted a visit from his wife. The ever-practical Alice addressed him bitterly:

> I marvel that you, that have been always hitherunto taken for so wise a man, will now so play the fool to lie here in this close filthy prison,

and be content to be shut up among mice and rats, when you might be abroad at your liberty, and with the favour and good will both of the King and his Council, if you would but do as all the bishops and best learned of this Realm have done. And seeing you have at Chelsea a right fair house, your library, your books, your gallery, your garden, your orchards, and all other necessaries so handsomely about you, where you might, in the company of me your wife, your children, and household be merry, I muse what a' God's name you mean here still thus fondly to tarry.[6]

More answered gently, 'Is not this house as nigh heaven as mine own?'

In October a further Act of Parliament, the Act of Supremacy, 'confirmed and corroborated' the King's position as 'the only supreme head in earth of the English Church'. Yet more legislation followed. The Acts of Supremacy and Treasons prescribed the form of oath and made it a capital offence to 'maliciously wish, will or desire, by words or writing' to deprive the royal family of 'their dignity, title or name of their royal estates'. More's last avenues of escape were now cut off.

THE INTERROGATION IN THE TOWER

Even so, the case against the former Chancellor was thin; further efforts would have to be made if he was to be convicted. A year after he had been first imprisoned More, now greatly enfeebled, was interrogated in the Tower by Cromwell and four others, but he still refused to answer their questions, commenting bitterly to Margaret, 'I do nobody harm. I think nobody harm, but wish everybody good. If this is not enough to keep a man alive, in good fayth I long not too lyve.' A few days later the Pope enraged Henry further by conferring a cardinal's hat upon the saintly John Fisher, Bishop of Rochester and a fellow prisoner in the Tower: it led to his death on the block. As the chronicler Holinshed wryly remarked, 'The hat came as far as Calais, but the head was cut off before the hat was on.'[7] What followed was to be the subject of perhaps the greatest betrayal in the whole affair.

On 12 June the Solicitor General, Sir Richard Rich, came to More's cell along with two others, ostensibly to remove his books. Roper records what happened:

And while Sir Richard Southwell and Mr Palmer were busy in trussing up of his books, Mr Rich pretending friendly talk with him, among other things of a set course, as it seemed, said thus unto him: 'Forasmuch as it is well known (Mr More) that you are a man both wise and well learned, as well in the laws of the Realm, as otherwise, I pray you therefore, Sir, let me be so bold as of good will to put unto you this case. Admit there were, Sir,' quoth he, 'an Act of Parliament, that all the Realm should take me for the King, would not you (Mr More) take me for the King?' 'Yes, Sir,' quoth Sir Thomas More, 'that would I'.

'I put the case further' (quoth Mr Rich) 'that there were an Act of Parliament that all the Realm should take me for the Pope; would then not you, Mr More, take me for the Pope?' 'For answer,' quoth Sir Thomas More, 'to your first case, the Parliament may well (Mr Rich) meddle with the state of temporal princes; but to make answer to your second case, I will put you this case. Suppose the Parliament would make a law, that God should not be God, would you then, Mr Rich, say God were not God?'

'No, Sir,' quoth he, 'that would I not, since no Parliament may make any such law.' 'No more' (said Sir Thomas More, as Mr Rich reported of him) 'could the Parliament make the King supreme head of the Church'.

The key words here are 'as Mr Rich reported'.

THE TRIAL IN WESTMINSTER HALL

A month later Thomas More was put on trial for high treason before the Court of King's Bench in Westminster Hall. The court comprised eighteen special commissioners including Chancellor Audley and Cromwell, as well as Thomas and George Boleyn, respectively the new queen's father and brother. Sir Richard Rich prosecuted. More, who after fifteen months' imprisonment could stand only with the aid of a stick, was allowed to sit before the court. He remained impassive and composed throughout. At the outset he rejected an offer of mercy in exchange for his compliance with the King's wishes.

The indictment alleged, in summary, that the defendant 'falsely, treasonably and maliciously' had refused to accept the royal supremacy of the Church of England; had engaged in treasonable correspondence with John Fisher, Bishop of Rochester, while they were both prisoners in the Tower of London, maliciously upholding his attitude and acquainting him with his own silence when examined; had described the Act of Supremacy as a two-edged sword, so that by accepting it one saved the body and killed the soul and that by rejecting it one saved the soul but killed the body; in conversation with Richard Rich had spoken against the Act, denying that the Parliament had the authority to declare Henry the head of the Church in England and thus also denying the King his royal authority. More, who had been given no previous notice of this lengthy document, pleaded not guilty to all the charges and defended himself with vigour, even partial success.

As to the first count, if we may use that term loosely, More argued that no law could justly punish silence and cited in support the legal maxim that 'qui tacet, consentire videtur' (he who is silent seems to consent). As to the second, More claimed that the correspondence with Fisher, which had since been destroyed, contained nothing treasonable since he had not disclosed his mind to anyone on the King's matter. As to the allegation that the condemned Fisher had made use of More's simile of a double-edged sword, this was, said More, nothing more than a coincidence; in any event it was no evidence of a conspiracy between the two of them. On these three counts More seems to have been acquitted. (The record is not entirely clear on the point.[8]) The only issue remaining was the fourth charge, that of denying the King's authority. Everything was to turn on whom the court believed.

THE EVIDENCE OF RICH

The critical testimony against Thomas More was that of Sir Richard Rich, the prosecutor who gave evidence of their conversation in his cell. According to Rich, More had denied the King's authority as head of the Church in England.

Roper reports More's biting commentary on Rich's evidence:

If I were a man (my Lords) that did not regard an oath, I need not (as it is well known) in this place, at this time, nor in this case to stand as an accused person. And if this oath of yours (Mr Rich) be true, then pray I that I may never see God in the face, which I would not say, were it otherwise, to win the whole world.

Then recited he unto the discourse of all their communication in the Tower according to the truth, and said,

'In faith, Mr Rich, I am sorrier for your perjury than for mine own peril, and you shall understand that neither I, nor no man else to my knowledge ever took you to be a man of such credit as in any matter of importance I, or any other would at any time vouchsafe to communicate with you. And (as you know) of no small while I have been acquainted with you and your conversation, who have known you from your youth hitherto. For we long dwelled both in one parish together, where, as yourself can tell (I am sorry you compel me so to say) you were esteemed very light of your tongue, a great dicer, and of not commendable fame. And so in your house at the Temple (where hath been your chief bringing up) were you likewise accounted.

'Can it therefore seem likely unto your honourable Lordships, that I would, in so weighty a cause, so far overshoot myself, as to trust Mr Rich (a man of me always reputed for one of so little truth, as your Lordships have heard) so far above my sovereign Lord the

King, or any of his noble councillors, that I would unto him utter the secrets of my conscience touching the King's supremacy, the special point and only mark at my hands so long sought for? . . . Can this in your judgments (my Lords) seem likely to be true? And if I had so done indeed, my Lords, as Mr Rich hath sworn, seeing it was spoke but in familiar secret talk, nothing affirming, and only in putting of cases, without other displeasant circumstances, it cannot justly be taken to be spoken maliciously. And where there is no malice there can be no offence . . .'

When Rich's two companions were called to corroborate the conversation, both denied having heard it. (They answered respectively, 'I took no heed' and 'I gave no ear'.) We can only speculate why these two worthies did not do what was so evidently expected of them.

In other words, anything said to Rich about the King's great matter had been put hypothetically by one lawyer to another and not as a statement of More's actual views. This strikes true; More was far too experienced a lawyer to make any damaging statements to the King's Solicitor General while awaiting trial on a charge of making just such a statement. Rich's evidence was clearly perjured. More now made a number of cogent submissions to the effect that there was no case to put to the jury, mostly centring on the absence of proof of malice, an essential ingredient to the offence of treason. All were rejected by the court. After only fifteen minutes' deliberation, the jury found More guilty of high treason. There was no right of appeal.

'GOD KNOWETH HOW'

As Audley began to pass the dreadful sentence required by law, More interrupted him, saying, 'My Lord, when I was toward the law, the manner in such case was to ask the prisoner before judgment, why judgment should not be given against him.' Acknowledging the oversight, Audley allowed More to make what is called a motion in arrest of judgment. He used the opportunity to justify his conduct. With nothing to lose, he made an impassioned plea.

Seeing that ye are determined to condemn me (God knoweth how) I will now in discharge of my conscience speak my mind plainly and freely touching my indictment and your statute withal. And forasmuch as this indictment is grounded upon an Act of Parliament directly repugnant to the laws of God and his Holy Church, the supreme government of which, or of any part whereof, may no temporal prince presume by any law to take upon him, as rightly belonging to the See of Rome, a spiritual pre-eminence by the mouth of our Saviour himself, personally present upon earth, only to St Peter and his Successors, bishops of the same See, by special prerogative granted; it is therefore in law, amongst Christian men, insufficient to charge any Christian man.[9]

The Lord Chancellor, 'loathe to have the burden of judgment to depend wholly upon himself', turned to the Lord Chief Justice, Lord Fitzjames, who replied deviously,

'My Lords all, by St Julian, I must needs confess that if the Act of Parliament be not unlawful then is not the indictment in my conscience insufficient.' Whereupon the Lord Chancellor said to the rest of the Lords, 'Lo, my Lords, Lo, you hear what my Lord Chief Justice saith.'[10]

There was an embarrassed silence, which was filled at last only by the passing of the sentence required by law, that More should be hung, drawn and quartered. A final plea for clemency was refused.

THE WAY TO THE SCAFFOLD

More walked from Westminster Hall to the Tower with the blade of the executioner's axe now turned towards him. As he reached the gate his son John broke through the crowd and knelt at his father's feet to receive his blessing. His favourite daughter, Margaret, followed, repeating, 'Oh my father! Oh my father!' and kissing him all the while, so that even the warders were moved to tears.

Four days after his trial More wrote his last letter to Margaret saying, 'I never liked your manner towards me better than when you kissed me last; for I love when daughterly love and dear charity hath no leisure to look to worldly courtesy. Farewell my dear child, and pray for me, and I shall for you and all your friends, that we may merrily meet in heaven.' With the letter he sent his hair shirt that she had so often washed for him in secret. More was now informed that, in recognition of his long service to the Crown, the King had 'graciously' reduced his sentence to one of beheading.

The next day More was taken to Tower Hill. On the way a woman cried out that he had used her unjustly when Lord Chancellor. 'Woman,' he replied, 'I remember well the whole matter. If now I were to give sentence again, I assure thee, I would not alter it.' At the scaffold the enfeebled More asked the executioner, 'See me up safe and for my coming down let me shift for myself.' In accordance with the King's wishes he spoke only briefly to the throng, declaring that he died, 'The King's good servant, but God's first.'

More's body was buried in the Tower church of St Peter ad Vincula; the head was parboiled and stuck on a pike on Tower Bridge. After some months Margaret managed to bribe a worker to give it to her instead of throwing it in the river. She had it buried in the Roper family vault in Canterbury.

WAS THE TRIAL FAIR?

The presence on the court that tried Thomas More of a person who had contributed to his prosecution is objectionable only by modern standards; in those days the knowledge of such a person was seen as a positive advantage. The appearance of the prosecutor as witness was deemed acceptable, as was the failure to give the accused written notice of the charges against him. But there was never any question of More being acquitted by this far from independent court. The King wanted him dead and the members of the King's court knew it. It is idle too to talk of the presumption of innocence, because no such presumption existed in More's day. While justice demands that a prisoner should have the right to legal representation, there is no record of More having requested it. But then, there was probably no man in the kingdom better qualified to defend himself than More.

Those of us born into a more secular society may be uncomfortable with More's submission that the statute was void because it was contrary to the will of God, but More's court was not: it differed from him only in its interpretation of the will of God. In any event the argument was rejected by a court that knew exactly where earthly power lay. Everything rested on what More could be proved to have said to Rich in his cell. Four and a half centuries later More's scornful condemnation of the scoundrel Rich still rings true. In its dismissal of the first three charges the members of the court showed a proper discrimination that cannot be faulted. When it came to the most serious charge, however, they 'knew where their duty lay'. Their finding was a craven submission to the King's wishes, but how many of us finding ourselves in a similar position could be sure that we would have done differently?

It took more than blatant perjury and a weak court to bring about More's end; it also required the willing complicity of the man himself. What sort of person would accept the most terrible death rather than temporise his principles?

A MAN 'BORN AND FRAMED FOR FRIENDSHIP'

Thomas More was exceptionally fortunate in his private life. After deciding, in the words of his lifetime friend, the Dutch humanist

Desiderius Erasmus, to 'be a chaste husband rather than an impure priest', he married twice; both were love matches. His first wife, the sixteen-year-old Jane Colt, died within six years of the ceremony. A few weeks after her death, More, now encumbered by three daughters and a son, remarried, this time to the widow Alice Middleton, eight years his senior. But it was not a case of 'off with the old, on with the new'; More arranged for the bones of his first and 'well beloved' wife Jane to be brought to his own chosen resting place. And the memorial he composed in advance of his death makes a fitting comment on his second wife. Alice, he recorded, had 'been so good to my children (which is a rare praise in mothers-in-law) as scant any could be better to her own'.

The More household at Chelsea is widely known through Holbein's delightful study. It included, though not in the picture, those late medieval accessories, a fool and a small menagerie. More was the gentlest of men and hardly ever lost his temper. It was said that he never beat his children save with peacocks' feathers. Erasmus described him as a somewhat ascetic man but with 'a character better framed for gladness than severity . . . born and framed for friendship . . . full of jokes and banter'. Everyone, including the servants, was encouraged to play an instrument. It was a home filled with love and laughter.

More wrote extensively. His best-known work, *Utopia* ('nowhere' in Greek), condemned the social evils of his day. The wool trade, it argued, was destroying agriculture and driving the poor into the cities, where they were tempted into crime. The book purported to describe a model land in which the hanging of thieves was condemned and where people could practise religion according to their conscience. In the twentieth century it was memorialised in Red Square, Moscow, as a great reforming document; others have seen it, perhaps more realistically, as a satire. Whichever may be the case, there can be no doubt of More's concern for humanity.

As a judge, More was beyond reproach. Not only did he clear the lists of the Court of Chancery (a great achievement among Lord Chancellors[11]); he steadfastly refused the bribes that were then commonly offered to those sitting in judgment, leaving the Bench no richer than when he was appointed. He once told his son-in-law how as a judge he might properly assist a friend at court (as by taking his case earlier in the list, he said, or by urging the parties to come to an agreement). But this was as far as he would go: 'One thing I assure thee on my faith, that if the parties will at my hand call for justice, then were it my father stood on the one side and the devil on the other side (his cause being good) the devil should have right.'[12]

Only the impious could expect no mercy from More. The epitaph that he himself wrote claimed that he had been 'to thieves, murderers *and heretikes* grievous' (emphasis added). He even once wrote: 'There should have been more burned by a great many than there have been within this seven year last.' How could such a manifestly kindly man act so uncharitably towards his fellows? The answer is to be found in his religious beliefs.

In a vivid evocation of the late medieval world into which the baby Thomas was born Peter Ackroyd begins his classic biography of More by describing in detail the almost superstitious ceremonies that attended his baptism. We should remember that the Holy Catholic Church had existed for some fifteen centuries before More's birth and it was to be forty years more before Martin Luther nailed his ninety-five reforming theses to the church door at Wittenberg. More was conscious of the deficiencies of his Church but he feared the heretic more. More, the priest manqué, never lost sight of the Church's teaching that this world was simply a preparation for the next. The fear of hell and the hope of heaven dominated even the best minds of his generation. Papist or Protestant alike had no doubt that it was more charitable to burn a man briefly on earth than to allow him to burn for ever in hell. (More is known to have been responsible for only one burning, but he always denied having used torture.)

The other great influence on More was his father the judge. There are many stories of the respect More paid to his father, even when holding the highest judicial office. Thomas was as at home with the law as with his religion. Both are essentially authoritarian disciplines, and More's fate was to be caught in a conflict between the two.

In the broad sum of things, the legal propriety of Henry's marriage to Catherine was a matter of little moment to anyone except the parties themselves; it was certainly not an issue worth dying for, as More well knew. The supremacy of the Church was a different matter in his eyes. It was only after he had been sentenced that More told his daughter Margaret what he had steadfastly withheld from his interrogators – that he had refused to take the oath because of its implications for the Church. Acceptance, not merely of the Act of Succession but of 'all other Acts and Statutes made since the beginning of the present Parliament', would have been to deny the Pope's authority over the Church in England. But More miscalculated badly when he wrote, 'I may tell thee, Meg, they that have committed me hither for refusing of the oath, not agreeable with the statute, are not able by their own law to justify my imprisonment.'

But power does not have to justify.

More hoped that the subtleties of the law that he knew so well could save his life without risking his soul. In the end it was only the King's will that counted. More told his inquisitors, 'I do no body harm, I say none harm, I think none harm, but I wish everybody good. And if this be not enough to keep a man alive, in good faith I long not to live.' It was not, and so he died.

After a trial presided over by her uncle, the Duke of Norfolk, Anne Boleyn was executed in 1536 for adultery, incest and plotting to murder the King. Cromwell was executed for heresy in 1540 and Cranmer was burned at the stake for the same reason sixteen years later. Shortly afterwards, the villain, Rich, who is said to have particularly enjoyed putting women to the rack, died in his bed, loaded with honours.

Thomas More was long considered a liberal by some Roman Catholics, and it was not until 1886 that he was beatified by the Church for which he had given his life. He was canonised in 1935. His chapel is in Chelsea Old Church, which stands behind what was once the orchard of his house. It was in this church, just a few days after Anne Boleyn was executed, that Henry was to marry his third wife, Jane Seymour.

CHAPTER TWELVE

The Martyrs

The Trial of the Tolpuddle Martyrs, 1834

In the year 1831–32, there was a general movement of the working classes for an increase of wages, and the labouring men in the parish where I lived gathered together, and met their employers, to ask them for an advance of wages, and they came to a mutual agreement, the masters in Tolpuddle promising to give the men as much for their labour as the other masters in the district. The whole of the men then went to work, and the time that was spent in this affair did not exceed two hours. No language of intimidation or threatening was used on the occasion. Shortly after we learnt that, in almost every place around us, the masters were giving their men money, or money's worth to the amount of ten shillings a week – we expected to be entitled to as much – but no, nine shillings must be our portion. After some months we were reduced to eight shillings per week. This caused great dissatisfaction, and all the labouring men in the village, with the exception of two or three invalids, made application to a neighbouring magistrate . . .

I was one nominated to appear, and when there we were told that we must work for whatever our employers thought fit to give us, as there was no law to compel masters to give any fixed sum of money to their servants. In vain we remonstrated that an agreement was made . . . From this time we were reduced to seven shillings per week, and shortly after our employers told us they must lower us to six shillings per week.

George Loveless, 'The Victims of Whiggery' [1837][1]

England in the first decade of the nineteenth century was not the contented society that a cursory reading of Jane Austen might suggest. Throughout the country the enclosure of common land had turned freeholders into labourers and turned labourers into casual hands. The situation had only been made worse by the introduction of industrial machinery. Beginning in Nottingham around 1810, violent resistance to industrialisation took hold throughout the mill towns. It was known as Luddism after a mythical Ned Ludd who destroyed industrial machinery. Secret meetings were held and mills were attacked by gangs of armed men. The government reacted by calling out the army. Pitched battles took place with deaths on both sides. Eventually, the problem died down, only to reappear in different form two decades later.

The bad winters and poor harvests of 1829 and 1830 led to thousands more being thrown onto poor relief. The cost to the taxpayer began to spiral out of control, and the ensuing reductions in benefit caused great resentment among the poor. Large-scale riots occurred across the south led by the mythical 'Captain Swing'. Landowners received threatening letters, barns were fired and machinery smashed. The pattern seemed chillingly reminiscent of events over the Channel, where, only four years before, barricades had been erected in Paris and King Charles X had been deposed. Across the country 600 rioters were imprisoned, 500 sentenced to transportation and 19 executed. A special commission of judges had to be set up to try the prisoners across the Home Counties, where poverty was at its worst. Many working men turned for support to the recently legalised trade unions.

In November 1833 beneath a giant sycamore tree in the little village of Tolpuddle, 9 miles east of Dorchester, a small group of men formed a Lodge of the Friendly Society of Agricultural Labourers. Early the following year the Lodge members resolved not to accept work for less than 10 shillings a week. The local magistrates were rattled. Chief among them was James Frampton JP. Frampton had been in Paris during the bloody revolution of 1789 and understood well the implications of social unrest allowed to get out of hand. Nor was he without experience of such problems in his own country. He had seen off rioting crowds at Bere Regis and had read the Riot Act at Winfrith. Now he was being told that strangers were recruiting for the union in Dorset and that meetings of between twenty and thirty men at a time had been held at night in various houses on the Great Heath, a wild place well away from prying eyes. Anyone who refused to join the union was likely to have his windows broken.

For some time the Dorset justices had been doing what they could to find out what the unions were up to. (The Tolpuddle prosecution rested partly on the evidence of at least one informer.) It was time to seek advice.

At the end of January 1834 Frampton wrote to the Home Secretary, Viscount Melbourne, expressing on behalf of a number of his colleagues concern at the formation of societies in Dorset that urged labourers to enter into 'dangerous combinations' involving the administration of 'clandestine oaths'. In fact, trade unions – or combinations, as they were then known – were no longer illegal as such. But, although the Combination Acts had been repealed, union activities were still severely circumscribed by law, and unionism was regarded with distrust by those in authority. The Home Office suspected that what was going on in Dorset was only part of a wider conspiracy designed to overturn the established order and advised the justices that 'measures of spirit and firmness' were necessary to suppress it. Their words fell on willing ears.

Acting on Melbourne's advice, printed notices, signed by nine magistrates, including Frampton, appeared in the Tolpuddle area on 22 February. Under the bold heading 'CAUTION', they warned that the taking or administration of unlawful oaths was a felony punishable by seven years' transportation. However, as the magistrates well knew, five initiates had already been sworn into the new union Lodge on 9 December.

THE SKELETON

Oaths counted for a lot in early nineteenth-century England; they were lawfully taken by soldiers, constables, magistrates; indeed, all manner of men. To break an oath was to put the oath-taker's immortal soul at peril. It was not surprising, therefore, that working men should turn to oaths to keep their still barely legal activities hidden from the authorities. Some of the oaths were pretty blood-curdling. The Luddites, for example, swore 'never [to] reveal any of the names of any one of this secret Committee, under the penalty of being sent out of this world by the first Brother that may meet me. I furthermore do swear, that I will pursue with unceasing vengeance any Traitors or Traitor, should there any arise, should he fly to the verge of . . .'.[2] What had actually taken place at that night-time meeting in the cottage on the Great Heath? No record of the swearing-in ceremony survives, but its outlines have been reconstructed from evidence given at their trial.

The five initiates were brought into the upper room of the cottage, blindfolded by their own handkerchiefs. 'A paper' was read to them, the purport of which they claimed not to remember. They were then made to kneel while more words were pronounced, possibly, they thought, from the Bible. Their eyes were uncovered and they saw in a corner of the room what appeared to be a skeleton. (In fact, it was a painting of a skeleton.) The person officiating, who was dressed in a white sheet, looked at the skeleton and said, 'Remember your end.' The initiates were again blindfolded and knelt while further words were said. They were then made to recite an undertaking that their souls would be condemned to perdition if they did not keep secret. The oath-takers kissed a book, which, again, they presumed to be the Bible. Finally, their blindfolds were removed for the last time, and the rules of the Lodge were explained, seemingly without much of the content lodging in their heads.

THE ARRESTS

Two days after the posting of the warning notices, six Tolpuddle men were arrested by the village constable on the order of a magistrate and marched to nearby Dorchester. Believed to be the ringleaders of union activity in the area, they were closely related to each other. Their names were James Brine (not to be confused with the constable of the same name who arrested them), James Hammett, George Loveless and his brother James, as well as Thomas Standfield and his son John. Although the oath-taking had taken place in John Standfield's cottage, the leading light was James Loveless, who, dressed in the white sheet, had sworn in the new initiates that fateful night in December.

George and James Loveless were no strangers to activism. In the 1830 riots George had been heard to say that anyone who accepted work at a rate lower than he demanded should have his head cracked. For what it is worth, Thomas Standfield (spelled 'Stanfield' in all official documents) was described by the Justices as 'a very discontented man'; his 21-year-old son John was considered a 'very saucy fellow', which probably meant no more than that he was prone to stand up for himself. James Hammett was stigmatised as 'a very idle man and ready for mischief'. This may be true: in 1829 he had been convicted of stealing iron and sentenced to four months' imprisonment. James Brine's only occupation seems to have been as a union recruiter. Whatever the justices may have thought of the men, however, the witnesses at their trial described most of them as hard-working. But there was something that put them in bad odour with authority: they were all Nonconformists.

The Loveless brothers were both Methodist preachers, each of them married and with a young family. As George was to write later, 'I am from principle, a dissenter.' And Thomas Standfield was an occasional preacher. The propertied classes, by contrast, were almost all Anglicans to whom dissent, as membership of the Nonconformist sects was then described, seemed to strike at the heart of established religion. Few dissenters were more despised than the Methodists. To the rich and powerful, a Methodist unionist was someone doubly suspect; the Loveless brothers and their friends fitted the bill well.

Following their arrest, the men were taken to the house of Frampton's half-brother, C.B. Wollaston JP, the Recorder of Dorchester, where, after formal evidence had been given of their presence at the oath-taking, they were committed to custody. When he was searched, a copy of the justices' warning notice was found in George Loveless's pocket and in his house was discovered a locked box containing the rules of the union. A curious feature that came to light only much later was that, although one of the witnesses at the trial, Andrew Legg, identified James Hammett as having been present at the ceremony, he was almost certainly not there. The brave James appears to have kept his silence and accepted his fate in order to protect his younger brother.

The prisoners were taken before a bench of magistrates that committed them to Dorchester jail to stand trial at the next Assizes. George Loveless's last chance of escaping justice came a few minutes later when his attorney conveyed to him a message from the magistrates offering him his freedom in return for informing on the union and its members; he courageously rejected the offer.

But on what charges were the prisoners to be tried? Not much thought appears to have been given to this before their arrest. Only after consultation with the government law officers were the indictments framed, under an Act of Parliament of 1797.

On Saturday 15 March the prisoners were brought before a grand jury in the courtroom of the Old Shire Hall, Dorchester, which is still there today. The purpose of a grand jury was to decide whether there was sufficient evidence to commit the defendant for trial. (The institution has been abolished in England but continues to serve in the United States.) It would be difficult to describe the Dorchester grand jury as wholly impartial. According to the custom of the time, it consisted of local justices, including James Frampton and three other signatories of the warning notice – effectively the prosecutors. Its foreman was W.S. Ponsonby MP, brother-in-law of the Home Secretary who had advised on the prosecution and the drawing-up of the charges. There was nothing illegal in any of this, however; all of it was accepted practice in those days.

The judge was the recently appointed Mr Baron Williams (a judicial, not an aristocratic title). He began the proceedings by charging the jury, as the business of instructing them on the law is called. The Incitement to Mutiny Act 1797, he declared, despite its title and original purpose, was not restricted to seditious actions but extended to all unlawful combinations. It was, he said, a serious matter to trifle with the sanctity of any oath, particularly where the purpose was to bind men to the irresponsible will of strangers. He referred to the evils of trade unions (without naming them as such), whereby men lost the right to work for whom they pleased and put themselves at danger of life and limb if they incurred the displeasure of their self-elected superiors. The grand jury did what was expected of them and returned a true bill.

DORCHESTER QUARTER SESSIONS

The trial proper began on the following Monday, this time with the judge sitting with what was then known as a 'petty' jury. It consisted of eleven yeomen and one farmer, people who might be expected to 'know where their duty lay'. When one of the jurymen turned out not to be a farmer, he was rejected, albeit under what was then, as it is now, a perfectly proper procedure. However unfortunate such an unrepresentative jury may appear today, it was customary then when it was thought that only men with a substantial stake in the community could be trusted to do justice. The Lovelesses and Standfield were represented by a

Mr Derbishire and the other accused by a Mr Butt, both of counsel and paid for, seemingly, by the union.

The union's rules, when they were produced to the court, proved to be less than revolutionary. Rule 23, for example, stated: 'The rules of the society can never be promoted by any act or acts of violence, but, on the contrary, all such proceedings must tend to hinder the cause and destroy the society itself. This order will not countenance any violation of the laws.' The centrepiece of the prosecution case, however, was the oath-taking. The two principal witnesses to this were John Lock, the son of James Frampton's gardener, and Edward Legg. Whether from poor memory, reluctance to incriminate the prisoners or fear of retribution from their 'brothers', both Lock and Legg seemed curiously vague about what had happened that night in Standfield's cottage; they professed not to recall the words or even the substance of the oath they had taken. The only fact they were clear on was, as Legg told the court, 'We were to keep it secret, and not to reveal anything that was done or said there.' Disclosure of the union's secrets, they had been warned, could result in death.

By the law of the day the defendants had no right to give evidence on their own behalf, but at the prisoner's request the judge read to the jury a short but dignified statement from George Loveless:

If we have violated any law, it was not done intentionally; we have injured no man's reputation, character, person or property: we were uniting together to preserve ourselves from utter degradation and starvation. We challenge any man, or number of men, to prove that we have acted, or intended to act, different from the above statement.[3]

Defence counsel suggested, somewhat weakly, that the purpose of the union was no more than to provide a fund, 'a kind of Agricultural Savings Bank'. This was clearly not the case, since the rules of the union provided for the use of strikes in support of better wages. But it was not union membership that was at stake. On the critical question the defence submitted that, while there undoubtedly had been a ceremony, there was no sufficient evidence of any illegal oath having been taken at it. They also raised an objection that even now has its supporters – namely, that the Act of 1797 was confined to cases of mutiny and sedition and had no application to trade unions.

THE MAXIMUM SENTENCE

The judge ruled against the defence on the law and the jury found against them on the facts – and it did not take them long to do so. For reasons that are still not clear, the judge then put the case back for a few days. This adjournment, though customary now, was unusual in its day. Why it was ordered and what discussions took place in the interim and between whom we can only speculate. What is known for sure is that, when the court resumed, the judge passed the maximum sentence of seven years' transportation on each of the accused. He then went on to make a statement, for which he has been much criticised: 'The object of all legal punishment is not altogether with a view to operating on the offenders themselves, it is also for the sake of offering an example and a warning.' Some have thought this unjust; the censure is misconceived. The deterrence of others is and always has been a proper objective of sentencing and one that the judge was certainly entitled to take into account. What is problematic is Williams's further statement that he 'had no discretion in the matter but was bound to pass the sentence which the Act of Parliament had imposed'.

What the Act of 1797 actually provided was that persons convicted under it '*may* be transported for any term of years *not exceeding* seven years' (emphasis added). In other words, seven years was the maximum sentence that the judge could pass, not a mandatory sentence that he had to pass. It is possible that the judge had meant to say that he 'had no discretion *in the circumstances of this case*, but was bound to pass the *maximum* sentence which the Act of Parliament *permitted*', but this was not what he is reported as having said. If it was an error, it was an egregious one, and Williams, though newly appointed to the Bench, does not appear to have been a sloppy lawyer. One is left with the uneasy feeling that an injustice, and a gross one at that, may just possibly have occurred.

And there is another problem. The maximum sentence provided by law is intended for use only when the crime in question is committed in the gravest possible circumstances. It is difficult to see what aggravating features could possibly be thought to have brought the Tolpuddle men's flimflam ceremony within this category so as to justify the imposition of the maximum sentence allowed by law – a fact that only tends to support the appalling possibility that the judge misread his powers.

BOTANY BAY

Immediately following sentence, the prisoners, with the exception of George Loveless, who had fallen ill, were taken in chains to a prison hulk moored in Portsmouth and thence to the convict ship *Surrey*, which was to take them to the penal colony of New South Wales. As soon as he recovered, Loveless joined his friends on the *Surrey*, but, in a move designed to separate him from his fellows, was later transferred to another ship headed for a different part of the colony.

Apart from the normal privations of a long journey under sail in the early nineteenth century, conditions on the convict ships were especially hard, due in no small measure to the primitive sanitation arrangements for the convicts. In 1790, for example, out of 938 men on one ship, 251 died at sea and a further 50 after landing. On board, the discipline was harsh, sometimes involving flogging and branding. Fortunately, none of the Tolpuddle men seems to have been brutalised in this way, seemingly on account of their good behaviour.

After fourteen weeks at sea the bulk of the men arrived at Botany Bay, now Sydney, then a convict settlement. Convicts not needed for government work were assigned by lot at £1 a head to masters who, for good or ill, had complete control over their lives. Although punishment could be brutal, the exemplary behaviour of the Tolpuddle men seems once again to have helped them escape the worst. After a time John Standfield was even given permission to visit his father, Thomas, who was living in a nearby settlement and weak from the rigours of colonial life. (At forty-four, he was the oldest of the Tolpuddle men.) Later, the two Standfields were recalled to Sydney and put on government labour, apparently on orders from London.

George Loveless found himself in the penal settlement of Port Arthur in Tasmania, which was reserved for the more difficult prisoners and escapees. Questioned about the activities of his fellow unionists, he stoutly refused to give anything away, but does not seem to have suffered for this. Once, when charged with neglect of duty as a cattleman, he escaped punishment when his overseer confirmed his diligence as a worker.

PROTEST IN ENGLAND

Protest against the Tolpuddle men's sentences began almost immediately after their conviction, and a fund was set up to support them. (Their families had been refused poor relief on the ground that they were being financially assisted by the union.) Lawyers drew attention to the supposed uncertainty of the law. Even Members of Parliament antipathetic to the unions supported the men's cause. Committees were formed and public meetings held. The biggest, at Copenhagen Fields in London, attracted a turn-out of over 50,000. Fearing disorder, the government called out the army and swore in additional special constables, but the event passed off without trouble.

With pressure mounting on the government to do something for the prisoners, the government offered George Loveless's wife a free passage to Australia. When she arrived, her husband was declared exempt from compulsory labour and, with some difficulty, found an ordinary job for himself.

After various changes in government Lord Melbourne became Prime Minister for the second time in April 1835. His Home Secretary was Lord John Russell, who while out of office had supported the pardoning of the Tolpuddle men. He now proposed that Hammett, the Standfields and Brine should be pardoned after two years but that the Lovelesses, as ringleaders, should never be allowed to return. This was not enough to satisfy public opinion. One Member of Parliament suggested, perhaps tongue in cheek, that, if the Tolpuddle men had been prosecuted, the Orange lodges, whose ceremonies were not dissimilar to theirs and whose president was the Duke of Cumberland, a prince of the royal blood, should also be suppressed.

Further concessions followed that pleased no one, and it was not until March 1836 that full and unconditional pardons were granted to all six men. The necessary papers arrived in Botany Bay in August of that year and delays occurred before the men were told. Fortunately, George Loveless had read of the pardon in an old newspaper of his employer. After various vicissitudes, he left for England in January 1837, arrived unnoticed and settled down in Tolpuddle to write a brief account of his experiences from which the quotation at the beginning of this chapter has been taken. Brine, James Loveless and the Standfields followed him in September of that year. The captain of their ship was so touched by their plight that he gave each of them £5 out of his own pocket to help them start afresh in their home country.

The men's homecoming in March 1838 was marked by great celebrations in London and Dorset, after which they went to live on farms in Essex that had been bought for them by public subscription. Eventually, in August 1839, Hammett too returned to England and settled in one of the farms. (Working up-country in Australia, he had lost touch with the others and had not been contacted.) The flame of radicalism was undimmed in their breasts and, to the horror of the local gentry, the six soon formed a Chartist association in their area. (The Chartists were a radical political party with ideas well in advance of their time.)

ENVOI

Whether their exile had unsettled them or perhaps simply for the same reasons as many others at the time, most of the Tolpuddle men emigrated to Canada in 1844, where they lived and prospered for the rest of their lives. An intelligent, brave, even noble man, George Loveless helped build a Methodist church in his new home town. His brother James became sexton of his local church. John Standfield ran a hotel and ended up as the mayor of his district. Hammett alone remained in England, returning to Tolpuddle in 1841; his grave is in the churchyard. James Brine married Elizabeth, John Standfield's sister, in 1839 and they had eleven children. He was the last of the Martyrs to die, in 1902.

WERE THEY PROPERLY CONVICTED?

Controversy has long surrounded the use of the Incitement to Mutiny Act 1797 to prosecute the Tolpuddle men. It certainly involved a tortuous piece of reasoning, which, so far as the present writer can make out, went as follows:

1. It was an offence under the Act of 1797 to administer an unlawful oath in an unlawful combination.
2. By the time of the trial trade unions had ceased to be unlawful combinations.
3. But an Act of 1799 had made a trade union an unlawful combination if an unlawful oath was administered in it.
4. Therefore it was an offence to administer an unlawful oath in a trade union.

An agricultural labourer of the time could perhaps be excused for failing to understand so complex a law, even if he was aware of it. What the Tolpuddle men did know, however, is that what they were doing was wrong. (Why else meet at night in a remote area?) But was the scope of the Act of 1797 as wide as the government thought and the judge ruled?

The Act of 1797 had been passed as an immediate reaction to the naval mutinies that had taken place at Spithead and the Nore, and that had involved the taking of unlawful oaths. That this was the case was recognised in the Preamble to the Act (the explanation of why it had been enacted). Many, including the one-time Labour Solicitor-General, Sir Stafford Cripps KC, have expressed the view that the effect of the Preamble was to confine the Act to incitement to mutiny or the like. Was this right?

The argument was not a new one; it had been rejected by Baron Williams at the trial on good legal authority and legal opinion of the day supported his view. A Preamble to an Act of Parliament may be used as a guide to its meaning, but, as a contemporary authority comments, 'The courts are reluctant to allow a Preamble to override inconsistent operative provisions.'[4] The operative provisions of this Act were not in any way limited to the Preamble and were certainly wide enough to cover the Tolpuddle oath. It follows that the law under which the men of Tolpuddle were prosecuted, though hideously complex, was applicable to the circumstances of the case and not, as is often suggested, a piece of legal sleight of hand.

There was, however, a curious lacuna that does not appear to have been noticed at the trial. The indictments alleged that the oaths had been taken by the six on 24 February, whereas the date was in fact 9 December. The point is probably immaterial, however, since the accuracy of the date was relevant in law only if time was of the essence of the criminal act, and that was not the case here.

DID THEY GET A FAIR TRIAL?

But was there, as the defence denied, sufficient evidence before the court of an oath actually having been taken in that upper room in Standfield's cottage? There was certainly evidence of a strange ritual, accompanied by the kissing of what may or may not have been a Bible and an injunction to secrecy – but little more. Evidence of the terms of any oath was vague at best. It is difficult to resist the conclusion that on this central issue the jury 'applied their common sense' to a situation in a way that a lawyer might, perhaps, not have done. In this, they were probably wiser than the lawyers.

The judge has also been criticised for pressing the jury in favour of conviction and for his criticism of trade unions. There may be force in these complaints and if there was it might have been sufficient to nullify the proceedings, but our patchy record of the trial is wholly inadequate to make a firm judgement on the point. This has not, of course, stopped many from doing so.

All in all and judged solely by the standards of the day, there is little that can be criticised in the trial of the Martyrs. The same cannot be said about the sentence imposed. The judge's words strongly implied that he misunderstood his duty. Even if he had not, the maximum sentence he imposed was wholly unwarranted by the facts of the case. If there had been a true system of appeals in those days, the sentence should have been overturned.

WHAT WENT WRONG?

The Tolpuddle six, as the present-day media would surely describe them, are rightly regarded as the foremost 'martyrs' of the early trade union movement, and rallies are held regularly in the village, attracting large crowds. But the story is not as black and white as some would paint it.

Academics have recently challenged the extent of rural poverty in early nineteenth-century Dorset,[5] but that poverty existed in both relative and absolute terms there can be no doubt. Coupled with a lack of security of tenure and the propensity of many landowners to treat their tenants cavalierly, the lot of the rural labourer cannot have been one of unalloyed content. And change was in the air. Better communications and improved education had led to a new willingness on the part of the poor to demand a larger share of the national wealth. With unrest and violence fresh in the memories of the government and the gentry, it would have been strange indeed if they had not been fearful of the taking of secret and seemingly blood-curdling oaths by barely legalised combinations of the working poor, particularly when there were suspicions that the practice might be part of a wider conspiracy threatening the very fabric of society. Unless this development was nipped in the bud, they must have thought, might not England go the way of less fortunate lands? When viewed through today's egalitarian spectacles, it is easy to see the selfish element in such attitudes. But, while this reaction to early labour militancy may be criticised as unimaginative, in contemporary eyes it would have been seen as no more than a sensible reaction to those who appeared to seek society's destruction.

The Dorset Society of Labourers may well have turned out to be as 'Friendly' as its name suggested; it did not look so to the justices at the time. It was the ill luck of Loveless and his friends – nonconformists in every sense of the word – to find themselves at the centre of this struggle. Whatever their intent, they surely could not have realised that the somewhat absurd ceremony in which they had taken part constituted a transportable offence. We can only speculate whether, had the justices' warning notices appeared earlier, the men would have been deterred from the oath-taking; possibly not.

The consultations that took place between the justices and the Home Office seem to modern eyes to betray an unacceptable lack of independence in those who were to try the case, but at that time the distinction between government and justices of the peace was nowhere near as clear-cut as it is today. Justices then had many duties other than the purely judicial, of which the maintenance of public order was probably the most important. They were in a very real sense part of the administration of their areas. As to the trial itself, much of the criticism it has received has been wide of the mark.

Nevertheless, we are left with an impression of a flawed judicial process presided over by an inexperienced judge who, for whatever reason, imposed a sentence far more severe than the circumstances warranted. Although the journey to the Antipodes must have been awful, the men's sufferings when they got there were probably little worse than those experienced by many voluntarily indentured labourers in that new land. Their four years' exile – five in Hammett's case – was made longer than it should have been through bureaucratic foot-dragging. Tolpuddle may be summed up as shaky justice, harsh sentencing, moderate hardship and commutation of sentence – followed by rehabilitation with honour. If it was martyrdom it was a very English sort of martyrdom.

CHAPTER THIRTEEN

The Anarchists

The Trial of Sacco and Vanzetti, 1921

Fifty years to the day after two young men had been electrocuted for the brutal murder of a payroll official and his guard, a proclamation was issued by the governor of the State of Massachusetts:

> I, Michael S. Dukakis . . . do hereby proclaim Tuesday, August 23 1977, 'NICOLA SACCO AND BARTOLOMEO VANZETTI MEMORIAL DAY'; and declare, further, that any stigma and disgrace should be forever removed from the names of Nicola Sacco and Bartolomeo Vanzetti, from the names of their families and descendants, and so . . . call upon all the people of Massachusetts to pause in their daily endeavors to reflect upon these tragic events, and draw from their historic lessons the resolve to prevent the forces of intolerance, fear, and hatred from ever again uniting to overcome the rationality, wisdom, and fairness to which our legal system aspires.[1]

Interestingly, while the proclamation stigmatised the trial as unjust, it stopped short of declaring the defendants innocent.

Few trials have given rise to more controversy in twentieth-century America than that of two Italian immigrants sentenced to death for a crime they vehemently denied committing. The cause of Nicola Sacco and Bartolomeo Vanzetti was taken up by writers and intellectuals around the world, helped in no small part by the defendants' own writings.

Whether in the halting English of the newly arrived immigrant or in the more polished language that Vanzetti in particular acquired over his seven years in prison, their letters never fail to move. Scores of books have been written portraying them as the innocent victims of corrupt law-enforcement officers, a prejudiced judge and an intolerant society. Much their most impressive advocate was the distinguished Harvard law professor and subsequent Supreme Court Justice, Felix Frankfurter, who, five months before the condemned men's execution, published an article arguing forcefully that the trial failed 'to observe the standards of Anglo-American justice'.[2] His views, which were followed up in a book, naturally commanded great respect. But were they right? Before making any assessment of this most fascinating of cases it is necessary to understand the background to the trial.

Anarchism, or the rejection of state authority, was a popular movement in nineteenth-century Italy, where its philosophy of 'propaganda by the deed' evolved into a campaign of bombing and murder. In the early years of the twentieth century mass immigration of poor Italians brought this violent philosophy to the New World. Foremost among the new arrivals was Luigi Galleani.

Galleani's journal *Cronaca sovversiva* (Subversive Chronicle) was suppressed in 1918 because of its opposition to the war with Germany. His supporters were not slow to react. Fly posters appeared in the mill cities of New England proclaiming, 'The senile fossils ruling the United States see red! . . . The storm is within and very soon will leap and crash and annihilate you in blood and fire. You have shown no pity on us! We will do likewise. *We will dynamite you!*' The authors of these notices kept their promise. Businessmen, judges and officials in eight American cities nationwide received bombs and acid through the post. One of the bombs blew off the hands of a former Senator's maid and burnt his wife about the face and head. Galleani was arrested in May 1919, but another wave of explosions took place in June, this time destroying the homes of judges and officials and killing a nightwatchman. The home of the US Attorney General himself was torn apart by an explosion that also killed the bomber. In the ensuing crackdown, which came to be known as the 'Red scare', over 10,000 suspected communists and anarchists – the distinctions were little understood at the time – were arrested in raids around the country. The vast majority were released, but over 200, including Galleani, were deported.

A few months after the explosions a violent crime occurred in a quiet Massachusetts town that was to result in one of the most notorious trials of the century.

THE ATTEMPTED ROBBERY AT BRIDGEWATER

It was early morning, Christmas Eve in 1919. A payroll truck was making its routine delivery of over $30,000 to the LQ White Shoe Company in the little town of Bridgewater, some 25 miles south of Boston, Massachusetts. As well as the driver, the truck contained the company paymaster and an armed policeman. As it slowly crossed the tramway, three men got out of a car parked nearby and called on the truck to stop. Getting no reaction, one of the three, a man with a black moustache, knelt down and began shooting at the vehicle with a shotgun, while the other two fired their pistols. The guard returned fire and the truck swerved into a telegraph pole. A passing trolley car now got between the attackers and the pay truck. Realising that the game was up, the attackers jumped back in their car and drove off in the direction of the nearby town of Cochesett. Witnesses described them as 'dark and foreign' and driving either a Buick or a Hudson Overland car.

Michael E. Stewart, the Bridgewater chief of police, told the press that he believed that the hold-up was the work of an out of town band of Russians and ordered a search for Buick and Overland cars. Three and a half months later, with no one having been arrested for the Bridgewater job, a robbery took place in the nearby town of South Braintree. This time the consequences were to be far more serious.

THE SOUTH BRAINTREE ROBBERY

Every Thursday morning the local agent of American Express went to the railway station at the town of South Braintree to collect cash that had been sent to pay the wages at two local shoe factories. On 15 April 1920 he took nearly $16,000 to the office of the Slater & Morrill Shoe Factory, where it was sorted into payroll envelopes and packed into two steel cashboxes. At about three o'clock in the afternoon, when this task was finished, the boxes were collected from the office by Frederick Parmenter, the company paymaster and an armed guard, Alessandro Berardelli.

As Parmenter and Berardelli walked towards the factory, each carrying one of the boxes, they passed two men wearing dark clothes and caps leaning against a fence. One of them, who seemed to know Berardelli, reached out as if to touch him. Suddenly shots rang out. The first bullet hit Berardelli in the abdomen, severing the artery to the heart. His attacker was seen to bend and pick up the guard's discarded gun. The other robber fired a shot that hit Parmenter; he dropped the box he was carrying and staggered away across the road. Instead of making off with the money, as he could easily have done, the second gunman followed Parmenter, bent down and shot him again. The two robbers then returned to Berardelli, now on his hands and knees and begging for his life. After firing three more shots into him they left the guard dead on the road.

A seven-seater blue Buick car containing two more men now pulled up. (It had been seen earlier in the day cruising around the district.) The gunmen seized the money boxes, threw them into the car and leapt in after them, as did a third man who had been hiding behind a pile of bricks. The car sped out of town, a shotgun poking from its rear window. At a railway crossing one of the men waved a pistol and ordered the gate to be raised. Strips of rubber with nails in them were thrown from the car to puncture the tyres of pursuing vehicles.

The Buick disappeared into thickly wooded country. Two days later it was found abandoned in woods. Leading away from the scene were the tracks of a smaller car.

The day after the Braintree robbery, in a seemingly unconnected matter, the Bridgewater police were asked by the immigration authorities to find out why an Italian anarchist Ferrucio Coacci had failed to appear at a deportation hearing. When an officer went to his house, he found Coacci packing a trunk, apparently about to leave. The story he had told the authorities about his wife being ill proved to be a fabrication and he was arrested.

Tyre tracks were found inside a shed in Coacci's garden resembling those of a Buick car. The house was less than 2 miles from the wood where the abandoned car had been found, and Chief Stewart jumped to the conclusion that Coacci had been preparing to leave with the proceeds of the Braintree robbery. (In fact, the contents of his car turned out to have nothing to do with the robbery.) Coacci shared his house with another anarchist, Mike Boda, formerly Mario Buda. Learning that Boda's Overland car had been towed to a garage in Cochesett for repair, the police instructed the garage proprietor, a Mr Johnson, to call them when anyone came to pick up the vehicle.

On the evening of 5 May Boda and yet another anarchist, Riccardo Orciani, arrived at the garage on a motorcycle and sidecar. At the same time Sacco and Vanzetti turned up on foot. When asked for the car, Mr Johnson tried to delay the men by pointing out that the car's licence plates were out of date, while his wife went next door and phoned the police. Apparently realising what was going on, Boda and Orciani made off on their motorcycle, while Sacco and Vanzetti walked away. (Orciani, who was arrested later, was released when he was able to establish alibis for both the Bridgewater and the Braintree robberies. Boda was never arrested.)

Not long after, police found Sacco and Vanzetti riding on a trolley car. Vanzetti was searched and found to be carrying in his hip pocket a loaded .38 revolver of the type normally carried by the murdered guard and four 12-gauge shotgun shells. At the police station Sacco was found to have a fully loaded Colt .32 automatic tucked in the front of his waistband and twenty-three extra cartridges in his pockets. He was also in possession of the draft of a handbill for an anarchist meeting at which Vanzetti was to be the main speaker.

That night, when asked why they had gone to the garage and why they were carrying weapons, Sacco and Vanzetti told what turned out to be a pack of lies. They also denied knowing Boda and Coacci, despite the fact that the four men had long been friends and comrades. The next day the two men were questioned by the District Attorney, Frederick Katzmann. Asked where he had been on the day of the Braintree robbery, Sacco replied that he had been at work, a story that he was to change later. He also claimed never to have been in Braintree; in fact he had worked there three years before under an assumed name. Vanzetti claimed that on the day of the robbery he had been selling fish in Plymouth, some 25 miles away. During the course of the day around thirty witnesses to the two robberies were brought to the police station to see whether they could identify the arrested men.

Next day, Sacco and Vanzetti pleaded guilty to a charge of carrying concealed weapons. When further evidence came to light, however, they were charged with the armed robbery and murders at South Braintree. Nevertheless, it was only Vanzetti who was charged with the attempted robbery at Bridgewater after Sacco's alibi for that day had been corroborated.

Who were these two young men who were so shortly to burst onto the world stage?

SACCO AND VANZETTI

In 1908 the sixteen-year-old Nicola (born Ferdinando) Sacco and his elder brother Sabino had emigrated to the United States and settled in Massachusetts, Sabino returning to Italy the following year. In 1912 Sacco married an Italian girl, Rosina, by whom he was to have a son the following year and a daughter born in 1920 after his arrest. In 1913 Sacco started attending anarchist meetings and, like Vanzetti, contributed to and raised funds for the anarchist journal *Cronaca sovversiva*. At the time of his arrest Sacco was in steady employment as a shoe trimmer (or edger) in a local factory. He was twenty-nine years old.

The twenty-year-old Bartolomeo Vanzetti's history was much the same. A pastry shop worker from Piedmont, Vanzetti had also emigrated to the United States in 1908 following the death of his mother after a long illness. Nine years later he applied for US citizenship. It was at about this time that he met Sacco at an anarchist meeting. Shortly after, along with sixty or so other Italian anarchists, the two men left for Mexico under assumed names in order to avoid conscription for the war in Europe, against which they had conscientious objections. One member of this party was later to become the bomber who blew himself up outside the home of the US Attorney General.

Once the armistice had been declared in 1918 Sacco and Vanzetti returned to America. Vanzetti, who up to then had had a variety of labouring jobs, acquired a handcart from which he sold fish. (He described himself as a fish peddler.) At the time of his arrest he was aged thirty-two.

THE VANZETTI TRIAL

Vanzetti's first trial – for the attempted robbery at Bridgewater – took place in the summer of 1920. The prosecution case rested on three legs: eye-witnesses who identified the defendant as 'the shotgun bandit';

evidence of his possession of shotgun shells at the time of his arrest on the trolley car; and the many indisputable lies that he told the police after his arrest. In his defence, some of Vanzetti's close friends gave evidence that he was selling eels on the day of the robbery. (Eating eels is an Italian Christmas Eve tradition.) They were not believed. Most damning of all, however, was the failure of the accused to give evidence on his own behalf. (Years later, Vanzetti was to complain that he had been persuaded against doing so by his lawyer for fear of his radical background coming to light.)

With such strong evidence of guilt it is not surprising that Vanzetti was convicted of assault with intent to rob.[3] Contrary to local practice and notwithstanding his good character, he was given the maximum sentence of ten to fifteen years. Despite some inconsistencies in the identification evidence he did not appeal against conviction or sentence, and the proceedings aroused little public interest at the time.

Shortly afterwards, in apparent revenge for the decision to prosecute Sacco and Vanzetti, a horse-and-buggy bomb exploded outside the offices of the bankers J.P. Morgan in New York, killing thirty-three people, injuring hundreds more and causing extensive damage to property.

DEDHAM COURT HOUSE

The trial of Sacco and Vanzetti for the Braintree robbery and murders began under heavy guard on 31 May 1921 at Dedham, a quiet residential suburb of Boston. The presiding Judge, Webster Thayer, and prosecuting counsel, Frederick Katzmann, were the same as for Vanzetti's earlier trial.

A radical attorney, Fred H. Moore from California, was instructed for the defence by the anarchist newspaper editor Carlo Tresca; it was a disaster for his clients. Moore's tactics throughout were thoroughly unscrupulous. As his assistant Eugene Lyons was to write later, 'Moore had no conscience once he decided his client was innocent. He would stop at nothing, frame evidence, suborn witnesses, have his people work on witnesses who had seen the wrong things – I pity anyone he went after.'[4] Nor was Moore a good prosecutor; his lack of preparation of his witnesses resulted in their being easily discredited by the able Katzmann. In the words of Felix Frankfurter, Moore was 'a factor of irritation and not of appeasement . . . In opinion, as well as in fact, he was an outsider. Unfamiliar with the traditions of the Massachusetts bench, not even a member of the Massachusetts bar, the characteristics of Judge Thayer unknown to him, Fred H. Moore found neither professional nor personal sympathies between himself and the Judge.' Most important of all, his decision to politicise the trial was controversial and, ultimately, self-defeating.[5]

On 14 July, after a trial lasting nearly seven weeks and involving fifty-nine Commonwealth, that is to say prosecution, witnesses and ninety-nine defence witnesses, both accused were found guilty of robbery and murder in the first degree. But this was only the beginning.

SIX YEARS OF APPEALS

Over the next couple of years the defence was to make eight motions for a new trial on such grounds as an alleged prejudicial remark by a juror, a new witness, the retraction of a witness's statement and fresh forensic evidence. Accusations of prejudice were made against the Judge and the District Attorney; it was even suggested that there had been a conspiracy between the prosecution and the Department of Justice to convict the accused. Under Massachusetts law such motions had to be heard by the trial Judge. Webster Thayer denied them all.

Sacco, who, like Vanzetti at a different time, was for a period committed by his own counsel to a hospital for the criminally insane, now dismissed Moore as his counsel, accusing him of using the trial as an 'instrument of infamous speculation', specifically that he was milking the defence fund for his fees. He was replaced by a respected Boston lawyer.

In May 1926 the Supreme Court of Massachusetts rejected appeals against all of Judge Thayer's rulings. It is important to note that this was not a retrial; the appeal court could intervene only if the Judge's rulings were vitiated by errors of law or abuse of discretion. This has sometimes been portrayed as devaluing the decision of the appeal court, but it should be stressed that their findings necessarily implied that the Judge's decisions were, not only legally correct, but also within the bounds of reasonableness.

THE MADEIROS CONFESSION

A startling development now occurred, not in the courtroom but at Dedham jail, where Sacco and Vanzetti were being held. In November 1925 Celestino F. Madeiros (also Medieros), a young Portuguese immigrant with a bad criminal record, was awaiting the result of an appeal against his conviction and sentence of death for murder. After reading a press report of the Braintree robbery he sent the following rough note, first to the newspaper, and then to Sacco:

> I hear by confess to being in the South Braintree shoe company crime and Sacco and Vanzetti was not in said crime.
> Madeiros

Madeiros had been a member of what was known as the Morelli Gang that had been involved in the stealing of shoes from freight cars, including the property of the Slater & Morrill Company of South Braintree. He claimed that on the day in question he had been part of a group of five, including three Italians, who had taken part in the Braintree robbery. When arrested, Madeiros had a sum of money on him equal to about one-fifth of the South Braintree payroll. The gang's leader, Joe Morelli, looked not unlike Sacco. His brother drove a Buick and another gang member owned a Colt .32 such as had been used in the robbery.

This 'confession' was naturally the subject of a further appeal by the defence. In October 1926 in an opinion that ran to some 25,000 words, Judge Thayer rejected the motion for a fresh trial. Statements from a 'thief, a robber and a liar' with nothing to lose, he said, had to be examined with the greatest care. Madeiros seemed to him strangely ignorant of matters that a participant in the robbery would be expected to know, he had refused to give information about the other members of the gang and his story was inherently improbable. Once again, the Supreme Court of Massachusetts reviewed Thayer's judgment and declined to upset it.

The mandatory sentence of death by electrocution was passed on Sacco and Vanzetti on 27 April 1927. In court both continued to maintain their innocence, Vanzetti declaring,

> I am suffering because I am a radical and indeed I am a radical; I have suffered because I was an Italian, and indeed I am an Italian; I have suffered more for my family and for my beloved than for myself; but I am so convinced to be right that if you could execute me two times, and if I could be reborn two other times, I would live again to do what I have done already.

A worldwide storm of protest followed.

THE LOWELL COMMITTEE

A month after sentence had been passed, Vanzetti petitioned the Governor of Massachusetts, Alvan T. Fuller, for clemency. Sacco refused to sign the petition, but the Governor decided to treat it as if he had.

Fuller took his duties seriously and, with the assistance of his legal counsel, Joseph Wiggin, interviewed Vanzetti, Madeiros and many others involved. As a result, he set up an Advisory Committee consisting of A.L. Lowell, President of Harvard University, former Judge Robert Grant and Samuel W. Stratton, President of Massachusetts Institute of Technology. The Lowell Committee, as it came to be called, interviewed 102 witnesses in addition to those who had given evidence at the trial. Two months later the Committee reported to Governor Fuller that in its opinion

'Sacco was guilty beyond reasonable doubt' and that 'on the whole, we are of opinion that Vanzetti also was guilty beyond reasonable doubt'.[6] (The qualification 'on the whole' was later explained by Lowell as indicating 'a putting together of circumstances no one of which alone would be conclusive'.[7])

On 3 August Governor Fuller, who, it will be remembered, had also carried out his own investigation, announced that he found 'no sufficient justification for executive intervention. I believe with the jury, that these men, Sacco and Vanzetti, were guilty, and that they had a fair trial.'

The accused now applied to the Supreme Court of Massachusetts for a writ of error, alleging judicial prejudice and errors of fact and law. It was too late; the motion had been filed more than a year after the verdict and was out of time. The following day, in a desperate attempt to delay proceedings, applications were made to a Supreme Court Justice, to a Judge of a circuit court of appeals and to a circuit Judge. All declined to intervene.

Sacco and Vanzetti went to the electric chair on 23 August 1927. Sacco's last words were:

[In Italian] Long live anarchy! [Then, quietly in English] Farewell my wife and child and all my friends. [Looking at the witnesses] Good evening, gentlemen.[8]

Vanzetti said,

I wish to say to you that I am innocent. I have never done a crime, some sins, but never any crime. I thank you for everything you have done for me. I am innocent of all crime, not only this one, but of all, of all. I am an innocent man.[9]

Madeiros, who had also lost his appeal, had been executed earlier the same day.

Some 8,000 people followed the anarchists' funeral procession. At the funeral parlour a floral tribute proclaimed, 'Aspettando l'ora di vendetta' (Awaiting the hour of vengeance). Worldwide protests followed.[10] In England crowds sang 'The Red Flag' outside Buckingham Palace. Demonstrations in the Weimar Republic resulted in the deaths of six people. Six months later, the executioner's house was bombed. Four years on Judge Thayer's home suffered the same fate, and his wife was injured. He moved to his club in Boston, where he died seven months later. Few men have fought as tenaciously as Sacco and Vanzetti to establish their innocence, but were they in fact innocent or guilty?

At the trial the prosecution's case had been that Sacco had fired the bullet from a Colt automatic that had killed Berardelli, while Vanzetti remained in the car, and that some other person unknown had shot

Parmenter. The evidence for this was of three broad categories: from eyewitnesses who placed the accused at the scene of the crime; expert testimony linking the crime to the pistols found on the accused at the time of their arrest; and evidence of what Massachusetts law described as 'consciousness of guilt'.

THE EYEWITNESSES

Seven witnesses gave evidence to the effect that Sacco was in or near Braintree at the time of the crime; some of them said he resembled one of the robbers. One witness described him as a 'dead image', but he only saw the attack from a second-floor window (presumably first floor in British usage). No witness placed Vanzetti near the crime scene, but two identified him as being in the getaway car and two said that he was in the vicinity of the town that morning. All the identifications were made without the benefit of a formal identity parade. For the defence, five witnesses swore that Vanzetti had been in Plymouth selling fish on the day of the robbery and seven claimed that they had seen Sacco at the restaurant in Boston. Before the shooting Berardelli's murderer was seen to be wearing a dark cap of a salt and pepper design, but it was not on him when he fled the crime. Sacco accepted that a cap picked up by a witness at the scene of the crime looked like one he had owned and when he tried it on in court it fitted. However, the prosecution placed little reliance on the cap and the Lowell Committee agreed with them.

Young and Kaiser's careful analysis of the trial casts serious doubt on the identification evidence and points to the difficulties in relying solely on such evidence. For its part the Lowell Committee agreed that the identification evidence alone was insufficient to convict the two defendants, but observed that it was only part of the prosecution case.

One of the arresting officers told how, after his arrest, Vanzetti had 'put his hand in his hip pocket and I says, "Keep your hands on your lap, or you will be sorry"'. At the police station a revolver was found in the arrested man's hip pocket. When the officer gave evidence in court, Vanzetti protested, 'You are a liar.' Nevertheless, Judge Thayer later placed some importance on this incident.

The problem is that the principal witness to this seemingly significant incident had made no mention of it when giving evidence at Vanzetti's earlier trial, nor had he done so when giving evidence before the Sacco and Vanzetti grand jury. And another officer appears to have changed his account to accord with the 'threatening gesture' story. It is difficult to resist the conclusion that, for whatever reason, the witness had 'embroidered' his evidence on this point.

GUNS AND BULLETS

Forensic evidence had established that Berardelli had been killed by a bullet from a Colt automatic. Judge Thayer had over-egged the pudding by instructing the jury that there was evidence that 'it was [Sacco's] pistol that fired the bullet that caused the death of Berardelli'. This was not strictly accurate; all that the (somewhat in-)expert witness for the prosecution had said was that the condition of the bullet was 'consistent with' being fired from that pistol – which means no more than 'it could have been'. (Two defence experts testified otherwise.) Over two years later, the prosecution witness, who by then had fallen out with Katzmann over the payment of his bill,[11] claimed that he had deliberately given his evidence in an ambiguous way at the request of the District Attorney. After interviewing everyone concerned, the Lowell Committee concluded that there was no good ground to suppose that the witness's answer was designed to mislead the jury.

The court heard that the bullet that killed Berardelli was of a type no longer manufactured. The cartridges found in Sacco's pockets at the time of his arrest were of the same obsolete type.

More advanced tests conducted in 1961 concluded that the fatal bullet had in fact been fired from Sacco's gun, and this was confirmed by yet more tests in 1983.[12] Those convinced of Sacco's innocence have drawn the conclusion that the fatal bullet must have been substituted by someone anxious to secure a conviction, but this theory was rejected by the Lowell Committee as being unsupported by any credible evidence. 'Such an accusation,' the committee concluded, 'devoid of proof, may be dismissed without further comment . . .'. But what about the weapons found on the accused at the time of their arrest?

Vanzetti had had a .38 revolver on him that resembled the gun normally carried by the guard Berardelli and that had apparently been picked up by one of the robbers. He claimed that he had bought it for fear of hold-ups and called the seller to confirm the purchase, but he was unable to tell the court how many chambers the gun contained. Furthermore, the only ammunition he had for it was in the gun. There was evidence that the hammer of the guard's gun had been repaired shortly before the killings and the hammer of Vanzetti's revolver showed signs of having been repaired. Finally, Vanzetti had lied to the police about how much he had paid for the weapon and where the bullets had come from and he had been unable to give any explanation for these untruths.

CONSCIOUSNESS OF GUILT

By far the most damaging evidence against the defendants, however, was what was known to Massachussetts law as 'consciousness of guilt'. Judge

Thayer correctly instructed the jury that 'intentional false statements, deception and concealment of truth are evidences of consciousness of guilt and can be used against a defendant when and only when, such consciousness relates to the crime charged in the indictment'. The fact that both defendants gave totally untruthful answers to numerous questions from the police and the District Attorney was undisputed. The only question was, why did they do so?

Sacco's and Vanzetti's explanation for their lack of frankness turned on an event that occurred in New York the day before the crime. Andrea Salsedo, an anarchist comrade of Boda, Sacco and Vanzetti, either had jumped or, as some of his comrades would have had it, been pushed out of a window on the fourteenth floor of the offices of the Department of Justice, where he was being held for questioning about the bombing atrocities. Following this incident they had been warned to 'hide the literature and notify the friends against the federal police'. Sacco and Vanzetti claimed that they had gone to the garage to get Boda's car for this purpose. They had lied to the police, they said, because they assumed that their arrest was in connection with their anarchist activities, rather than with a charge of robbery and murder.

Such an explanation might possibly have accounted for the two men's lies on the night of their arrest, when the police questioning had been directed principally at their political beliefs. (Remember that it was the police hypothesis that Braintree had been a robbery designed to provide funds for anarchism.) The same could not be said of the questioning on the following day. Not only were numerous witnesses to the two robberies paraded before the arrested men, but the District Attorney's questions were clearly directed at the Braintree crimes. And there was another way in which Sacco's and Vanzetti's explanation did not stand up. As the Lowell Committee observed, 'The difficulty with this excuse is that it by no means explains all their falsehoods, some of which had no connection whatever with their being Reds, but did have a very close connection with the crime at South Braintree.' This was particularly true of Sacco's first untruthful alibi.

THE ALIBIS

On the day after his arrest, Sacco had told Katzmann – more than once and perfectly clearly – that he had been at work on the day of the robbery and had read about it in the paper the day after it had taken place. In court he told a completely different story: he had taken the day of the robbery off work in order to go to Boston (some 40 minutes away by train) to obtain a passport from the Italian consulate because his mother had died and his father had written urging him to return home. Arriving in Boston at 9.35 that morning, he had met a friend and had lunch with him. At the consulate at two o'clock in the afternoon, he was refused a passport on the ground that the photograph he had brought with him was too large. This took some 10 minutes. He had then bought some groceries and gone to a restaurant for a coffee, where he saw two more friends. He left at about four o'clock, getting home some two hours later. No documentary evidence was produced to establish the visit to the consulate, but seven defence witnesses testified that they had seen him at the restaurant. (One of these was to admit later that he had perjured himself at the request of the anarchist group to which he belonged.) The passport – a one-way passport for Sacco, his wife and daughter – was eventually obtained the day before his arrest. It was not to be used.

Vanzetti gave evidence to the court that he had been selling fish in Plymouth at the time of the crime and called six witnesses to support this, most of them friends of his. The prosecution suggested that they had been confused about the date.

The jury rejected the alibis of both men and the Lowell Committee agreed with them. Of Vanzetti's evidence they wrote:

The alibi of Vanzetti is decidedly weak. One of the witnesses, Rosen, seems to the Committee to have been shown by the cross-examination to be lying at the trial; another, Mrs Brini, had sworn to an alibi for him in the Bridgewater case, and two more of the witnesses did not seem certain of the date until they had talked it over.[13]

AND THE MADEIROS CONFESSION?

But what about the Madeiros confession that Judge Theyer had dismissed so contemptuously? Frankfurter was scathing in his views:

Let us compare the two hypotheses. The Morelli theory accounts for all members of the Braintree murder gang; the Sacco–Vanzetti theory for only two, for it is conceded that, if Madeiros was there, Sacco and Vanzetti were not. The Morelli theory accounts for all the bullets found in the dead men; the Sacco–Vanzetti theory for only one out of six. The Morelli explanation settles the motive, for the Morelli gang were criminals desperately in need of money for legal expenses pending their trial for felonies, whereas the Sacco–Vanzetti theory is unsupported by any motive. Moreover, Madeiros's possession of $2,800 accounts for his share of the booty, whereas not a penny has ever been traced to anybody or accounted for on the Sacco–Vanzetti theory. The Morelli story is not subject to the absurd premise that professional holdup men who stole automobiles at will and who had recently made a haul of nearly $16,000 would devote an evening, as did Sacco and Vanzetti the night of their arrest, to riding around on suburban street cars to borrow a friend's six-year-old Overland. The character of the Morelli gang fits the opinion of police investigators and the inherent facts of the situation, which tended to prove that the crime was the work of professionals, whereas the past character and record of Sacco and Vanzetti have always made it inherently incredible that they should spontaneously become perpetrators of a bold murder, executed with the utmost expertness. A good mechanic, regularly employed at his trade, but away from work on a particular day which is clearly accounted for, and a dreamy fish peddler, openly engaged in political propaganda, neither do nor can suddenly commit an isolated job of highly professional banditry.[14]

Frankfurter dismissed Judge Thayer's written opinion on the confession as 'a farrago of misquotations, misrepresentations, suppressions, and mutilations . . . literally honeycombed with demonstrable errors, and a spirit alien to judicial utterance permeates the whole'.[15] Not everyone agreed: John H. Wigmore, Dean of Northwestern University Law School, for example, argued that Frankfurter had misstated his first point and had taken advantage of a trivial slip in his second.[16]

After an exhaustive examination of the evidence, including a visit to Madeiros in prison, the Lowell Committee came down in favour of Judge Theyer's view. It had no time for the argument that the crime demonstrated a 'professionalism' that the prisoners lacked: 'To the Committee both this crime and the one at Bridgewater do not seem to bear the marks of professionals, but of men inexpert in such crimes.' Governor Fuller took a similar view, adding: 'I give no weight to the Madeiros confession . . . In his testimony to me he could not recall the details or describe the neighborhood . . . I am not impressed with his knowledge of the South Braintree murders.'[17]

THE PREJUDICE OF THE TIME

Perhaps the most problematic criticism of the trial was that it had been conducted against a background of public prejudice against people of the defendants' nationality and political views, a background that the prosecution did its best to emphasise. Frankfurter claimed: 'By systematic exploitation of the defendants' alien blood, their imperfect knowledge of English, their unpopular social views, and their opposition to the war, the District Attorney invoked against them a riot of political passion and patriotic sentiment.' Harvard professor, Arthur Schlesinger put it this way:

It must be remembered that Sacco and Vanzetti were immigrants, they were poor, they were atheists, they were draft dodgers, they were anarchists. They were exactly the kind of person who 100% Americans felt might be guilty of anything. And they were anarchists who believed, as many anarchists did, in violence as a way of remedying what they regarded as the injustices of society.

The argument of a prejudicial atmosphere is always a difficult one; if upheld, it would mean that people charged with committing crimes that are repugnant to a majority of people could never be tried. The same cannot be said of the specific allegations of prejudice made against the Judge, the jury and the prosecuting attorney.

WAS JUDGE THEYER PREJUDICED?

Born in 1857, Webster Thayer was a graduate of Dartmouth College and a former newspaperman. He was appointed a Judge of the Superior Court of Massachusetts in 1917 and was aged sixty-three at the time of the Braintree trial. He is said to have asked to preside over that case.

The principal accusation against Judge Thayer was that he had improperly allowed prejudicial evidence of the defendants' radical opinions to be introduced into the case. This is a serious criticism that, if true, would have been good reason for quashing the conviction; however, it was the complete opposite of the truth. Before the trial began Thayer had called counsel together and told them he could see no reason why the defendants' radicalism should be mentioned. When the prisoners' political views were introduced at the trial, it was by Vanzetti himself while giving evidence. The Lowell Committee had its own view as to why the defence adopted this tactic:

> There had been presented by the Government a certain amount of evidence of identification, and other circumstances tending to connect the prisoners with the murder, of such a character that – together with their being armed to the teeth and the falsehoods they stated when arrested – would in the case of New England Yankees, almost certainly have resulted in a verdict of murder in the first degree, a result which the evidence for the alibis was not likely to overcome. Under these circumstances it seemed necessary to the defendants' counsel to meet the inferences to be drawn from these falsehoods by attributing them to a cause other than consciousness of guilt of the South Braintree murder.

In other words, it was the defence that, realising the strength of the prosecution case, had introduced evidence of their clients' anarchist beliefs in an attempt to explain their conduct. Once the issue of their anarchism had been introduced, it is difficult to criticise the prosecutor for making what use he could of it. While one can perhaps argue about the degree of latitude permitted to the prosecutor, this criticism of the Judge is without foundation.

Judge Thayer was also criticised for having made a number of ill-judged comments out of court that betrayed prejudice against the defendants. After looking into these in some depth, the Lowell Committee was 'forced to conclude that the Judge was indiscreet in conversation with outsiders during the trial. He ought not to have talked about the case off the bench, and doing so was a grave breach of official decorum. But we do not believe that he used some of the expressions attributed to him, and we think that there is exaggeration in what the persons to whom he spoke remember.' In any event, it was not the Judge's views or even his comments in private to friends that counted, but his conduct of the trial.

There are no obvious signs of bias in the Judge's charge to the jury. Viewed through twenty-first-century spectacles, the language appears orotund, even overblown at some points, but Massachusetts law prevented Judge Thayer from giving any lead to the jury (as an English judge would be permitted to do), and such guidance as he did give was peppered with proper warnings against prejudice. Apparently unable to find fault in what the Judge said in court, the defence claimed that he had resorted to facial gestures to indicate his disbelief of the defence. If he did, the jury noticed nothing of the kind. Governor Fuller was later to write of the Judge, 'I see no evidence of prejudice in his conduct of the trial. That he had an opinion as to the guilt or innocence of the accused after hearing the evidence, is natural and inevitable.' This was hardly surprising when the associate counsel for the defendants, Jeremiah J. McAnarney, had said in his closing argument at the trial, 'I want to say on behalf of these men – I say it to those men and to their friends – that they have had every opportunity here, and that they have had every patience, every consideration.'[18] And after the jury had retired, Fred Moore himself had told Judge Thayer that, no matter what they might decide, no one could say that the defendants had not had a fair trial.

WERE THE 'MEN OF NORFOLK' PREJUDICED?

The issues of the composition and impartiality of the jury were also raised during the course of Sacco's and Vanzetti's many appeals. What had happened was that, after the panel of jurymen had been exhausted in the normal process of jury selection, the Sheriff's deputies were instructed by the Judge to obtain more. The defence later suggested that the additional jurymen had been chosen by the Sheriff's officers as people predisposed to convict. There is no evidence of this whatever: Judge Thayer upheld the deputies' selection, and the composition of the jury had been subject at the trial to the usual right of challenge by the defence. It is little wonder that the Supreme Judicial Court found nothing wrong in principle on this point. The members of the Lowell Committee, who talked with all the available members of the jury, reported that they seemed to them 'an unusually intelligent and independent body of men, and withal representative'.

The District Attorney was attacked for having made in the course of his closing address to the jury a reference calculated improperly to appeal to their local patriotism when faced with two alien defendants, the so-called Men of Norfolk remark. There is no doubt that Katzmann sought to use every weapon in his forensic armoury in order to secure the conviction of men he believed guilty of two brutal murders. But what he said to the jury in his closing statement is difficult to fault:

> A jury must decide the facts judicially . . . Leave any consideration of sympathy for Mrs Berardelli or sympathy for Mrs Parmenter out of the case . . . The question is one of fact, gentlemen, arrived at under the rules of law . . . You are the consultants here, gentlemen, the twelve of you, and the parties come to you and ask you to find what the truth is on the two issues of guilt or innocence. Gentlemen of the jury, do your duty. Do it like men. Stand together you men of Norfolk.[19]

Norfolk was the county from which the jury had been drawn.

After the case was over, one of the jurymen confirmed, 'The so-called radicalism of the defendants played absolutely no part in the verdict.'

'A STRANGER IN A FOREIGN COUNTRY'

Even before it was over the Sacco–Vanzetti case had become an icon of the left. No small part of the reason for this was the power of the two men's writings, which can still move the reader over three-quarters of a century later. Take, for example, what might be called the inarticulate eloquence of Sacco's explanation at his trial for his flight to Mexico:

> What is war? The war is not shoots like Abraham Lincoln's and Abe Jefferson, to fight for the free-country, for the better education, to give chance to any other peoples, not the white people but the black and the others, because they believe and know they are mens like the rest, but they are war for the great millionaire. No war for the civilization of men.[20]

Or consider Vanzetti's more polished words in his letter to Governor Fuller shortly before his execution:

> I am an Italian, a stranger in a foreign country, and my witnesses are the same kind of people. I am accused and convicted on the testimony of mostly American witnesses. Everything is against me – my race, my opinions, and my humble occupation. I did not commit either of these crimes, and yet how am I ever going to show it if I and all my witnesses are not believed, merely because the police want to convict somebody, and get respectable Americans to testify against us? I suppose a great many Americans think that it is all right to stretch the truth a little to convict an anarchist; but I don't think they would think so if they were in my place.

Vanzetti's anti-establishment feeling burned strongly. In a letter from prison to a fellow anarchist, after describing the atrocities he believed the 'oppressors' had inflicted upon the 'oppressed', he declared, 'I will ask for revenge – I will tell that I will die gladly by the hands of the hanger after having known to have been vindicated. I mean "eye for an eye, ear for an ear", and even more since to win it is necessary that 100 enemies fall to each of us.' The idea of revenge features strongly in Vanzetti's writings.

A firm belief in the justice of your cause is, of course, no more proof of guilt than of innocence, but the cause that Sacco and Vanzetti supported was not a charity or even an ordinary political party; it was a movement that, as they were fully aware, was dedicated to what the attorney Montgomery called 'revolution and the destruction of America', its chosen instruments the bullet and the bomb.

Nor were the accused the simple sober citizens they claimed to be. On the twenty-seventh day of the trial the defence stipulated (without giving reasons) that the jury should ignore any evidence to the effect that Sacco or Vanzetti were 'peaceful and law abiding citizens'. Exactly what lay behind this admission is still disputed, but there certainly must have been some cause. After his clients' executions, their counsel Fred Moore was to tell the writer Upton Sinclair that on the day of their arrest the two men had gone to Bridgewater to get Boda's car to collect dynamite from comrades; for what purpose we can only imagine. On that day both were armed to the teeth with lethal weapons and ammunition for which they could give no good explanation. Sacco claimed that he had taken his pistol for shooting in the woods and that, following an argument, he had completely forgotten that he was carrying spare cartridges and a loaded gun stuffed in his waistband. (This is an unlikely story, as anyone who has held such a weapon will know.) Vanzetti claimed that he carried a revolver, which he had bought under an assumed name, 'because it was a very bad time, and I like to have a revolver for self-defence'. Is it not more likely that these murderous weapons were carried for use against the authorities or anyone else who attempted to frustrate their plans? While the two young anarchists no doubt saw themselves as humanitarians, they were at the time of their arrest equipped for and prepared to use violence, even lethal violence, against anyone who got in their way.

Sacco and Vanzetti have been consistently portrayed as underdogs ground down by the subservient judiciary of a capitalist state. In fact, they were represented by expensive lawyers paid for out of a large fighting fund, supported in part by the Soviet Union. Their trial was no swift rush to judgment; it lasted some two and a half months (a long time in those days) and was followed over the next six years by countless appeals to every available judicial body, as well as a clemency review by a governor and a distinguished commission. It is true that the commission's chairman has been anathematised by the noted attorney and academic Alan Derschowitz as 'an anti-Italian bigot and an avowed racist',[21] but whatever the character of the president of Harvard University, the idea of a retired judge and the president of MIT both rolling over at his behest is hard to swallow. In any event, Lowell was later to tell a friend that he had begun the investigation convinced of the anarchists' innocence. In 1936, four years after he had retired from Harvard, he still stood by his committee's conclusions.

WAS THE TRIAL FAIR?

It may be doubted whether a legal system can ever be described as humane that allows a man to be incarcerated for some seven years in the expectation of an unpleasant death. (Governor Fuller concluded that the 'inexcusable delay' in this case was caused by 'the persistent, determined efforts of an attorney of extraordinary versatility and industry, the judge's illness, the election efforts of three District Attorneys, and dilatoriness on the part of most of those concerned'.) Of the many objections taken to the fairness of the trial, however, the only one that warrants serious examination is the extraordinary provision of Massachusetts law whereby the trial Judge was obliged to rule on objections to his own impartiality.

The most fundamental right of a person accused of a crime is to a fair trial before an independent and impartial tribunal. It is manifest nonsense to expect anyone to rule impartially on an allegation that he himself lacked impartiality. The fact that Judge Thayer's ruling on this point was subject to appeal did not fully remedy that fault since the appellate court was not empowered to substitute their judgment for his. To this extent, therefore, and only to this extent, the trial of Sacco and Vanzetti was defective. But this is a technical point; it is impossible to believe that any of those who did review the issue of the Judge's impartiality (the appellate court, the governor and the review committee) would have kept quiet if they had found reason to suspect Theyer's impartiality. The fact is that none of them expressed the slightest qualms; quite the contrary.

The most trenchant criticisms of the trial had come from the pen of Felix Frankfurter, who rose, more than a decade after the deaths of Sacco and Vanzetti, to become one of the most respected Justices of the US Supreme Court.[22] What Frankfurter did not reveal in his article was that he had been a leading, if unofficial, adviser to the defence of Sacco and Vanzetti – which rather mars any claim of his to disinterestedness in that case. (Could the great man's apparent lack of candour have had anything to do with the fact that he himself had arrived in America a twelve-year-old immigrant with no English?)

Judge Thayer may or may not have been a brilliant trial judge but he has not been proved to be a prejudiced one. At bottom, this was a case where no single piece of prosecution evidence established the defendants' guilt to the high degree required in criminal cases. The jury's decision to convict must have been based on the aggregate or cumulative effect of the evidence it had heard. Such decisions, while neither improper nor uncommon, are often controversial. The verdict could very easily have gone the other way if the defendants had been represented by a competent lawyer prepared to treat the case as an ordinary criminal trial, instead of an incompetent lawyer who sought to convert it into a revolutionary *cause célèbre*. But was there another reason why these two men went to their deaths?

THE BLOOD OF THE MARTYRS

Brutal murderers or innocent victims? We are unlikely ever to know for sure. The case against Sacco was so strong that, during the trial, his attorney suggested that he should plead guilty and Vanzetti not guilty.[23] Vanzetti rejected the suggestion, saying, 'Save Nick. He have the wife and child.' In 1941, just two years before his assassination, Carlo Tresca, that great icon of the left, is said to have told a communist friend, 'Sacco was guilty, but Vanzetti was not.'[24] And in 1982, Francis Russell, the author of a book on the trial, received a letter from the son of Giovanni Gamberi, one of four members of the Sacco–Vanzetti defence group and a member of *Il Gruppo Autonomo*, the anarchist cell of which Sacco, Vanzetti, Coacci and Boda were all members. It claimed that '[e]veryone [in the Boston anarchist circle] knew that Sacco was guilty and that Vanzetti was innocent, as far as the actual participation in the killing'. According to the same source, the defence group had rejected an offer of deportation in favour of a trial because it was thought likely to give greater publicity to the anarchist cause.[25] And this may be at the heart of the matter.

From childhood, Vanzetti had been familiar with the adage of the early Christian writer Tertullian that the blood of the martyrs is the seed of the Church. Standing on the brink of eternity, the condemned man said to a reporter,

> If it had not been for these things, I might have lived out my life talking at street corners to scorning men. I might have died, unmarked, unknown, a failure. Now we are not a failure. This is our career and our triumph. Never in our full life could we hope to do such work for tolerance, for justice, for man's understanding of man as now we do by accident. Our words, our lives, our pains – nothing! The taking of our lives [– lives of a good shoemaker and a poor fish peddler –] all! That last moment belongs to us – that agony is our triumph.[26]

In their deaths Sacco and Vanzetti may have achieved more for their unpleasant cause than they could ever have hoped to achieve in life.

Notes

Introduction

1. Radically different views have been expressed about how much the criminal process should be weighted in favour of the accused. Voltaire espoused 'that generous Maxim, that 'tis much more Prudence to acquit two Persons, tho' actually guilty, than to pass Sentence of Condemnation on one that is virtuous and innocent' (*Zadig*, 1749). In this country Lord Chief Justice Hale had earlier claimed that 'it is better five guilty persons should escape unpunished than one innocent person should die' (2 Hale PC 290, 1678). The great jurist Sir William Blackstone was later to assert that 'it is better that ten guilty persons escape than one innocent suffer' (*Commentaries*, 2 Bl. Com. c. 27). Sir John Fortescue, chief justice of the Court of King's Bench, put the ratio at 20:1, admittedly in relation to the sentence of execution (*De Laudibus Legum Angliæ*, 1470). The palm, however, must go to that Renaissance man Benjamin Franklyn, who upped the stakes to 100:1 (letter to Benjamin Vaughan, 14 March 1785, in *The Writings of Benjamin Franklin*, ed. Albert H. Smyth (New York, Macmillan, 1906), vol. 9, p. 293). It would be interesting to know on what bases these examples of the felicific calculus were arrived at. (For an uncharacteristic instance of divine flexibility on this point, compare Genesis 18: 20–32.)

Chapter One: The Divine Ruler

1. Originally imposed in ports for the support of the navy, the unpopular ship money was gradually extended to the whole country. It was the poll tax of its day.
2. Quoted in A.S.P. Woodhouse (ed.), *Puritanism and Liberty* (London, J.M. Dent, 1966), p. 53.
3. Formerly, the lowest commissioned rank in the cavalry.
4. Graham Edwards, *The Last Days of Charles I* (Stroud, Sutton Publishing, 1999), p. 59.
5. Robert B. Partridge, *'O Horrable Murder'* (London, Rubicon Press, 1998), p. 39.
6. *Sydney Papers*, ed. R.W. Blencowe (London, J. Murray, 1825), p. 237.
7. C.V. Wedgwood, *The King's Peace, 1637–1641* (4th edn, London, Collins, 1964), p. 72.
8. *Ibid.*, p. 63.
9. Partridge, *'O Horrable Murder'*, p. 53.
10. Geoffrey Robertson (*The Tyrannicide Brief* (London, Chatto & Windus, 2005)) paints a persuasive picture of Cook (who, some years earlier, had offered Strafford assistance with his legal defence) as an embryonic human-rights lawyer.

11. John Rushworth, *Historical Collections,* quoted in Austin Lovill (ed.), *Notable Historical Trials* (London, Folio Society, 1999), p. 107.
12. Despite what C.V. Wedgwood describes as his 'violent royalist prejudice' (*The Trial of Charles I* (2nd edn, London, Collins, 1964), p. 227), the account of the trial that follows is taken, unless otherwise stated, from J.G. Muddiman, *The Trial of King Charles the First,* Notable British Trials (London, William Hodge, 1928).
13. A locket worn round the neck was part of the regalia of the Order of the Garter.
14. Partridge, *'O Horrable Murder',* p. 83.
15. The extracts from the King's speech are from Edwards, *The Last Days of Charles I,* pp. 178 ff.
16. Wedgwood, *The Trial of Charles I,* p. 193.
17. Muddiman, *The Trial of King Charles the First,* p. 231. The King was prevented from tendering this defence in court, and it was published after his death.
18. *State Trials,* vol. 5, pp. 1090, 1127, quoted in Wedgwood, *The King's Peace,* p. 134.
19. Quoted in Muddiman, *The Trial of King Charles the First,* p. 232.
20. The story may be true, but, as Wedgwood remarks, 'When history fails to supply the moment of drama, human invention will often fill the gap' (*The King's Peace,* p. 202). Sir Roger Manley tells a different and more prosaic version. See Edwards, *The Last Days of Charles I.*

Chapter Two: The Diarist

1. Martin Booth, *The Doctor and the Detective: A Life of Sir Arthur Conan Doyle* (London, Hodder & Stoughton, 1997).
2. This and the succeeding quotations from Casement's Congo Report are taken from Arthur Conan Doyle, *The Crime of the Congo* (London, Hutchinson, 1909). See also *The Eyes of Another Race: Roger Casement's Congo Report & 1903 Diary,* ed. Seamas O'Siochain (Dublin and Chester Springs, Pa., University College Dublin Press, 2003).
3. Brian Inglis, *Roger Casement* (Harmondsworth, Penguin, 1973), p. 255.
4. 'Address to the Irish POWS at Limburg, May 15th, 1915', published in Roger Casement, *Objects of an Irish Brigade in the Present War* (1915).
5. H.M. Hyde, *The Trial of Roger Casement* (London, William Hodge, 1960), p. xxvii.
6. In 1908 the Sunday Chronicle published a light article featuring a fictional character of doubtful reputation named Artemus Jones. Despite the fact that he bore no resemblance to the newspaper character, the barrister of the same name sued the paper for libel and won.
7. Hyde, *The Trial of Roger Casement,* p. lxxi.
8. *Ibid.,* p. lxiii.
9. This account of the trial, the evidence and speeches is taken from *ibid.*
10. This strange incident is known, misleadingly, as the Curragh mutiny.
11. A metonym for the office of Lord Chancellor.
12. Inglis, *Roger Casement,* p. 348.
13. Hyde, *The Trial of Roger Casement,* p. cxxxii.
14. Sir Arthur Conan Doyle, *Memories and Adventures* (London, Greenhill Books, 1988).

15. Hyde, *The Trial of Roger Casement*, p. cxxii.
16. *Ibid.*, p. cxiii.
17. A. Hochschild, *King Leopold's Ghost* (London, Macmillan, 1999), p. 287.
18. Hyde, *The Trial of Roger Casement*, p. cxvi.
19. *The Amazon Journal of Roger Casement*, ed. Angus Mitchell (Dublin, Anaconda Editions, 1997).
20. Audrey Giles, *Examination of Casement Diaries*, Report, 8 February 2002.
21. Hyde, *The Trial of Roger Casement*, p. xl.

Chapter Three: The Broadcaster

1. See Mary Kenny, *Germany Calling* (Dublin, New Island, 2003), p. 40.
2. The following account of the trial is based on J.W. Hall (ed.), *The Trial of William Joyce*, Notable British Trials (London, William Hodge, 1946).
3. Rebecca West, *The Meaning of Treason* (London, Phoenix Press, 1982), p. 14.
4. The date on which Joyce's passport expired.
5. West, *The Meaning of Treason*, p. 38.
6. Hall (ed.), *The Trial of William Joyce*.
7. H. Lauterpacht, 'Allegiance, Diplomatic Protection and Criminal Jurisdiction over Aliens', *Cambridge Law Journal*, 9 (1947), 330.
8. Glanville Williams, 'The Correlation of Allegiance and Protection', *Cambridge Law Journal*, 1 (1948), 54.
9. William Joyce, *Twilight over England* (London, Imperial War Museum, 1992).

Chapter Four: The Atom Spies

1. Ronald Radosh and Joyce Milton, *The Rosenberg File: A Search for the Truth* (London, Weidenfeld & Nicolson, 1983).
2. *Ibid.*, p. 98.
3. *Ibid.*, p. 270.
4. Hiss, a former law clerk to the great Supreme Court Justice Oliver Wendell Holmes, had enjoyed a distinguished career in the US government, being at different times Roosevelt's adviser at the Yalta conference and a significant figure in the setting-up of the United Nations. In 1948 he was denounced by the journalist Whittaker Chambers as a Russian spy. Hiss was called before the House Committee on Un-American Activities, where his testimony led to a charge of perjury and a prison sentence of five years. He spent the rest of his life seeking to prove his innocence. Even today, his case is a touchstone of political affiliations in America.
5. A food product congealed with gelatine.
6. Louis Nizer, *The Implosion Conspiracy* (New York, Doubleday, 1973), p. 210.
7. Radosh and Milton, *The Rosenberg File*, p. 339.
8. Nizer, *The Implosion Conspiracy*, p. 395.
9. *United States* v. *Rosenberg*, 195 F. 2d 583 (2d Cir. 1952). For a criticism of the court's acceptance of evidence of the defendants' communism, see 'The Rosenberg Case: Some Reflections on Federal Criminal Law', *Columbia Law Review*, 54 (1954), 219.
10. Douglas worked hard to secure a reputation as the legal champion of the individual, but history (and his somewhat odd later life) has not confirmed it.
11. *Rosenberg et al.* v. *United States* (1953) 346 US 273.

12. See Robert L. Stern, 'The Rosenberg Case in Perspective: Its Present Significance', in *The Supreme Court Historical Society Yearbook* (1990).
13. Radosh and Milton, *The Rosenberg File*, p. 449.
14. Quoted in *ibid.*, p. 160.
15. CBS News, *60 Minutes II*, broadcast 5 December 2001.
16. Not all Greenglass's admissions were favourable to the Rosenbergs. In particular, he claimed to Roberts that he had, at the request of Julius, made the metal clamp that supposedly attached the spy camera to the table.
17. Alan M. Dershowitz, *America on Trial* (New York, Warner Brothers, 2004), p. 323.
18. Radosh and Milton, *The Rosenberg File*, p. 450.
19. A. Feklisov, *The Man behind the Rosenbergs* (New York, Enigma Books, 2004).
20. There are two other interesting snippets in Feklisov's account. First, that all the information he received from Julius was handwritten. And, secondly, that the insecure password phrase was in fact 'I come from Julius' and that it had been ordered 'from the Centre'.
21. The following extracts are taken from N. West, *Venona: The Greatest Secret of the Cold War* (London, HarperCollins, 1988).
22. Ilene Philipson, *Ethel Rosenberg: Beyond the Myths* (New York, Franklin Watts, 1988), p. 318.

Chapter Five: The Maid

1. For this extract from the trial I have used the translation of the Joan of Arc museum, Rouen, and W.S. Scott (ed. and trans.), *The Trial of Joan of Arc* (London, Folio Society, 1956).
2. Régine Pernoud, *Joan of Arc* (London, Macdonald, 1964), p. 125.
3. *Ibid.*, p. 148.
4. *Ibid.*, p. 199.
5. See the verbatim report in Scott, *The Trial of Joan of Arc*, from which the ensuing account of Joan's trial and death is taken.
6. *Ibid.*, p. 84.
7. Pernoud, *Joan of Arc*, p. 216.

Chapter Six: The Starry Messenger

1. Georgio De Santillana, *The Crime of Galileo* (London, Heinemann, 1958), p. 183.
2. Joseph de Maistre, quoted in *ibid.*, p. 205.
3. De Santillana, *The Crime of Galileo*, p. 252.
4. *Ibid.*, p. 289.
5. www.catholic.net/rcc/Periodicals/Issues/GalileoAffair.html.
6. De Santillana comments: 'Urban VIII and his court may be considered much less the oppressors of science than the first casualties of the scientific age.'

Part Three: Introduction

1. *Liversidge v. Anderson* [1942] AC 206, at p. 244.
2. History has a habit of repeating itself. At the time of writing, over 600 suspected Taleban and Al Quaeda prisoners have been held at the American

military base at Camp X-ray in Guantanamo Bay, Cuba, for over three years in highly dubious circumstances. The detainees have been refused access to lawyers, have not been told what charges they will face or when and, in the early stages of their confinement at least, were shackled and hooded. Comparison with the treatment of Lincoln's assassins is compelling.

Chapter Seven: The Scapegoat

1. Dudley Pope, *At Twelve Mr Byng Was Shot* (London, Secker & Warburg, 1962), p. 292.
2. *Ibid.*, p. 35.
3. 'The Blue' referred to the colour of the officer's flag.
4. The Duke of Cumberland was later to characterise this as 'an infamous council of war infected with terrors and void of obedience'.
5. Given in evidence by Captain Gardiner at Byng's courtmartial. This and all other extracts from the trial are taken from *The Trial of the Hon. Admiral Byng at a Court-Martial, Held on Board His Majesty's Ship the St George in Portsmouth Harbour, Tuesday, Dec. 28, 1756* (London, J. Lacy, 1757).
6. Quoted in *ibid.*, appendix XXV.
7. Pope, *At Twelve Mr Byng Was Shot*, app. IV.
8. *Ibid.*, p. 111.
9. *Ibid.*, p. 208.
10. I have used the translation of the Voltaire Society of America.
11. *The Trial of the Hon. Admiral Byng at a Court-Martial, Held on Board His Majesty's Ship the St George in Portsmouth Harbour, Tuesday, Dec. 28, 1756.*
12. Pope, *At Twelve Mr Byng Was Shot*, p. 240.
13. *R* v. *G* [2003] UKHL 50.
14. The Hon. G. French, *The Martyrdom of Admiral Byng* (Glasgow, McLellan, 1961).
15. The good doctor had previously written two pamphlets in support of the Admiral.

Chapter Eight: The Assassins

1. Carl Sandberg, *Abraham Lincoln*, vol. 4, *The War Years* (Boston, Harcourt, Brace and World, 1939), p. 244.
2. Carl Sandberg, *Abraham Lincoln*, vol. 2, *The Prairie Years* (Boston, Harcourt, Brace and World, 1939), p. 103.
3. When asked about their policies, members of the Know-Nothing Party were expected to reply, 'I know nothing'.
4. Sandberg, *Abraham Lincoln*, vol. 4, p. 318.
5. The British equivalent of Secretary of State is Foreign Secretary.
6. One of them, General Wallace, was later to write the famous novel, *Ben Hur: A Tale of the Christ.*
7. For this account of the trial I have used the Surratt House Museum's proceedings (available on their website), which are taken from the original Pittman trial transcripts.
8. *Thomas B. Mudd, son of Richard D. Mudd and great-grandson of Samuel Mudd, deceased* v. *Thomas A White, Secretary of the Army et al.* (2002) US DC Circuit Court of Appeal, 8 November.
9. *Ex parte Milligan* 71 US 2 (1866). The decision has never been repudiated.

10. The state song of Maryland (composed 1861, adopted 1939) still exhorts its citizens to:

> Avenge the patriotic gore
> That flecked the streets of Baltimore,
> And be the battle queen of yore,
> Maryland! My Maryland!

11. Atzerodt's confession may be found in full at the website of the Surratt House Museum.
12. John Paul Jones (ed.), *Dr Mudd and the Lincoln Assassination: The Case Reopened* (Pennsylvania, Combined Books, 1995), p. 244.
13. *Ibid.*, p. 247.
14. *Ibid.*, p. 246.
15. Sandberg, *Abraham Lincoln*, vol. 4, p. 94.
16. *Ibid.*, p. 264.

Chapter Nine: The Nazis

1. Gdansk, German name, Danzig, was then a free city within the Polish free tariff area.
2. Winston S. Churchill, *The Second World War*, vol. 6, *Triumph and Tragedy* (London, Cassell & Co., 1954), p. 605.
3. Britain removed this defence from its *Manual of Military Law* only in April 1944.
4. *The Times*, 11 July 2004.
5. This and all other extracts from the trial testimony are taken from the Avalon Project of Yale Law School.
6. The Kellogg–Briand pact, on which the Tribunal relied, had been signed by all major nations in 1928 with a view to outlawing war. However, the treaty provided no means of enforcement in the event of breach, and by 1940 the existence of a crime of aggressive war had come to be widely doubted in legal and diplomatic circles.
7. Paul Schmidt, *Hitler's Interpreter: The Secret History of German Diplomacy* (New York, Macmillan, 1951).
8. Minutes of the Hossbach conference, 5 November 1937. See German Foreign Policy, series D, I, no. 19. The significance of the memorandum has been challenged by A.J.P. Taylor, *The Origins of the Second World War* (London, Hamish Hamilton, 1961), pp. 131 ff.
9. Robert E. Conot, *Justice at Nuremburg* (New York, Harper & Row, 1983).
10. Albert Speer, *Inside the Third Reich* (London, Weidenfeld & Nicolson, 1970), p. 31.
11. The claim is now doubted; it was most likely a lie for the purposes of the trial or a corrupted memory of something he had once contemplated.
12. Gitta Sereny, *Albert Speer: His Battle with Truth* (London, Macmillan, 1995), p. 570.
13. *Ibid.*, p. 708.
14. Ironically, Jodl was posthumously acquitted by a German de-Nazification court.
15. All prisoners had been thoroughly searched before and during incarceration. It is now believed that Goering was given a suicide pill by a sympathetic American soldier.

16. A.J.P. Taylor, *The Second World War: An Illustrated History* (London, Hamish Hamilton, 1975), p. 233.

Part Four: Introduction

1. Using the term in a very narrow sense. In those days no one found it surprising that women and slaves should be disenfranchised.

Chapter Ten: The Gadfly

1. *Henry V*, Act I, Scene iii.
2. A plant of the family, Umbelliferae. Exactly which, has given a great deal of innocent pleasure to historically inclined pharmacologists.
3. Apart from a brief note from one of Socrates' pupils, Xenophon, the only report of the trial is a Dialogue (or conversation piece) written by another pupil, Plato. Plato was no ordinary pupil. As the mathematician A.N. Whitehead remarked, 'The safest general characterization of the European philosophical tradition is that it consists of a series of footnotes to Plato.' Nevertheless, both Plato and Xenophon had axes to grind and both have to be read against the habit of classical writers putting words into the mouths of their subjects. The great classicist Dr Jowett described the *Apology* as 'an ideal rather than a literal truth'. Others are prepared to be more accepting. To a lawyer, Plato's account carries the assurance of having been written only a few years after the event, when it could have been read by those present at the trial, which, Plato claimed, included himself. It is for that reason that I have relied mainly on this source.
4. The god of healing. Was this request, as some have suggested, a way of diverting his friends from their grief or, as the present writer prefers to think, the last act of a scrupulously honest man?
5. Plato, *Phaedo*. I have used Benjamin Jowett's translation in *The Four Socratic Dialogues of Plato* (Oxford, Clarendon Press, 1903).
6. Thomas Cahill, *Sailing the Wine Dark Sea* (New York, Anchor, 2003). The description is based on a statue of the philosopher that is thought to be authentic.
7. Diogenes of Laerte, *Lives of the Philosophers: Socrates*.
8. I.F. Stone, *The Trial of Socrates* (Boston, Little, Brown, 1988), p. 28.
9. This and the following extracts from the trial are taken from Plato, *Apology*.
10. Plato, *Apology*.
11. *Ibid.*
12. Stone describes his address to the jury as 'offensively boastful and arrogant' (*The Trial of Socrates*, p. 184).
13. Plato, *Phaedo*.
14. Plato, *Apology*. Stone speculates that Socrates' later years may have been overshadowed by the murder of his favourite pupil, Alcibiades, by another pupil, Critias (*The Trial of Socrates*, p. 66).
15. Stone, *The Trial of Socrates*, p. 80.
16. Aeschines, *Against Timarchus*, 346 BC.

Chapter Eleven: The Good Servant

1. *Foxe's Book of Martyrs* describes Bainham as having been tied to a tree and whipped and thereafter racked in the Tower. More denied this, and there is

no independent confirmation of these allegations, which are inconsistent with More's known character.

2. For the following account of More's interrogations and trial I have principally relied on William Roper, *The Life of Sir Thomas More, Knight* in E.E. Reynolds (ed.), *Lives of Saint Thomas More* (London, Everyman's Library, 1963), and John Farrow, *The Story of Thomas More* (New York, All Saints Press, 1963). We should remember that Roper's knowledge of the trial must have been second hand.

3. Roper tells the story that, after his resignation as Lord Chancellor, More came to his wife in church and said, in parody of one of his former aide's announcements, 'Madam, my lord has gone'.

4. Thomas Edward Bridget, *Life of Blessed Thomas More* (London, Burns Oates & Washbourne, 1924), p. 340.

5. Farrow, *The Story of Thomas More.*

6. *Ibid.*

7. Bridget, *Life of Blessed Thomas More*, p. 368.

8. J. Duncan M. Derrett (to whose scholarly account of the trial, 'The Trial of Sir Thomas More', *English Historical Review*, 312 (July 1964), pp. 409 ff., I am greatly indebted) suggests that the Attorney General presented the case for the Crown on the fourth count in the indictment only.

9. Farrow, *The Story of Thomas More.*

10. Roper, *The Life of Sir Thomas More, Knight.*

11. A feat commemorated by the rhyme:
> When More some time had Chancellor been
> No more suits did remain.
> The like will never more be seen,
> Till More be there again.

12. Farrow, *The Story of Thomas More.*

Chapter Twelve: The Martyrs

1. George Loveless, 'The Victims of Whiggery', in *Trade Unions in the 1830s* (New York, Arnos Press, 1934).

2. Fitzwilliam MSS, in A. Aspinall and E. Anthony Smith (eds), *English Historical Documents*, vol. 11, *1784–1832* (Oxford, Oxford University Press, 1959).

3. This and all succeeding quotations from the trial are taken from Walter Citrine (ed.), *The Book of the Martyrs of Tolpuddle*, Trades Union Congress (London, Odhams Press, 1934).

4. Francis Bennion, *Interpretation of Statutes*, 3rd edn (London, Butterworths, 1997), p. 563.

5. See B. Reay, *Microhistories: Demography, Society and Culture in Rural England, 1800–1939* (Cambridge, Cambridge University Press, 1996).

Chapter Thirteen: The Anarchists

1. William Young and David E. Kaiser, *Postmortem: New Evidence in the Case of Sacco and Vanzetti* (Amherst, MA, University of Massachusetts Press, 1985), p. 3.

2. Felix Frankfurter, 'The Case of Sacco and Vanzetti', *Atlantic Monthly* (March 1927), p. 409.

3. The Governor of Massachusetts was later to examine the evidence and write: 'I believe with the jury that Vanzetti was guilty and that his trial was fair.'

4. Francis Russell, *Sacco and Vanzetti: The Case Resolved* (New York, Harper & Row, 1986).

5. In 1983 the son of one of the group that had hired him claimed that Moore was a cocaine addict who had to be supplied with the drug throughout the course of the trial.

6. Transcript of the Record, 5378.

7. Quoted in Russell, *Sacco and Vanzetti*, p. 201.

8. *Ibid.*, p. 141.

9. *Ibid.*

10. From such luminaries as Anatole France, H.G. Wells, Walter Lippman, H.L. Mencken and John Dos Passos.

11. The prosecutor refused to pay because it was the police officer's duty to give evidence.

12. Russell, *Sacco and Vanzetti*, ch. 11.

13. This and other excerpts come from Osmund K. Fraenkl, *The Sacco–Vanzetti Case* (London, George Routledge & Sons, 1931), pp. 165–77.

14. Frankfurter, 'The Case of Sacco and Vanzetti', 409. See also Felix Frankfurter, *The Case of Sacco and Vanzetti: A Critical Analysis for Lawyers and Laymen* (Boston, Little, Brown, 1969).

15. 'J.H. Wigmore Answers Frankfurter Attack on Sacco–Vanzetti Verdict: A Fair Trial: Facts as Well as Law Reviewed by Supreme Court', *Boston Evening Transcript*, 25 April 1927.

16. Frankfurter described the evidence placing Vanzetti at the scene of the crime as 'bordering on the frivolous' and poured scorn on the evidence of a newsboy who said that he 'knew by the way [the gunman] ran he was a foreigner'. But Montgomery points out that this comment was by the way; the boy clearly identified the man in the dock as the man with the shotgun, as did other witnesses.

17. Governor Fuller's report is printed at Fraenkl, *The Sacco–Vanzetti Case*, pp. 161–5.

18. Robert H. Montgomery, *Sacco and Vanzetti: The Murder and the Myth* (New York, Devin-Adair Company, 1960).

19. Fraenkl, *The Sacco–Vanzetti Case*, p. 88.

20. Nicola Sacco, *The Letters of Sacco and Vanzetti*, ed. Marion Denman Frankfurter and Gardner Jackson, Twentieth-Century Classics (repr. New York, Penguin, 1997).

21. Alan M. Derschowitz, *America on Trial* (New York, Warner Books, 2004), p. 252.

22. Frankfurter made two cogent points well ahead of his time: visual identification evidence is notoriously unreliable and accused persons may lie for reasons quite unconnected with the crime of which they are accused.

23. Russell, *Sacco and Vanzetti*, p. 216.

24. *Ibid.*, p. 27.

25. *Ibid.*, p. 12.

26. *Ibid.*, p. 222. The words in brackets were the invention of the journalist who reported these comments.

Select Bibliography

For the lives of those involved in the trials in this book I have relied principally on the following sources. I must also acknowledge the benefit I have received from two excellent compendia, Justin Lovell (ed.), *Notable Historical Trials* (London, Folio Society, 1999), and 'Famous Trials', a website prepared by Prof. Doug Linder of the University of Missouri, Kansas City Law School.

Chapter One: The Divine Ruler

Carlton, C., *Going to the Wars* (London, Routledge, 1992)
Edwards, Graham, *The Last Days of Charles I* (Stroud, Sutton Publishing, 1999)
Fraser, Antonia, *Cromwell: Our Chief of Men* (London, Weidenfeld & Nicolson, 1973)
Hyde, Edward, *The History of the Rebellion and Civil Wars in England begun in the Year 1641* (Oxford, Oxford University Press, 1993)
Kishlansky, M., *A Monarchy Transformed* (Harmondsworth, Penguin, 1996)
Muddiman, J.G., *The Trial of King Charles the First, Notable British Trials* (London, William Hodge, 1928)
Partridge, Robert B., *'O Horrable Murder'* (London, Rubicon Press, 1998)
Robertson, Geoffrey, *The Tyrannicide Brief* (London, Chatto & Windus, 2005)
The Trial of Charles The First: A Contemporary Account Taken from the Memoirs of Sir Thomas Herbert and John Rushworth (London, Folio Press, 1974)
Wedgwood, C.V., *The King's Peace, 1637–1641* (London, Collins, 1964)
—— *The Trial of Charles I* (London, Collins, 1964)

Chapter Two: The Diarist

Dudgeon, J., *Roger Casement: The Black Diaries* (Belfast, Belfast Press, 2002)
Hochschild, A., *King Leopold's Ghost* (London, Macmillan, 1999)
Hyde, H.M., *The Trial of Roger Casement* (London, William Hodge, 1960)
Inglis, B., *Roger Casement* (Harmondsworth, Penguin, 1973)
Weale, Adrian, *Patriot Traitors* (London, Viking, 2001)

Chapter Three: The Broadcaster

Hall, J.W. (ed.), *Trial of William Joyce*, Notable British Trials (London, William Hodge, 1946)
Joyce, William, *Twilight over England* (London, Imperial War Museum. 1992)
Kenny, M., *Germany Calling* (Dublin, New Island, 2003)
Lauterpacht, H., 'Allegiance, Diplomatic Protection and Criminal Jurisdiction over Aliens', *Cambridge Law Journal*, 9 (1947), 330–48
West, R., *The Meaning of Treason* (London, Phoenix Books, 1982)
Williams, Glanville, 'The Correlation of Allegiance and Protection', *Cambridge Law Journal*, 1 (1948), 54

Chapter Four: The Atom Spies

Feklisov, A., *The Man behind the Rosenbergs* (New York, Enigma Books, 2004)

Meeropol, R., and Meeropol, M., *We Are Your Sons*, 2nd edn (Chicago, University of Illinois Press, 1986)

Nizer, Louis, *The Implosion Conspiracy* (New York, Doubleday, 1973)

Philipson, Ilene, *Ethel Rosenberg: Beyond the Myths* (New York, Franklin Watts, 1988)

Radosh, R., and Milton, J., *The Rosenberg File: A Search for the Truth* (London, Weidenfeld & Nicolson, 1983)

Roberts, S., *The Brother: The Untold Story of the Rosenberg Case* (New York, Random House, 2003)

West, Nigel, *Venona: The Greatest Secret of the Cold War* (London, HarperCollins, 1988)

United States of America v. *Julius Rosenberg, Ethel Rosenberg, Anatoli A. Yakovlev, David Greenglass, and Morton Sobell*, US District Court, Southern District of New York, C.134–245, 6 March–6 April 1951 (republished in 8 vols, 1952).

Chapter Five: The Maid

Michelet, Jules, *Joan of Arc*, ed. and trans. Albert Guerard (Ann Arbor, University of Michigan Press, 1957)

Pernoud, Régine, *The Retrial of Joan of Arc: The Evidence at the Trial for her Rehabilitation*, trans. J.M. Cohen (New York, Harcourt, Brace and Co., 1955)

—— *Joan of Arc* (London, Macdonald, 1964)

Scott, W.S. (ed. and trans.), *The Trial of Joan of Arc* (London, Folio Society, 1968)

Warner, M., *Joan of Arc: The Image of Female Heroism* (London, Weidenfeld & Nicolson, 1981)

Chapter Six: The Starry Messenger

Finocchiaro, Maurice A., *The Galileo Affair*, vol. 1 (Berkeley and Los Angeles, University of California Press, 1990)

Machamer, Peter (ed.), *The Cambridge Companion to Galileo* (Cambridge, Cambridge University Press, 1998)

De Santillana, Georgio, *The Crime of Galileo* (London, Heinemann, 1958)

Sobel, Dava, *Galileo's Daughter* (London, Fourth Estate, 1999)

Westfall, Richard S., *Essays on the Trial of Galileo* (Indiana, Ind., University of Notre Dame Press, 1989)

Chapter Seven: The Scapegoat

Clowes, W.L., assisted by Markham, Sir C., Mahan, Captain A.T., Wilson, H.W., Roosevelt, Theodore, Langton, L.C., and others, *History of the Royal Navy of England: From the Earliest Times to the Present Day*, vol. 5 (Boston, Little, Brown & Co., 1898)

Fortescue, Sir J., *A History of the British Army*, vol. 2 (London, Macmillan, 1913)

The Newgate Calendar (1846)

Pope, Dudley, *At Twelve Mr Byng Was Shot* (London, Secker & Warburg, 1962)

The Trial of the Hon. Admiral Byng at a Court-Martial, Held on Board His Majesty's Ship the St George in Portsmouth Harbour, Tuesday, Dec. 28, 1756 (London, J. Lacy, 1757)

Tunstall, B., *Admiral Byng and the Loss of Minorca* (London, Philip Allan, 1928)
Wragg, H., *Letters Written in our Time* (Oxford, Oxford University Press, 1915)

Chapter Eight: The Assassins

Carter III, Samuel, *The Riddle of Dr Mudd* (New York, Putnam, 1974)
Chamlee, Roy Z., *Lincoln's Assassins: A Complete Account of their Capture, Trial and Punishment* (Jefferson, NC, McFarland, 1990)
Sandburg, Carl, *Abraham Lincoln* (New York, Harcourt Brace and World, 1939)
Swanson, James, and Weinberg, Daniel, *Lincoln's Assassins: Their Trial and Execution* (Santa Fe, Arena Editions, 2001)
Trindal, Elizabeth Stegner, and Trindal, Mary, *Mary Surratt: An American Tragedy* (Gretna, LA, Pelican, 1996)
Winkler, H. Donald, *Lincoln and Booth* (Nashville, TN, Cumberland House, 2003)

Chapter Nine: The Nazis

Conot, R.E., *Justice at Nuremberg* (London, Weidenfeld & Nicolson, 1983)
Elliot, G., *Twentieth Century Book of the Dead* (Harmondsworth, Penguin, 1972)
Kagan, D., *On the Origins of War* (London, Pimlico, 1995).
Goerlitz, W., *Hitler's Generals*, ed. C. Barnett (London, Weidenfeld & Nicolson, 1989)
Overy, R., *Interrogations: Inside the Minds of the Nazi Elite* (Harmondsworth, Penguin, 2002)
Sereny, Gitta, *Albert Speer: His Battle with Truth* (London, Macmillan, 1995)
Speer, Albert, *Inside the Third Reich* (London, Weidenfeld & Nicolson, 1970)
Taylor, A.J.P., *The Origins of the Second World War* (London, Hamish Hamilton, 1961)
Taylor, Telford, *The Anatomy of the Nuremberg Trials* (London, Bloomsbury, 1993)
Tusa, Ann, and Tusa, John, *The Nuremberg Trial* (London, Macmillan. 1983)

Chapter Ten: The Gadfly

Cahill, T., *Sailing the Wine Dark Sea* (New York, Anchor Books, 2003)
Plato, *The Four Socratic Dialogues of Plato*, trans. B. Jowett (Oxford, Clarendon Press, 1903)
Stone, I.F., *The Trial of Socrates* (Boston, Little, Brown, 1988)

Chapter Eleven: The Good Servant

Ackroyd, Peter, *The Life of Thomas More* (London, Chatto & Windus. 1998)
Bridget, Thomas Edward, *Life of Blessed Thomas More* (London, Burns Oates & Washbourne, 1924)
Derrett, J.D.M., 'The Trial of Sir Thomas More', *English Historical Review*, 312 (July 1964)
Farrow, John, *The Story of Thomas More* (New York, All Saints Press, 1963)
Harpsfield, Nicholas, 'The Life and Death of Sir Thomas More', in E.E. Reynolds (ed.), *Lives of Saint Thomas More* (London, Everyman's Library, 1963)
Roper, William, 'The Life of Sir Thomas More, Knight', in E.E. Reynolds (ed.), *Lives of Saint Thomas More* (London, Everyman's Library, 1963)

Select Bibliography

Chapter Twelve: The Martyrs

Select Bibliography

Chapter Twelve: The Martyrs

Citrine, Walter (ed.), *The Book of the Martyrs of Tolpuddle*, Trades Union Congress (London, Odhams Press, 1934)

Evatt, H.V., *Injustice within the Law* (Sydney, Law Book Company of Australia, 1937)

Loveless, George, 'The Victims of Whiggery', in *Trade Unions in the 1830s* (New York, Arnos Press, 1972)

Marlow, J., *The Tolpuddle Martyrs* (London, André Deutsch, 1971)

Chapter Thirteen: The Anarchists

Ehrmann, H.B., *The Case That Will Not Die* (London, W.H. Allen, 1970)

Fraenkl, Osmund K., *The Sacco–Vanzetti Case* (London, George Routledge & Sons, 1931)

Frankfurter, Felix, 'The Case of Sacco and Vanzetti', *Atlantic Monthly* (March 1927), p. 409

Joughin, Louis, and Morgan, Edmund M., *The Legacy of Sacco and Vanzetti* (repr. Princeton, Princeton University Press, 1978)

Montgomery, Robert H., *Sacco and Vanzetti: The Murder and the Myth* (New York, Devin-Adair Company, 1960)

Russell, Francis, *Sacco and Vanzetti: The Case Resolved* (New York, Harper & Row, 1986)

The Sacco–Vanzetti Case: Transcript of the Record of the Trial of Nicola Sacco and Bartolomeo Vanzetti in the Courts of Massachusetts and Subsequent Proceedings, 1920–7. 5 Volumes. With a Supplemental Volume on the Bridgewater Case. Prefatory Essay by William O. Douglas (Mamaroneck, NY, Paul P. Appel, 1969)

Young, Willia and Kaiser, David E., *Postmortem: New Evidence in the Case of Sacco and Vanzetti* (Amherst, MA, University of Massachusetts Press, 1985)

234

Index